BROTHER BRIGHAM

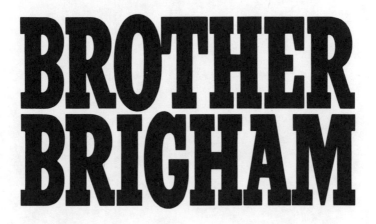

BROTHER BRIGHAM

Eugene England

Copyright © 1980 by Bookcraft, Inc.

All rights reserved. This book or any part thereof may
not be reproduced in any form whatsoever, whether by
graphic, visual, electronic, filming, microfilming, tape
recording or any other means, without the prior written
permission of Bookcraft, Inc., except in the case of
brief passages embodied in critical reviews and articles.

Library of Congress Catalog Card Number: 79-57136
ISBN 0-88494-394-1

First Printing, 1980

Lithographed in the United States of America
PUBLISHERS PRESS
Salt Lake City, Utah

Contents

Preface

Too many books about Brigham Young have been written without love or faith. And they have suffered from the lack of insight into human character that only sympathy, even empathy, can bring. They have thus not provided much penetration into the most profound springs of feeling and motivation for a man such as Brother Brigham: the hand of God on his life and his own transforming conviction that the true gospel of Christ had been restored—that, however inadequate he might be, he was called to serve Jesus Christ as one of his latter-day apostles. Such books, from the early exposés to the latest biography, Stanley Hirshson's *The Lion of the Lord*, in some cases provide useful information and perspectives. But they have failed to put us in touch with the complete Brother Brigham; even in relating fact and truth they have created a stereotype—the stoic polygamist and tough, practical administrator who conquered the desert—that has tended to hide the real man even from Mormons who accept him as a prophet.

But what about those books written by Mormons, such as Preston Nibley or Elder S. Dilworth Young or Brigham Young's own daughters? These books were certainly motivated by love and faith, and as a result have much to offer. They were written as acts of piety, aimed specifically at fostering a certain image of a beloved prophet and father, rather than at critical appreciation. And they were of course limited by the lack of certain primary materials, which have only recently been made available even to a Church historian or family member.

One reason, then, for offering another book on Brigham Young is that I have been able to read through many of the primary sources only quite recently catalogued in the LDS Church Archives—from the early holograph diaries and letters through the manuscript history and later office journals and letterbooks. I have also had access to numerous unpublished diaries and letters by Brigham Young's contemporaries which give important details and assessments from those who knew him best. The efforts of Ronald Esplin, research historian in the Historical Department of the LDS Church, in helping to select and assess those materials, reduced this book's writing time by at least half; he also generously shared with me—through suggested secondary readings, his own fine essays, and many hours of his time for discussions and criticism—the benefit of his excellent insights and skills as a professional historian. Without him I could not have written the book. I am also indebted to Leonard J. Arrington, director of the History Division of the Historical Department, for his own knowledge and love of Brigham Young and for providing resources that have made this book possible, to the assistance, attentive reading, and suggestions of other members of his staff (I will mention here Davis Bitton, James B. Allen, Maureen Ursenbach Beecher, Dean Jessee, and Debbie Lilenquist, though others also gave helpful suggestions and criticism), and to the support of History Division fellowships part of the time during the writing. And I am grateful to the Humanities College of Brigham Young University for a fellowship which enabled me to do a careful final rewriting after meticulous reading and forthright suggestions of my colleagues Richard Cracroft and Clifton Jolley.

A small volume of rather personal essays can only begin to touch a few of the dimensions of such a large life. There are two areas of that life I have not even approached. President Young's unique achievements and relationships in his work with American Indians, which were quite far ahead of the times but based on faith in that people's ancient calling and destiny as a part of the House of Israel whose ancestors wrote the Book of Mormon, are being fully explored in two books now in process: Lawrence C. Coates's carefully researched work on Mormon Indian policy in the nineteenth century and a volume edited by Dean Jessee of President Young's correspondence with Indian chiefs. Brigham's staggering achievements as a good husband to sixteen plural wives and an excellent father to forty-six children, his unique understanding of what a family kingdom can be and admirable success in creating one, and the complex history of his ideas and feelings about polygamy—from his first reaction ("I'd rather be dead") to spending a day in jail over a divorce suit by his last wife, spanned by thirty-five years of vigorously living and defending "The Principle"—all this I find too important and difficult to try to include here.

One great excitement in my own rediscovery of Brigham Young, and one that has made him able to move me emotionally and to change my life for good, has been to see him as a warm, fallible, humorous, loving father, husband, friend—that is, as a man, as well as a prophet of God. I am convinced that those who knew him in this way were compelled to respect Brother Brigham

—and often to love him. And they were moved, the better they knew him, to faith in God and themselves and to courage and energy to be better and build better than they had before. These essays attempt to bring us, through the special means of language, to reach back more than a hundred years and to know that man— one made of the same common clay as each of us, and yet a man transformed into a vessel of honor by a divine fire that is available to us all.

Note: Parts of the first three chapters were published in the *New Era* in September, November, and December 1977, and the chapter, "Brigham's Gospel Kingdom," was published in a more complete form in *Brigham Young University Studies,* Spring 1978. Readers may wish to see the many valuable photographs accompanying the *New Era* essays, particularly those of Brigham Young's craftsmanship and of the landscape of his early life in the September 1977 *New Era,* and to consult the *BYU Studies* article for additional information and perspective.

Young Brigham   1

When Brigham Young died, on August 29, 1877, he was the leader of a commonwealth of 350 towns and cities blossoming in a desert, and the prophet—the literal spokesman of God—to over a hundred thousand people. But for some years after his birth in 1801 he may well have thought of himself as insignificant—and without a future. Two persistent efforts made all the difference in the first half of his life and determined the direction of the dramatic changes and struggles and achievements of the latter half: In his teens and early twenties Brigham became a first-rate carpenter, painter, and glazier—skills he would always take pride in; in his early thirties he carefully examined the newly proclaimed Latter-day Saint faith for two years and finally embraced it with undeviating commitment, as he said, "For all day long." Those early developments are difficult to analyze because we have almost no contemporary sources about the years before young Brigham joined the Church and so must depend on reminiscences recorded by President Young and others long afterwards. But his early life must be carefully examined if we are to understand his later life, which has heretofore preoccupied most of his biographers.

Brigham's parents were devout, puritanic Methodists, trapped for many years in a precarious struggle with poverty. He remembered of his father, "It used to be a word and a blow, with him—but the blow came first."[1] Brigham's daughter reported that his mother mellowed this stern, emotionally narrow effect somewhat with her "tender solicitude" and gave the children "what schooling she could."[2] At any rate, Brigham responded to the strict, humorless piety of his parents by neither adopting nor totally rejecting it. Instead, he developed a remarkable independence that led to careful and long consideration before making his own religious commitments. Later he could reflect on that early experience with mature insight, revealing both his own success in avoiding the rebelliousness that often follows a repressed childhood and also what kind of parent — and leader — he had learned to be:

> When I was young, I was kept within very strict bounds, and was not allowed to walk more than half-an-hour on Sunday for exercise. The proper and necessary gambols of youth having been denied me, makes me want active exercise and amusement now. I had not a chance to dance when I was young, and never heard the enchanting tones of the violin, until I was eleven years of age; and then I thought I was on the highway to hell, if I suffered myself to linger and listen to it. I shall not subject my little children to such a course of unnatural training, but they shall go to the dance, study music, read novels, and do anything else that will tend to expand their frames, add fire to their spirits, improve their minds, and make them feel free and untrammeled in body and mind.[3]

As we will see later, a central part of Brigham's conversion to Mormonism was his finding in it a philosophy, a way of life, and a model — in Joseph Smith — that would complete his long quest to become "free and untrammeled," yet healthily disciplined, in body and mind.

But for a long time he had to struggle. He later recalled:

> Brother Heber [Kimball] and I never went to school until we got into "Mormonism:" that was the first of our schooling. We never had the opportunity of letters in our youth, but we had the privilege of picking up brush, chopping down trees, rolling logs, and working amongst the roots, and of getting our shins, feet, and toes bruised. . . . I learned to make bread, wash the dishes, milk the cows, and can make butter; and can beat the most of the women in this community at housekeeping. Those are about all the advantages I gained in my youth. I know how to economise, for my father had to do it.[4]

Brigham's father had to economize because he moved his family from Vermont, where Brigham was born, to a series of frontier homesteads in the New York Finger Lakes country on the road west from Albany — first near present-day Smyrna and then north of Ithaca on Cayuga Lake. The whole family worked to clear the forest, build successive log cabins, and plant corn, grain, and slips of sugar maples. Brigham had less than a year of formal schooling because, as he noted in his own history with typical terseness, "At an early age I labored with my father, assisting him to clear off new land and cultivate his farm, passing through many hardships and privations incident to settling a new country."[5] Late in his life he still remembered, "I used to work in the woods logging and driving team, summer and winter, not half clad, and with insufficient food until my stomach would ache."[6]

The work and privation were intensified for the entire family when Brigham's mother died of tuberculosis soon after his fourteenth birthday. His father then moved west again to a new homestead on a hundred acres of timber on Sugar Hill, near present Tyrone but then fifteen miles from any large settlement. He was sometimes away working or getting supplies in the nearest towns, and at these times the children were left to clear land and care for the maple trees by themselves. Brigham's younger brother who was named after the well-known Methodist preacher, Lorenzo Dow, recalls that one time when he and Brigham were left alone for a few days while their father went for food, they began growing faint from living only on the insubstantial maple sugar. Brigham finally shot a robin that lit near the house and while it was cooking they managed to thump a little flour out of the cracks of the flour barrel and thus "thickened the broth."[7] The grimness of such an existence was intensified by the father's continuing insistence that the children not indulge in any pastimes or amusements. Brigham remembers that his brother Joseph, older by four years, seemed never to smile "during some four or five years."[8]

Brigham himself, soon after his father's remarriage in 1817, began to be exposed to freedoms and opportunities that released and satisfied deep energies and needs in him. He was apprenticed out to John C. Jeffries, a chairmaker and housepainter in the town of Auburn on Owasco Lake, where some of Brigham's relatives already lived. By the time he was eighteen Brigham was skilled and mature enough to go into business for himself. He set up a small woodworking shop in Aurelius, a tiny village on the turnpike west of Auburn, noted mainly for its three inns which provided food and board for the emigrants going west and gathering places for the local frontiersmen. Suddenly Brigham was free of all restrictions from parents and masters and was at the same time exposed to ample temptation; but the independence that had kept him from joining his parents' church also kept him from serious evil. Though he later said that "like other young men, I was full of weakness, sin, darkness and ignorance,"[9] in that mature confession he was setting exceptionally high standards for his former self, because he refers specifically to losing control of his temper and his tongue. At the inns he learned to enjoy dancing, and that lifelong love was a major influence in making the dance an expression of joy and a solace in times of trouble for the Latter-day Saints he came to lead.

The dances that were held in the second stories of the inns were attended by the surrounding farmers and young girls of the township. Local tradition has it that at one of these dances in 1823 Brigham met Miriam Angela Works, then only eighteen and nearly five years younger than he was. The next year they were married and for their honeymoon traveled west along the nearly completed Erie Canal to Mendon, where some of Brigham's family had settled and where he at that time apparently first met Heber C. Kimball, who was later married to his niece and who eventually became his closest friend.

Brigham and Miriam established their home at Haydenville, north of Auburn, and Brigham developed into a fine craftsman. According to Mary Van Sickle Wait, a non-Mormon who wrote an appreciative history of Brigham's early years, he had even earlier "established himself as the skilled artisan who is [still famous in Western New York] for the beauty of his stairwell decorations, fan-light doorways, door frames, stair rails, louvered attic windows and, above all—fireplace mantels."[10] Mrs. Wait said she had derived "keen delight" from living much of her life in one of the homes west of Auburn that Brigham worked on during this period. She described it as "distinguished by its fan-shaped doorway, . . . a small but perfect example of Colonial architecture"[11] that had been praised by visitors and regarded with pride by the community for over 150 years. Mrs. Wait also described in detail other homes and particular articles of furniture that are still preserved, such as a cherry desk, "plain and sturdy, rather chaste in design, and the wood . . . beautiful."[12] She quotes, with full agreement based on her own careful study and close observation, a statement of Brigham's daughter Susa:

> He excelled when the interiors were planned and finished, with a keen feeling for minor decorations of a chaste and substantial nature. . . . He had that care for detail, that appreciation for form and proportion that gave the classic touch to simple models. His mantels, fireplaces, doorways, and cupboards are worthy of the study of trained architects today.[13]

Simple beauty, sturdiness, usefulness—it would be hard to find better standards for a person's work in the world. But what is perhaps most interesting is the way Brigham gradually transferred these ideals from cabinets to people, and included his craftsman's integrity in a total perspective of life's meaning, as he found the religious conviction that unified the various elements of his life.

Not long before he died, one of Brigham's friends from this early period, Captain George Hickox, wrote him recalling how kind Brigham had been to him when he was ill almost fifty years before —and inviting Brigham to the centennial celebration of the town, where "the most interesting [item] will be one of the chairs you made for me."[14] President Young replied:

> I felt amused and interested in your statement that a chair, made by me, would occupy a place in your Centennial supper. . . . I have no doubt that many other pieces of furniture and other specimens of my handiwork can be found scattered about your section of the country, for I have believed all my life that that which was worth doing was worth doing well, and have considered it as much a part of my religion to do honest, reliable work, such as would endure, for those who employed me, as to attend to the service of God's worship on the Sabbath.[15]

Brigham's daily work gradually changed after he became a Mormon; but even as he came to labor with words and organizations and souls rather than glass and paint and wood, the emphasis on honest, reliable, and enduring work remained. The goal of helping shape a thing, without violating the integrity (or agency) of the material—whether oak plank or immigrant English millworker— into something more useful, strong, and beautiful endured and intensified. And Brigham never lost his love of seeing good handwork or of doing some himself (such as he did on the St. George Temple), even as a busy prophet.

Brigham's search for religious integrity was a long one. Despite the orthodox piety of his parents, despite, like Joseph Smith, being "brought up from my youth amid those flaming, fiery revivals so customary with the Methodists," Brigham, also like Joseph, as a boy held aloof from actually joining a church:

> Priests had urged me to pray before I was eight years old. On this subject I had but one prevailing feeling in my mind—Lord, preserve me until I am old enough to have sound judgment, and a discreet mind ripened upon a good solid foundation of common sense.[16]

Those were the keys—judgment, discretion, common sense. Of the Methodist camp meetings Brigham said, "I had seen men and women fall, and be as speechless and breathless as that stove before me" as a result of "what they called the power of God." But though Brigham was unwilling to deny their sincerity, because of their excesses these people's ideas "did not commend themselves to my understanding":

Before I embraced the Gospel, I understood pretty well what the different sects preached, but I was called an infidel because I could not embrace their dogmas. . . . there were some things they preached I could believe, and some I could not. . . . As far as their teachings were in accordance with the Bible, I could believe them, and no further.[17]

He continued to seek new possibilities:

I used to go to meetings — was well acquainted with the Episcopalians, Presbyterians, New Lights, Baptists, Freewill Baptists, Wesleyan and Reformed Methodists, — lived from my youth where I was acquainted with Quakers as well as the other denominations, and was more or less acquainted with almost every other religious ism.

. . . I understood the Scriptures tolerably well, and my whole mind and reflections were to seek for every particle of truth with regard to doctrine.

I always admired morality, and never saw a day in which I did not respect a good, moral, sensible, man far more than I could respect a wicked man.[18]

It seems that Brigham, like many in modern times, turned from the arid contentions of the traditional churches and the self-indulgent extremes of the dissenting groups and tried simply to be a moral, hard-working, loving husband and father. Susa Young Gates tells us of her father:

He once remarked that after marriage he worked for half a crown [about 65 cents] a day when he could not get more; got breakfast for his wife [ill with tuberculosis], himself, and the little girls, dressed the children, cleaned up the house, carried his wife to the rocking-chair by the fireplace and left her there until he could return in the evening. When he came home he cooked his own and the family's supper, put his wife back to bed and finished up the day's domestic labours.[19]

During the mid-1820s, after his first daughter was born, Brigham farmed in the summer, pursued his various hand skills in the winter, and was even employed for a while in a carding mill and also in a paint factory, where, to grind the paint, he used the cannonball his father had carried home from the Revolutionary War. Elder S. Dilworth Young (a grandson) reports family tradition that Brigham invented an ingenious "water-powered pigment crusher" with the cannonball "as the pestle to an iron pot mortar," thus saving a good deal of work and time.[20] But Brigham found

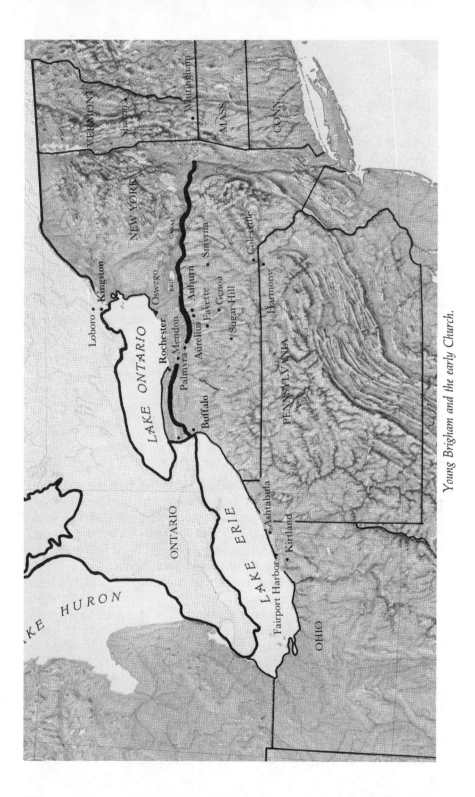

Young Brigham and the early Church.

that to succeed as a painter where he lived he would have to adulterate the linseed oil like his competitors. Unwilling to do so, he moved north to Oswego, on Lake Ontario, where he built a large tannery and again survived with farming and carpentry.

From later evidence, however, it seems clear that Brigham was *not* able to be satisfied with merely a moral, hard-working life. He yearned for spiritual and emotional fulfillment — for some response to nagging questions about life's meaning, about the potential and future of human beings. We know this because over thirty years later a Methodist minister, Hiram McKee, who had been his friend in Oswego, wrote reminding him of the times when Brigham had been his fellow seeker after truth there in western New York: "I have not forgotten your advise, counsel, prayers. My confidence was great in you, in view of your deep piety, and faith in God. You was one of my early spiritual friends, and guides." Reverend McKee went on to wonder, because of the scandalous reports in Eastern papers,

> if Brigham enjoyed as much piety now as then, or whether ambition, and love of power, and distinction did not hold some sway in that mind that was once so humble, contrite and devoted . . . O, my brother how is it? How sweet was our communion in Old Oswego, how encouraging our prayers, and enlivening our songs we used to sing. . . . Now Brother Brigham, before the allseeing God, who in the judgment will judge us, can you lay your hand on your heart and say that your hope of heaven is as good as then?[21]

President Young assured the good reverend that he was "as honest a seeker after truth as I was during our acquaintance in Oswego."[22] He and Miriam had apparently joined with McKee in a little group of independent "seekers" and may have associated with similar groups in the other towns where they lived. (We know they did later with Brigham's brothers and father when they moved to Mendon in 1829.) About this time Brigham and Miriam also shared a remarkable vision, a bright light in the nighttime western sky that for two hours formed itself into marching armies of men.[23] It is somewhat hard to imagine the down-to-earth and skeptical young Brigham being easily impressed in this way, and he must have been responsive in part to an inner hope; when he later learned that that night, September 22, 1827, was the night the Angel Moroni gave the gold plates of the Book of Mormon to Joseph Smith, and that Heber and Vilate Kimball and Brigham's sister Fanny had seen the same vision over at Mendon, he, like all of them, took it for an important preparatory sign.

It seems that, despite his revulsion at the emotional extremes of some groups, Brigham could not rest in the emotional and spiritual sterility of mere good works or traditional theology. Later, in 1871, he told a Mormon audience in Ogden, Utah, to take their children to hear the speakers at the Protestant camp meeting, then being held in Salt Lake City, and to accept all the truth they could learn; but he offered them little hope of benefiting much:

> I recollect when I was young going to hear Lorenzo Dow preach. He was esteemed a very great man by the religious folks. I, although young in years and lacking experience, had thought a great many times that I would like to hear some man who could tell me something, when he opened the Bible, about the Son of God, the will of God, what the ancients did and received, saw and heard and knew pertaining to God and heaven. So I went to hear Lorenzo Dow. . . . and when he got through I asked myself, "What have you learned from Lorenzo Dow?" and my answer was, "Nothing, nothing but morals." He could tell the people they should not work on the Sabbath day; they should not lie, swear, steal, commit adultery, etc., but when he came to teaching the things of God he was as dark as midnight. . . . But [the religious world] can explain our duty as rational, moral beings, and that is good, excellent as far as it goes.[24]

On the other hand, Brigham recalled the irrationality of frontier revivals:

> I have often prayed—if there is a God in heaven save me, that I may know all and not be fooled. I saw them get religion all around me—men were rolling and hollering and bawling and thumping but had no effect on me—I wanted to know the truth that I might not be fooled.[25]

It was that dissatisfaction with things that did not go far enough, and yet fear of things that went too far in the wrong direction, that drove and haunted Brigham Young in his long religious quest. When he moved from Oswego about sixty miles west to Mendon, in 1829, he joined the Congregational Church and also took part in another independent society of seekers led by his brother Phineas, who described it thus: "We opened a house for preaching, and commenced teaching the people according to the light we had; a reformation commenced, and we soon had a good society organized, and the Lord blessed our labors."[26] Such groups were, of course, common on the American frontier, and many tended to be "restorationist" in character, seeking through close study of the New Testament to learn what Christ's original Church was like and to conform exactly in teaching and practice. Brigham's group was one of those; he later recalled this time of searching in a way that indicates some of the fundamental things that attracted him to Mormonism:

> I read the Bible for myself; . . . When I was told to believe in Jesus Christ, and that was all that was required for salvation, I did not so understand the Bible. I understood from the Bible that when the Lord had a church upon the earth it was a system of ordinances, of laws and regulations to be obeyed, a society presided over and regulated by officers and ministers peculiar to itself to answer such and such purposes, and bring to pass such and such results. . . . Such a system answering the description given in the Bible I could not find on the earth. . . . When I would ask the ministers of religion . . . if that which is laid down in the New Testament is not the pattern, all the reply I could receive from them was; "but . . . these things are done away."[27]

Some of the groups seeking to pattern themselves after the New Testament coalesced in fairly large movements like the Campbellites, from which group came many of the early converts to Mormonism. This was in part because Mormonism, actually claiming to be the divinely authorized restitution of Christ's Church described in the Bible, was itself basically "restorationist." Of course, Mormonism embraced other important things as well, and those other things kept it from being accepted by or uniting with the other restorationist groups.

One of the most profound differences was the Book of Mormon. With one stroke that book distinguished Mormonism from the molds of traditional, even "reformed," Christianity as it opened up vistas of continuous and universal revelation. It revealed periodic dispensations of and apostasies from the gospel, going back into the ancient past and including the whole world. God's redemptive work was not limited to an evolution in Palestine from Moses through Christ and then down through essentially European Christianity. Thus Mormonism, in response to the widespread feeling that there had been a "falling away" from truth, could describe a number of ancient patterns, from both Palestine and America, for a restoration, and could also witness the reality of a modern dispensation of authority through the prophetic calling of Joseph Smith, who had translated the ancient scripture through divine means.

Phineas was the first of the Young family to see the Book of Mormon, though even before it was published they had all heard and read of the notorious "Joe Smith" and his "gold Bible" over in

Palmyra, which was less than fifteen miles away. In April 1830, while eating at an inn near Mendon, Phineas was shown one of the first copies of the Book of Mormon by Joseph's brother Samuel, who said to him, "I know the book to be a revelation from God, translated by the gift and power of the Holy Ghost, and that my brother Joseph Smith, Jun., is a Prophet, Seer and Revelator."

Phineas thought that kind of expression very strange, even ridiculous, and decided the young man must be deceived "and that the book was a production got up to lead people astray." But he determined to read it in order that he might "as a teacher in Israel, expose such errors and save the people from the delusion." After studying it for a week he could not find the errors he expected and even began to feel the book was true; he was called on to give his views on the matter at the meeting of the society the following Sabbath, at which Brigham was quite certainly present, and he reported of that experience, "I had not spoken ten minutes in defence of the book when the Spirit of God came upon me in a marvellous manner, and I spoke at great length on the importance of such a work, quoting from the Bible to support my position, and finally closed by telling the people that I believed the book."[28]

Phineas lent his copy of the Book of Mormon to his father, who thought it "the greatest work . . . he had ever seen," then to his sister Fanny, who declared it "a revelation." Fanny passed it on to Brigham, who was more reserved:

> though I had beheld, all my life, that the traditions of the people was all the religion they had, I had got a mantle for myself. Says I, "Wait a little while; what is the doctrine of the book, and of the revelations the Lord has given? Let me apply my heart to them;" and after I had done this, I considered it to be my right to know for myself, as much as any man on earth.
>
> I examined the matter studiously for two years before I made up my mind to receive that book. I knew it was true, as well as I knew that I could see with my eyes, or feel by the touch of my fingers, or be sensible of the demonstration of any sense. Had not this been the case, I never would have embraced it to this day; it would have all been without form or comeliness to me. I wished time sufficient to prove all things for myself.[29]

On a later occasion Brigham further explained this reserve:

> Upon the first opportunity I read the Book of Mormon, and then sought to become acquainted with the people who professed to believe it. . . . I watched to see whether good common sense was

manifest; and if they had that, I wanted them to present it in accordance with the Scriptures. . . .

. . . I could not more honestly and earnestly have prepared myself to go into eternity than I did to come into this Church; and when I had ripened everything in my mind, I drank it in, and not till then. From that day to this, it is all right with me.[30]

"Examine," "prove all things," "good common sense," "ripened." All were good, rational approaches, and were characteristic of Brigham, his Yankee skepticism and his well-learned wariness of religious extremes. But just as characteristic, though more hidden perhaps, was his need and desire to "apply his *heart*" to these new and attractive teachings, and after about a year and a half it was through his feelings that he was moved to action. He was visited by a group of Mormon missionaries from Columbia, Pennsylvania, one of whom sat Brigham down and "bore his testimony" to him:

If all the talent, tact, wisdom, and refinement of the world had been sent to me with the Book of Mormon, and had declared, in the most exalted of earthly eloquence, the truth of it, undertaking to prove it by learning, and worldly wisdom, they would have been to me like the smoke which arises only to vanish away. But when I saw a man without eloquence, or talents for public speaking, who could only say, "I know, by the power of the Holy Ghost, that the Book of Mormon is true, that Joseph Smith is a Prophet of the Lord," the Holy Ghost proceeding from that individual illuminated my understanding, and light, glory and immortality were before me. I was encircled by them, filled with them, and I knew for myself that the testimony of the man was true. . . . My own judgment, natural endowments, and education bowed to this simple, but mighty testimony. There sits the man who baptized me, (brother Eleazer Miller). It filled my system with light, and my soul with joy.[31]

Of course that is the remembrance, written twenty years after the event, by a man who had meanwhile had much experience with the Holy Ghost and who was trying to make a special point about its importance. But the original impact can be gauged by what we know of young Brigham's response. From President Young's many statements about this early experience, it is clear that Miller was so effective precisely because his "simple, but mighty testimony" *completed and fulfilled* — rather than crudely contradicted — what Brigham's own "judgment, natural endowments, and education" had already helped him to yearn for and now helped him to find in the Book of Mormon and the people who believed it. After all the partial fulfillments and disappointments of

his long search, the flood or famine of emotionality, the intellec-
tuality without common sense, the call to good works without
motivating power, the guilt and anxiety without any basis for the
self-esteem necessary for a successful process of repentance — after
all this, everything seemed to come together for him in Mormonism.

Shortly after his meeting with Eleazer Miller, Brigham went
with his brother Phineas and Heber Kimball to Miller's home
branch of the Church in Columbia:

> We conversed with them, attended their meetings and heard them
> preach, and after staying about one week we returned home, being
> still more convinced of the truth of the work, and anxious to learn
> its principles and to learn more of Joseph Smith's mission. The mem-
> bers of the Branch in Pennsylvania were the first in the Church who
> received the gift of tongues.[32]

Speaking in tongues may have been a severe test for the young
man who had earlier been repelled by the excesses of frontier
evangelical groups carried away by their religious ecstasy. But here
the context of edifying common sense and the balance of convincing rationality apparently made such emotional experiences
quite different. Brigham was not only able to accept speaking in
tongues as one of the appropriate signs that follow those who
believe but gradually responded personally, and even participated
in such expressions, as his suspicions concerning emotion and
ecstasy were calmed.

Phineas reports that when the group of them returned from
Pennsylvania they preached Mormonism along the way, though
from what he later said it seems the inexperienced Brigham took
no part; however, Brigham then took his horse and sleigh to
Canada to get his brother Joseph, a circuit-riding Methodist
preacher and missionary, and "told him what I had experienced of
the power of God."[33] Joseph and Phineas and their father actually
joined the Church a week before Brigham did, having traveled
again to the little Mormon branch in Columbia. But then Eleazer
Miller went from there to Mendon and baptized Brigham on April
15, 1832 — with dramatic results:

> I recollect the Sunday morning on which I was baptized, in my own
> little mill stream; . . . I passed the day in meeting, and one week
> from that day I had the pleasure of meeting with and preaching to a
> large congregation. I think there were present on that occasion four
> experienced Elders, formerly of the Methodist and Baptist persua-

sions, who had received the Gospel and had been numbered with us. I expected to hear them address the people on the principles that we had just received through the servants of the Lord. They said that the Spirit of the Lord was not upon them to speak to the people, yet they had been preachers for years. I was but a child, so far as public speaking and a knowledge of the world was concerned; but the Spirit of the Lord was upon me, and I felt as though my bones would consume within me unless I spoke to the people and told them what I had seen, heard and learned — what I had experienced and rejoiced in; and the first discourse I ever delivered I occupied over an hour. I opened my mouth and the Lord filled it.[34]

Much earlier than this recollection Brigham had included in his personal history a few more details concerning his feelings on the day of his baptism that suggest reasons for the powerful changes taking place: "Before my clothes were dry on my back [Brother Miller] laid his hands on me and ordained me an Elder, at which I marvelled. According to the words of the Savior I felt a humble, child-like spirit, witnessing unto me that my sins were forgiven."[35] It seems that the childlike meekness and sense of acceptance in God's universe — but also the virile joy in being called and authorized by divine sanction to *do* something through the authority and commission of a lay priesthood — combined to release enormous reserves of spiritual energy and ability in young Brigham. He not only soon preached his first sermon, feeling there the direct power of spiritual gifts, but a few weeks after his baptism, while with a group gathered at Heber Kimball's house for family prayer, he reports that "the Spirit came on me, and I spoke in tongues, and we thought only of the day of Pentecost."[36]

One of the most interesting, and most significant, changes was that release of language in Brigham, evidenced not only in his gift of tongues and his launching himself on a series of preaching missions to spread the gospel but also in his beginning his first diary a few days after his baptism. That first sketchy record, covering the years 1832-35, is our earliest "holograph" (personally handwritten) evidence of Brigham's experiences and feelings. It is a miracle, given the persecutions, travels, and sharp disruptions of Brigham's life, that the small notebook, and three others somewhat like it covering parts of the years until 1844, survived at all. The holograph diaries are even less introspective or reflective than the histories kept for him by various scribes after 1844; they primarily report places visited on his numerous missions, distances traveled, numbers baptized.[37] But they give us the most direct early evidence of how he perceived his work and some indirect evidence of what he sometimes felt. Together with the fairly large number of surviving holograph letters written after 1840, they reveal a man of tenderness, spiritual warmth, and insight, as well as the more commonly known Brigham of great energy and devotion.

These early writings in his own hand also show that Brigham Young, as one would expect an intelligent man without formal education to do and as most people in the nineteenth century who were not trained clerks also did, tended to spell words phonetically, the way they were spoken to and by him, rather than according to the arbitrary conventions of standard English (which in fact did not become rigid and a criterion of acceptability until the twentieth century). Having now recovered somewhat from the extreme pruderies of the genteel tradition, we are able to recognize in Brigham's phonetic spelling and his untutored early grammar instructive, and sometimes moving, indications of how he actually spoke. We can also gauge the progress of his remarkable self-education after his conversion. This dramatic, though as we shall see, rather painful, evolution into a man of words as well as action seems to me important and revealing—of both Brother Brigham and of Mormonism. Morris R. Werner, perhaps his best non-Mormon biographer, wrote, "Without Brigham Young the Mormons would never have been important after the first few years of their institutional life, but without the Mormons Brigham Young might have been a great man."[38] Despite the many virtues in his book, Werner has this exactly backwards. It can indeed be argued that Brigham Young saved the Church from disintegration at Joseph Smith's death, but he did so because of qualities and resources available to him only because he had embraced Mormonism. And he did in fact become a "great man," but not in spite of but precisely by means of what Mormonism did to him—especially in opening to him the Word and thus giving play to the great potential within him. *Without* Mormonism he would likely have continued to develop as a fine craftsman, probably becoming well known throughout one New York county at most and, perhaps, after ten or fifteen years winning election to a term or two of the state legislature. *Within* Mormonism his soul, formerly shut up or forced to find expression mainly through his hands, cascaded forth in a torrent of action and especially of words—writing, preaching, proselyting, speaking in tongues, even joyfully *singing* in tongues:

"Mormonism" has done everything for me that ever has been done for me on the earth; it has made me happy, it has made me wealthy and comfortable; it has filled me with good feelings, with joy and rejoicing. Whereas, before I possessed the spirit of the Gospel, I was troubled with that which I hear others complain of, that is, with, at times, feeling cast down, gloomy, and desponding; with everything wearing to me, at times, a dreary aspect.[39]

Brigham Young eventually became the most voluminous, wide-ranging, and, in my judgment, the most conceptually power-ful orator the Mormon Church has produced, and he is certainly one of the most original, entertaining, and personally expressive of all those who have used the English language. But he became such because of the impetus provided by his conversion and because of the continuing pressure of his excitement about the gospel, the duty it placed on him to develop himself and to share, and the courage it gave him to do his best.

Brigham was very conscious of his lack of training and experi-ence—and of the rejection, even ridicule, that he experienced (not only before he became a Mormon but among some of his brethren in the Church) because of his humble background and unpolished speech. Heber Kimball reports that when the Youngs moved to Mendon in 1829 "they were in lowly circumstances and . . . of course were looked down upon by the flourishing church where we lived . . . to them, my heart was united."[40] And Brigham much later remembered that when he and Heber were called as apostles "some of the knowing ones marvelled. . . . When they would meet brother Kimball and myself, their looks expressed, 'What a pity!' "[41] Brigham knew his deficiencies as compared with others ("I am personally as well acquainted with my own weaknesses as any other mortal is with them"[42]), but he also learned—in Mormonism —what responding to a sense of duty and constant effort can do:

> Men who understand language, who were taught it in their youth, who have had the privilege of schools and good education, [amaze me when they] get up and tell how they shrink from addressing this people.
>
> When I think of myself, I think just this—I have the grit in me, and I will do my duty any how. When I began to speak in public, I was about as destitute of language as a man could well be. But tell about being bashful, when a man has all the learning and words he can ask for! With scores and hundreds of thousands of words with which to convey one's ideas, and then tell about being bashful before a people! How I have had the headache, when I had ideas to lay before the people, and not words to express them; but I was so gritty that I always tried my best.[43]

Brigham's anxiety and effort to improve on his abilities persisted throughout his life. As late as 1863 he was telling the Saints, "I am limited in knowledge and in the ability to convey the knowledge that is within me and often resort to gestures to convey what my language fails to impart; neither am I mighty in writing."[44] His daughter Susa reports that "he had acquired the habit of copying the definition of any new word (or one new to him) on a slip of paper; and a conversation well guided, or a later public discourse would furnish a form in which to wrestle with the word and make it his own through use."[45] This general kind of effort to improve his vocabulary and knowledge, coupled, of course, with the huge number of discourses he delivered, had obvious results.

Brother Brigham apparently never prepared specifically for a speech:

> When I have endeavored to address a congregation, I have almost always felt a repugnance in my heart to the practice of premeditation, or of pre-constructing a discourse to deliver to the people, but let me ask God my heavenly Father, in the name of Jesus Christ, to give me His Spirit, and put into my heart the things He wishes me to speak whether they be for better or worse. . . . I would ask . . . that we might speak and hear with an understanding heart, that a hint, a key word, or a short sentence pertaining to the things of God, might open the vision of our minds, so that we might comprehend the things of eternity, and rejoice exceedingly therein.[46]

Yet it seems that despite the difficulties and continuing struggles, Brigham, as President of the Church, eventually became confident that he had grown able to succeed in what was for him the greatest purpose for words:

> I think that I tell you the words of the Lord Almighty every time I rise here to speak to you. I may blunder in the use of the English language; but suppose I should use language that would grate on the ears of some of the learned, what of that? God can understand it, and so could you, if you had the Spirit of the Lord. . . .
>
> If I do not speak here by the power of God, if it is not revelation to you every time I speak to you here, I do not magnify my calling. . . . I shall be removed from the place I occupy.[47]

He rejoiced in his God-given and self-developed ability that could be used to shape ideas and feelings for the benefit of others as his hands had shaped wood and glass:

> What is the best thing you have to devote to the kingdom of God? It is the talents God has given you. . . . What a beautiful gift! It is

more precious than fine gold that I can stand here and give you my ideas, and you can rise up and tell me what you think and feel, and thus exchange our ideas.[48]

Brigham Young particularly appreciated the speaking of Heber C. Kimball. A Jewish artist who visited Utah remarked that Heber "speaks fluently, his language is inornate, and indicates an original mind without cultivation." Fanny Stenhouse said, "Everyone likes Heber for his outspoken, honest bluntness." Heber said, "I can make grammar as fast as anybody."[49] And Brigham, whose language is also described by those comments, said it better than any of them:

> I rejoice in the words of brother Heber this day. He has spoken by the power of the Holy Ghost, and you are his witnesses. . . . and his ideas are as rich, I may say, as the flowers of eternity, and his ideas and his words are congenial to my feelings and spirit. He told you here to-day that we never differ — that I say, "Go ahead, say what you please."
> . . . You cannot, the best of you, beat brother Kimball's language. You may call up the college-bred man, and he cannot beat it.[50]

Heber came from a background as ungenteel as Brigham's; he made similar changes (he was baptized the day after Brigham); and he became Brigham's closest friend and advisor (from 1829 they were never apart more than a few weeks — except for Heber's one-year mission to England in 1837 — until Heber died in 1868 while serving as Brigham's counselor in the First Presidency). Heber reports that when he moved to Mendon in 1820 as an apprentice to his brother, a potter, he took great pains to get the best quality clay for his work, even hauling it a long distance; throughout his life, like Brigham, he was proud of the skill of his hands. He, too, let the imagery of that early vocation enrich his speech and inform his sense of the value of good, honest work and the supreme value of helping to shape people, even influencing Brigham (who may well have assisted Heber at the wheel or the kiln) to adopt some of his potter's terms as images in talking about people and religion.

Heber reports that after Brigham's father moved to Mendon in 1827 the old man used to come and see Heber and his wife Vilate (the old man's granddaughter) almost every day "and would sit and talk with us and pray and jump and sing and do anything that was good to make us lively and happy, and we loved him."[51] This helps balance the picture of a dour John Young we get from Brigham's childhood reminiscences, and it helps us understand that his father was able to grow beyond the harsh pressures of puritan training and frontier survival to become the first patriarch ordained in the Church.[52] When Brigham moved to Mendon in 1829, three of his brothers and two sisters, in addition to his father, were already there, and his sister Fanny was living with the Kimballs, helping her daughter Vilate. The Youngs and Kimballs quickly became close friends—working together, joining together in their religious searches, the Youngs naming their second daughter, born in 1830, after Heber's wife, and the Kimballs taking Miriam during her last illness to their home where, consoled, even exultant, in her new-found faith, she finally died of her tuberculosis in September 1832, only a few months after her baptism.

Brigham and Heber had occasionally visited nearby families and branches of the Church that summer of 1832 and had preached the gospel and baptized some. Like many others they were anxious to meet Joseph Smith, and about three weeks after Miriam's death they left both sets of children with Vilate and set out, with Brigham's brother Joseph, for Kirtland, visiting various Church groups on the way. Brigham records, "We exhorted them and prayed with them, and I spoke in tongues. Some pronounced it genuine and from the Lord, and other pronounced it of the Devil." They found the Prophet and his brothers-in-law chopping and hauling wood in the forest behind Newell K. Whitney's store, where Joseph and Emma were then living. To find a prophet thus employed reassured more than it surprised a laboring man like Brigham: "Here my joy was full at the privilege of shaking the hand of the Prophet of God, and received the sure testimony, by the Spirit of prophecy, that he was all that any could believe him to be, as a true Prophet. He was happy to see us, and bid us welcome."[53] They stayed for supper and for a gathering of some of the brethren that evening where they "conversed together upon the things of the kingdom." Heber recalled many years later that they "had a glorious time; during which brother Brigham spoke in tongues before brother Joseph, it being the first time he had heard any one speak in tongues. We had a precious season and returned with a blessing in our souls." Brigham himself related, in his Manuscript History:

> We tarried about one week in Kirtland, held meetings nearly every night, and the blessings of the Lord were extensively upon us. I baptized one man while in Kirtland, by the name of Gibson Smith, the father of Newel K. Whitney's wife, who had just come from Connecticut to learn the things that were being revealed. Being con-

vinced of the truth of the work, he requested me to go into the waters with him.[54]

Brigham and Heber continued with local preaching journeys that fall, and then in December, Brigham, again with his brother, went on his first real mission to Canada, where Joseph Young had earlier preached Methodism and was quite well known. The two brothers were given a specific assignment to convert a man by the name of Artemus Millett, whom Joseph Young had known during his earlier work in Canada and whom they had recommended when Joseph Smith talked with them in October about the need for a mason for the proposed Kirtland Temple. According to Millett's journal, the young Church President said to the brothers, "I give you a mission to go and baptize him into the church and tell him to bring $1,000 with him."[55] The Youngs traveled over five hundred miles on foot, "most of the way through snow and mud from one to two feet deep," and finally crossed six miles of thin ice on the east end of Lake Ontario (where the St. Lawrence River begins) to get to Kingston:

> We commenced preaching and bearing our testimony to the people. Proceeding [north] to West Loboro, we remained about one month preaching the Gospel there and in the regions round about. We baptized about 45 souls, and organized the West Loboro and other Branches. In the month of February 1833, we started for home, crossing from Kingston on the ice, just before it broke up.[56]

Artemus Millett had been baptized by Brigham on February 18 in Loboro; and that summer Brother Millett sold his property and moved to Kirtland with more than the requested one thousand dollars to help with the temple.

When Brigham returned to Mendon he lived with the Kimballs, where his daughters had been living since their mother's death. In April he took the children on a boat from Palmyra along the Erie Canal to stay with their Grandmother Works in Aurelius, also preaching for two weeks in the area of Auburn. Then he went to Canada again, preaching, baptizing, and encouraging the previously formed branches and organizing a new one—all with increasing confidence. Following is an exact transcription from his diary, which records more spontaneous feelings and reactions than the fully edited Manuscript History written over ten years later (as well as suggesting the sound of his voice):

> 29 Monday went to Lob[o]ro. Had a prair meting in the evning, found the Brotherin in good helth and in good Sperits. Their has been 17 Seventeen Baptized sence Brother Joseph and I left heir. . . .

. . . . 30 thursday went to Brother N. Lake. Held a meting at one o'clock. Had good liberty in preaching.

June 1,th 1833 preached at 10 A.M. at Peater Rice's — took Dinner at Brother Picksley's, then attended Reform Methodist quarteley meting in the afternoon.

2 Sunday held meting at Brother Daniel Wood at 10 A.M. At 4 P.M. at Stiles' barn and Baptized three. . . .

8 Saterday met in confrence with seven Elders . . . two teachers ordained. . . .

17 Preached at the Loge schoole house west of Brother Mil[l]et's.[57]

Following revelations in early 1833, commanding that a stake of Zion and a temple be established at Kirtland, Joseph Smith had begun to counsel the Saints to gather there. Accordingly, in July Brigham brought "Brother N. Lake's" family and other Canadian converts to Kirtland, where he helped them get permanently located and where they visited with the Prophet. Brigham returned home for a few months, but then went again on local preaching journeys throughout western New York, including an extended trip back along the Erie Canal to retrieve his children in Aurelius. In September, Brigham and Heber moved their own families to Kirtland, where, Brigham reports, "I tarried all winter, and had the privilege of listening to the teachings of the Prophet and enjoying the society of the Saints, working hard at my former trade."[58]

Apparently some of those who gathered in Kirtland had difficulty in finding the type of employment they wanted or getting paid on time, so they went off to surrounding towns for the winter. But during this time Brigham was beginning to develop and manifest an independent loyalty to Joseph and his teachings that was to become one of his most characteristic qualities and which would determine the course of his life:

> I told them I had gathered to Kirtland because I was so directed by the Prophet of God, and I was not going away . . . anywhere else to build up the Gentiles, but I was going to stay here and seek the things that pertained to the kingdom of God by listening to the teachings of his servants, and I should work for my brethren and trust in God and them that I would be paid. I labored for brother Cahoon and finished his house, and although he did not know he could pay me when I commenced, before I finished he had me paid in full. I then went to work for father John Smith and others, who paid me, and sustained myself in Kirtland, and when the brethren who had gone out to work for the Gentiles returned, I had means, though some of them were scant.[59]

For more important reasons than the material success his obedience brought, the winter was a significant and enjoyable one for Brigham. He began the shift from one vocation to another and deepened his personal relations and religious life. He slowly developed a close friendship with Joseph Smith, learning from him in direct conversation and maturing under the influence of such a powerful model. And that February, Brigham was married again, to Mary Ann Angell, a self-reliant and firm-minded convert from New England. Susa Young Gates, who was a daughter of one of Brigham's later plural wives and who knew Mary Ann well for over twenty years, describes her thus:

> She was a member of the Free Will Baptists and a Sunday School teacher. Her study of the Scriptures, especially the prophecies, so engrossed her mind, that she confidently looked for their fulfillment, in consequence of which she resolved never to marry until she should meet a "man of God," one in whom she could confide and with whom her heart could unite in the active duties of a Christian life. Thus it was that she remained single until nearly thirty years of age.[60]

Mary Ann's patience was not in vain, and she and Brigham built a remarkable marriage, one that moved Brigham often to make the homely pun that she was indeed an "Angell." The marriage not only survived but actually flourished under the series of persecutions and exoduses and Brigham's many long absences in response to calls from Joseph—even under the uniquely traumatic shock of being called to live "The Principle" of polygamy.

The first absence came only three months after the marriage. As part of a mission to the Plains Indians in 1831, Parley P. Pratt had established a branch of the Church at Independence in western Missouri and enthusiastically discussed it with Joseph; later the Prophet had received revelations that the long-prophesied new Zion upon the American continent should be established there. But persecution of the fast-growing colony developed very quickly—mainly because of the fears of the "old settlers" aroused by economic competition, inroads into struggling Protestant congregations, and especially the supposed threat of so many nonslaveholders. These causes were intensified by Mormon clannishness and by loose talk by some of the Saints about taking over the whole territory for their "promised land." After a series of increasingly violent incidents, the Mormons were driven north into Clay County in November 1833. In response to revelations received that winter (D&C 101 and 103) Joseph determined to take a force of men from Kirtland to demonstrate his support of the Missouri Saints (his concern had been questioned by some of them) and to seek legal redress and if necessary to effect a reinstatement by force with the help of state militia promised by letter from Missouri's Governor Dunklin. The Prophet organized two hundred volunteers for the thousand-mile march, using the pattern established by Moses for the exodus of the children of Israel—groups of hundreds broken down into fifties and then tens for delegation of leadership—that Brigham learned and later used in leading his own exodus.

Brigham decided to go and wanted Joseph Young to go with him, but he found that his brother was quite hesitant, knowing well the great dangers. Brigham later recorded:

> While walking together . . . we met the Prophet, who said to him, "Brother Joseph, I want you to go with us up to Missouri." I informed the Prophet that my brother was doubtful as to his duty about going, to which the Prophet replied, "Brother Brigham and brother Joseph, if you will go with me in the camp to Missouri and keep my counsel, I promise you, in the name of the Almighty, that I will lead you there and back again, and not a hair of your heads shall be harmed," at which my brother Joseph presented his hand to the Prophet, as well as myself, to confirm the covenant.[61]

Brigham did not keep his diary during the journey, but Heber Kimball and George A. Smith, Joseph Smith's seventeen-year-old cousin, both did. Heber tells of putting all his savings and surplus property into a general fund for the entire company (after finding that some could not pay their own way, the Prophet asked the group to consecrate and equally share all their resources for the trip) and says he left his family on May 5, not expecting to see them again. He tells of seeing angels guarding them on the way, of the spies sent out from curious or frightened towns en route and from the groups of citizens in Missouri planning to oppose them. He describes the night of June 19, 1834, soon after they arrived near Jackson County, when a fierce storm raged all around them and completely scattered large forces gathering to attack them; he tells of Joseph Smith's negotiating with leaders of the state and of local counties and finally receiving the Lord's instructions to depart peacefully, without using force to aid their Missouri brethren, since "I have heard their prayers, and will accept their offering; and it is expedient in me that they should be brought thus far for a trial of their faith."[62]

George A. Smith describes in greater detail the trial of faith that Brigham, along with others, passed so well. He tells of the Prophet's careful organization and instructions as they left, especially his emphasis that if they were humble and obedient to the Lord's commandments they would all be preserved and God would deliver them out of the hands of their enemies; but if, like the children of Israel, they forgot God "they would be vexed with sore displeasure." He gives graphic details of the sufferings of these literally tenderfoot "soldiers": of Joseph Smith's giving George A. his own pair of boots because the young man's feet hurt so much —and then suffering bloody blisters with his followers; of their being protected, according to Joseph's promise, from the fatal "milk sickness" that afflicted many settlers along their route; of continual trouble with a rebellious Sylvester Smith that grew into general faultfinding until Joseph prophesied that the camp would be visited with a scourge and "many would die like sheep with the rot." He describes mock battles and military exercises for diversion and training.

The diary tells of the various devices used to keep the nature of their journey secret in order to avoid alarm. One such camouflage was a Sunday meeting near Jacksonville, Illinois, for an audience from a town of three hundred, during which Joseph assigned a number of the brethren to assume various religious roles so they each could preach on an element of the gospel without being detected as Mormons. Joseph himself spoke as a "liberal freethinker," Orson Hyde, as a Campbellite, on restoration, Joseph Young on free grace as if a Methodist, and Brigham, as a Close Communion Baptist, on the necessity of baptism for salvation. George A. mentions that in the great storm of June 19 (when, as Heber expressed it, "the Lord fought in our defense") "one of our enemies was killed by lightning and another had his hand torn off by his horse."[63]

But then the young diarist relates how—in accord with Joseph Smith's prophecy—cholera began to afflict the camp on June 21, and by June 25 many, including himself and Joseph and Hyrum, were literally struck down to the ground by the disease. He reports Hyrum's description, "It seized us like the talons of a hawk." Brigham reports in his history, written later, that they remained in camp about a week, caring for nearly seventy who were sick and burying eighteen who died. Joseph then called them together and promised that the plague would stop immediately, with not another case, if they would covenant to humble themselves and obey the Lord's counsel, "whereupon the brethren with uplifted hands covenanted that they would from that very hour hearken to his counsel and obey his word, and the plague was stayed according to the words of the Lord through his servant." Brigham left for home, with his brother and a few others, on July 4. They arrived in Kirtland in August, "having performed a journey of about two thousand miles on foot in a little over three months, averaging forty miles per day while traveling."[64]

Brigham survived the physical and spiritual trials of that journey and learned much that confirmed his assurance of the Prophet's calling and reaffirmed his own willingness and ability to be loyal to Joseph. When challenged to explain what he had gotten out of such a difficult and apparently quixotic effort as that march to Missouri and back, Brigham said: "Just what we went for. I would not exchange the knowledge I received this season for the whole of [this] county; for property and mines of wealth are not to be compared to the worth of knowledge."[65] And Heber C. Kimball reminisced in 1845 about the effect on him and Brigham of the experience of "Zion's Camp":

> Since [then] we have never turned to the right or to the left. Neither of us was ever an enemy to Joseph Smith; we never pulled him back; we have always been ready to push him forwards; we never dictated to him in the first things, but we assisted him in carrying it out.[66]

Loyalty was clearly a central issue—and testing it for the developing Church organization was a central purpose of the journey. New members of the young organization, as yet without established traditions, were still learning how to relate to and rely upon a prophet. On the long march Brigham saw the disastrous results of contention and rebelliousness, and he formed a deep and permanent aversion to those attitudes. From the evidence of later events he also began on that journey to impress Joseph Smith with what he had learned.

Brigham was soon called on to use those lessons. That fall he effectively defended Joseph as a witness in a suit brought against the Prophet by a member of Zion's Camp who had apostatized, answering with precision and ready wit the questions put to him by the prosecutor. Such defenses against the growing spirit of disaffection, even rebellion, in Kirtland would become a prominent part of Brigham's life for the next three years. But that winter he continued using his time working on Church buildings, particularly the ambitious temple.

On February 14, 1835, Brigham and Heber were called to places in the first modern Quorum of Twelve Apostles, and from then on much of Brigham's time was taken up with meetings of instruction and counsel — and specific missions. He went on one mission in May to Indians living in New York (he called on a relative on the way and preached the gospel to him, but the man was "not inclined" to receive it, and, Brigham coolly notes, "To avoid calling on me to ask a blessing at table, he asked the blessing himself, probably for the first time in his life"[67]); he continued on into Vermont in June (where, as an evidence of growth and developing interest there, he preached to one responsive congregation of over two thousand); finally he went on to Massachusetts, where in September he visited many of his relatives. ("I found Grandmother alive and comfortably well for her. She expressed great joy for the privilege of seeing one of mother's children once more.")[68]

In the fall of 1835 Elder Young, as he was now called, had some time for his own family's needs, and that winter he was able to participate for a while in Joseph Smith's unusual Hebrew school, directed by a Jewish scholar, Joshua Seixas, who was hired to come from the Hudson (Ohio) Seminary to teach two groups of over twenty each. But then Brigham was asked to superintend the painting and finishing of the temple, enabling him to work with his early convert from Canada, Artemus Millett, who was supervising the masonry work. Millett gave primary attention to the exterior, for which he invented a hard plaster that sparkled brilliantly in the sun because of the glass and china dishes sacrificed by the Mormon sisters to be ground up in the plaster.[69]

For the new Church, with still less than five hundred members in the Kirtland area, many of whom had been uprooted by the "gathering" and were struggling for survival, the large, three-story, sixty-thousand-dollar building was a magnificent accomplishment, and their sacrifices and faith brought forth great spiritual manifestations at the time of the dedication services. To accommodate all the Saints, the dedicatory service of March 27 was repeated on March 31, with the Prophet repeating each time a richly comprehensive prayer that has been a model for such prayers in the temples built since. (See D&C 109.) Many who attended claimed in their journals that they felt the presence of angels and heard heavenly choirs participating. Heber wrote that he and many others *saw* an angel appear on the stand near Joseph.[70]

On April 3 one of the most magnificent and extensive contacts ever made between heaven and earth occurred: During a meeting in the temple, and while they were separated from the audience by curtains drawn in front of the pulpits, Joseph Smith and Oliver Cowdery saw the Savior appear, standing before them "upon the breastwork of the pulpit," and heard him announce:

> I am the first and the last; I am he who liveth, I am he who was slain. . . . Let the hearts of your brethren rejoice, and let the hearts of all my people rejoice, who have, with their might, built this house to my name. For behold, I have accepted this house, and my name shall be here; and I will manifest myself to my people in mercy in this house.[71]

Then Moses appeared "and committed unto us the keys of the gathering of Israel from the four parts of the earth, and the leading of the ten tribes from the land of the north." Then Elias came and "committed the dispensation of the gospel of Abraham, saying that in us and our seed all generations after us should be blessed." Finally Elijah stood before them, saying that he had come according to the prophecy of Malachi that he should be sent before the great and dreadful day of the Lord to turn the hearts of the children to the fathers, and he accordingly gave them the power to do saving ordinances for their dead ancestors and to seal families together in eternal union.

Brigham was in the temple, though on the other side of the curtains, when these visitations came to Joseph and Oliver, and he was greatly impressed and moved by such spiritual outpourings that went beyond normal empirical limitations and rational controls but retained a solid rationality and edifying content. In his own later history (his daily journal is silent through 1836) he defers to Joseph Smith's own account of these events and only adds:

> I attended the solemn assembly, and, with my brethren of the Twelve, received my washings and anointings, and was privileged to listen to the teachings and administrations of the Prophet of God. We also attended to the washing of feet, which ordinance was administered to me by the Prophet Joseph.[72]

No doubt to the new apostle one of the most impressive of the many incredible events was this last tender ordinance, initiated by Christ with his own Twelve and now practiced with the special, loving authority of the man Brigham had accepted as Christ's modern prophet.

Elder Young spent much of that year and the next on a series of very successful missions for the Church throughout New England, but when he returned to Kirtland in the fall of 1837 he found the Prophet in great trouble. In a manner Brigham later emulated as President of the Church (and which also brought Brigham misunderstanding and persecution), Joseph combined his religious role with practical efforts to build the kingdom of God in areas that are normally thought of as purely secular, in this case founding a bank which ultimately failed during the national "Panic of 1837." The shock to the Saints over failure of the bank was profound. Even though they had contributed to the difficulties with a spirit of speculation, many Church members blamed the Prophet, and apostasy ran wild. Even stalwarts like the apostle Parley P. Pratt, a dauntless early missionary and powerful thinker and writer, became disaffected—though some (like Elder Pratt) only temporarily.[73]

This crisis produced such antagonism that, at one time during October when Joseph was on a trip to Missouri, a council was held in the temple in which a number of Church leaders declared him a fallen prophet and moved to depose him in favor of David Whitmer. Brigham recorded:

> Father John Smith, Brother Heber C. Kimball and others were present, who were opposed to such measures. I rose up, and in a plain and forcible manner told them that Joseph was a Prophet, and I knew it, and that they might rail and slander him as much as they pleased, they could not destroy the appointment of the Prophet of God, they could only destroy their own authority, cut the thread that bound them to the Prophet and to God and sink themselves to hell. Many were highly enraged at my decided opposition to their measure, and Jacob Bump (an old pugilist) was so exasperated that he could not be still. Some of the brethren near him put their hands on him, and requested him to be quiet; but he writhed and twisted his arms and body saying, "How can I keep my hands off that man?" I told him if he thought it would give him any relief he might lay them on. This meeting was broken up without the apostates being able to unite on any decided measures of opposition.[74]

During the rest of 1837, Brigham was caught up in nearly constant, extremely dangerous, and at this point characteristically physical loyalty to his leader. On one occasion he learned of an attempt to be made on Joseph's life as the Prophet was returning by stagecoach to Kirtland from a trip to Michigan. Brigham took the Prophet's brother William out to the stagecoach by horse and buggy, substituted him in the coach, and took Joseph home safely.

This rather grim period was lightened somewhat by successful missionary work, in which the young apostle played an important part and through which he continued to mature. In October 1836 his cousin Willard Richards, who had read the Book of Mormon, came to Kirtland, lived with Brigham, and after thorough investigation of the gospel was baptized by him. A skilled doctor, for that time, and a fine thinker and writer, Willard came to have great influence on the developing Church as a missionary, later as President Young's secretary and historian, and finally as his counselor in the First Presidency. By March 1837, he went with Brigham on a mission to New England, where as part of their work they successfully preached to many other members of their related families. And in June, Willard was appointed by Joseph Smith to accompany Heber Kimball and Orson Hyde in the extremely important mission to England, the first one overseas.

In a later reminiscence Heber reports that when Joseph called him to go to England he felt great inadequacy, poured out his feelings to the Lord in the temple, and asked the Prophet if Brigham could go also. But the Prophet replied that he wanted Brigham to stay with him (possibly foreseeing Brigham's effective aid in the gathering storm in Kirtland) and promised Heber that he "would prove the source of salvation to thousands, not only in England but in America."[75] This prophecy was fulfilled literally. In fact it was the success of the mission to England—and the one three years later when Brigham and six others of the Twelve did accompany Heber—that counterbalanced the external persecutions in Missouri and the internal divisions in Ohio and literally saved the Church.

Brigham's own increasingly mature sense of inner peace and assurance, despite the constant decisive action demanded of him and the constant danger whirling around him, is revealed in his description of a mission on which he accompanied Joseph and other Church leaders in the summer of 1837. Barely out of Kirtland on their way east, Joseph was arrested five times; each time, after some harassment, he was released for lack of cause or after the payment of a small fine or the leaving of a watch or other property as security:

> Next day we started again, and travelled by land as far as Ashtabula, shunning Painesville and other places where we suspected our enemies were laying in wait to annoy Joseph. We tarried in Ashtabula through the day, wandering over the bluffs, through the woods and on the beach of the lake, bathing ourselves in her beautiful waters, until evening, when a steamboat arrived from the west. We went on board and took passage for Buffalo. I gave the Prophet my valise for a pillow, and I took his boots for mine, and we all laid down on the deck of the vessel for the night.[76]

But another kind of maturity apparent at this time evidences that Brigham's loyalty to Joseph and the Church had become intelligently effective as well as physically courageous, and that he had developed the qualities necessary for independent action:

> Sept. 3 [1837]—This day was appointed for the Saints to meet in Conference to reorganize the Church. Owing to the disaffection existing in the hearts of many, I went to the brethren whose votes could be relied on, early in the morning, and had them occupy the stand and prominent seats. At 9, a.m., the services commenced; Joseph and his first counsellor were received, his second counsellor: F. G. Williams, was laid over, not being present. The members of the Quorum of the Twelve in good standing, and the Authorities, generally, were sustained. We were also enabled to disfellowship those of the Twelve and others seeking to bring disunion and destruction upon the Church. The apostates and disaffected, not being united, were compelled to endure the chagrin of witnessing the accomplishment of the will of God and the Prophet.[77]

Such actions by Brigham, and his forceful public defense of the Prophet, so inflamed the apostates that on December 22, even before Joseph was forced to leave, he had to take his family and flee Kirtland for his life, leaving behind a home and property he valued at about four thousand dollars.

After wintering in Dublin, Indiana, with his brother Lorenzo, Brigham moved on to Missouri and settled on Mill Creek near Far West in Caldwell County (an area planned out for settlement by Joseph Smith in a journey there the year before). He quickly built up a home and valuable property again, though Mary Ann was sick for several months and required his care. Meanwhile, some of the Missourians, inflamed by growing resentments that had a variety of causes, and, especially in the fall with time on their hands after the corn harvest was in, began to persecute their Mormon neighbors, who were developing large, successful farming cooperatives and whose numbers were approaching fifteen thousand. Violence intensified as this lawless element became moved by a lust for looting and for eventually taking over the Saints' land and homes, as well as by understandable anxiety about Mormon economic success and opposition to slavery.

The governor sent militia in response to Joseph's requests, but these men joined with the mobs in the persecutions. Despite some effective resistance by a Mormon militia raised by Mormon Colonels Lyman Wight and George Hinkle—and the sympathetic assistance of non-Mormon Generals David Atchison and Alexander

Doniphan—superior numbers overwhelmed the outlying settle-ments, and refugees poured into Far West, the main settlement in predominantly Mormon-populated Caldwell County.

The Caldwell militia, made up of resident Mormons, pursued a group of apparent mobbers who had taken some Saints hostage, and a battle ensued in which one Missourian and three Mormons, including the apostle David W. Patten, were killed. Rumor spread that the Missouri group (which, unknown to the Mormons, was also enlisted as a militia) had been massacred, and the whole state was aroused. Large mobs moved toward Far West, and Governor Lilburn Boggs, who had taken political advantage of the earlier persecutions at Independence, after receiving only the reports of militia and mob leaders, issued his notorious "Extermination Order" to the field commander of the state militia: "The Mormons must be treated as enemies, and must be exterminated or driven from the state if necessary for the public peace—their outrages are beyond description." After receiving this order a militia of two hundred men attacked an unresisting settlement of Mormons at Haun's Mill, killing seventeen, including at least one child, wounding twelve and mutilating some of them, looting the homes and taking cattle and wagons, and raping a number of the women.

By October 30 the main militia had massed outside Far West, and the Mormons, with the news of the "Haun's Mill Massacre" fresh in their hearts, prepared for battle. The militia's leader, General Samuel Lucas, drew up terms which called essentially for unconditional surrender: The Saints were to give up all arms and the Church leaders were to surrender for trial and punishment; Mormon property was to be confiscated to raise appropriations to pay the costs of the "war"; and all Mormons were to immediately leave the state. In an action inexplicable except as treachery, the Mormon militia leader, George Hinkle, agreed to the terms and returned and told Joseph and other Mormon leaders that General Lucas wanted a conference. But when they went, Hinkle turned them over as prisoners. After taking away the Mormon militia's arms, Lucas dismissed his own forces, many of whom turned im-mediately into mobs. Brigham had watched Joseph and the others give themselves up and was an eyewitness to what followed:

They commenced their ravages by plundering the citizens of their bedding, clothing, money, wearing apparel, and every thing of value they could lay their hands upon, and also attempted to violate the chastity of the women in sight of their husbands and friends, under pretence of hunting for prisoners and arms. The soldiers shot down our oxen, cows, hogs and fowls, at our doors, taking part away and leaving the rest to rot in the street.[78]

Joseph Smith, Sidney Rigdon, Parley P. Pratt, and a number of other Church leaders who had been turned over by Hinkle were court-martialed on November 1 and sentenced by Lucas to be executed the next morning, but General Doniphan absolutely refused the order Lucas sent him to carry out the executions and threatened Lucas with prosecution if they were carried out by anyone else. The Church leaders were finally jailed at Richmond, then some, including Joseph, were taken to Liberty jail and remained there until April, when they were allowed to escape.

With David Patten killed and Thomas Marsh alienated from the faith, Elders Young and Kimball were suddenly left as the senior apostles, and the Prophet instructed them by letter to take charge and evacuate the Saints into then friendly Illinois. Brigham, being the slightly older of the two, was deferred to as the leader, and he immediately began to act with impressive effectiveness as well as energy. At a public meeting, called to discuss how they could respond to the governor's order to leave, the new chief apostle made the proposal

> that we this day enter into a covenant to stand by and assist each other to the utmost of our abilities in removing from this state, and that we will never desert the poor who are worthy, till they shall be out of the reach of the exterminating order.[79]

He also mobilized the help of a number of non-Mormons who were appalled by the circumstances of the Mormon refugees. Brigham had not been captured with the Church leaders, apparently because he was not yet well known to the Missourians or even thought important by Mormon traitors. But with this sudden leadership activity he came under attack and had to escape, so that the remainder of the exodus was carried out by committees he had organized and was led by Heber Kimball, who was even less well known, having just returned from England.

In the meantime the Mormon leader had been welcomed by citizens of Quincy, Illinois, and invited to settle the exiled Saints near there. After the large groups led by Heber had escaped, Brigham returned eleven times to help others until over twelve thousand were evacuated, leaving property and possessions worth in excess of two million dollars. Despite the hospitality of people in Quincy, who took many in, the Saints suffered much sickness and many deaths as they camped in tents and dugouts along the Iowa and Illinois shores of the Mississippi River.

During this time of transition and trouble, Brigham, through his actions and the spirit of his leadership, also inspired many others to action. He reports meeting with the Twelve in Quincy on March 17 to respond to a request for teams and money to remove fifty destitute families still in Far West:

> Though the brethren were poor and stripped of almost everything, yet they manifested a spirit of willingness to do their utmost, offering to sell their hats, coats, and shoes to accomplish the object. We broke bread and partook of the sacrament. At the close of the meeting $50 was collected in money, and several teams were subscribed to go and bring the brethren. Among the subscribers was widow Warren Smith, whose husband and son had their brains blown out, another son shot to pieces at Haun's Mill. She sent her only team on this charitable mission.[80]

Even when most of the Saints (other than those who had deserted the Church) had been successfully evacuated before the ultimate deadline, Brigham continued his forceful leadership; he inspired the Twelve to return to Far West to fulfill the Lord's revelation, given back in July 1838, which expressly commanded them to leave from there *the following April 26* for their missions to England. Despite the governor's ultimatum and the boasts of mob leaders that this was one "prophecy by Joe Smith" that would not be fulfilled because they would kill anyone who tried, Brigham led the apostles back to Far West, and they obeyed the Lord's instructions to the letter — in what seems a powerful indication of the maturity the new Church leader had reached. He was no longer young Brigham.

Brigham Young In England　　2

The two years between April 1839, when Brigham Young led a majority of the Twelve Apostles in a daring, necessarily secret, formal farewell ceremony, deep in enemy territory in Far West, and April 1841, when he triumphantly led them back from their mission in England, may have been the two most important of his life—in both accomplishment and personal development. Such a claim would, of course, be difficult to prove, but that period of Brigham Young's life has been neglected by historians and biographers—and many who think they know much about Brother Brigham are not aware that he participated in the justly famous mass conversions in Herefordshire usually associated primarily with Wilford Woodruff; or that he preached in London and visited St. Paul's Cathedral and the British Museum; or that in England he spoke in tongues, healed the lame and sick, compiled a book of hymns, published the Book of Mormon and prepared an index for it, established and for a time edited the *Millennial Star*—all while welding the Quorum of the Twelve into a unified, smoothly working executive and apostolic body, with himself firmly at its head.

Those two years were a chastening in the crucible for both the Quorum and Brigham, full of the most intense suffering of mind and body and great struggle against the opposition of man and nature and, as they believed, the very devil. And the obvious, tangible rewards were magnificent: the firm establishment of a foreign mission system that brought in over seven thousand converts the first year; the continuation of that missionary effort with great success under the organization and spiritual impetus set by the Twelve; and the development of a stream of immigrants which was immediately able to strengthen the severely wounded Church as it recovered from the flight from Kirtland and the Missouri expulsion and which eventually brought nearly a hundred thousand European Saints to settle the Great Basin Kingdom.

The changes in Brigham Young were perhaps as important for the future of the Church as those achievements. For one thing, the rather brash, uneasy Brigham was softened and mellowed, nurtured in self-confidence. He earned acceptance, by himself as well as by the Quorum, in his role as a leader, decision-maker and spiritual example. Of course, the trial that produced such changes was severe. Heber C. Kimball wrote his wife Vilate on September 19, 1840, one year after the difficult and poignant parting of the apostles from their sick and destitute families, who were left clinging to life in the swampy flats of Montrose and Commerce: "I have aged more in one year past than five years previous. . . . Brother Brigham and G.A. Smith has failed in the same way."

Brigham had not only aged; he had *matured* more in that year than in the five previous. And so had the Quorum. In April 1841, just before most of them departed for home, Wilford Woodruff describes, in the characteristic detail of his journal, the final meetings of the eight apostles who went to England (plus Orson Hyde, who had just arrived on his way to Palestine). He tells of all nine apostles bearing testimony to the general conference in Manchester: "It is seldom that any congregation is privileged with as much testimony as on this occasion for this is the first time that so many of the twelve have met together for about four years." And he comments again and again on the special spirit: "Perfect union and harmony prevailed in all the deliberations of our councils for the past four days."[1] The Quorum had indeed achieved a special spirit of cooperation and self-confidence through their labors together, through the success that had attended their decision-making and actions, and through the process of meeting regularly together in conferences and council meetings since arriving in England (about every three months in official conferences, along with much counseling together in smaller groups and writing to each other as they shared very similar experiences). As Heber C. Kimball reported to his wife not long after the arrival in England and the initial success, "The Twelve are one for they all draw together."[2] And just a few days later, while sitting at a table with Brigham Young and other brethren selecting hymns for the hymn book they had decided to publish, he wrote, "There never was better feelings among the Twelve than at this time; all things go on well."[3]

And indeed things *were* going on well. Only three years before, when Joseph Smith had, with similar prophetic daring, sent two members of the Twelve on a mission to England, it had been a dark hour for the Church and himself. Joseph had been in the midst of persecution and apostasy in Kirtland, Ohio, because of tensions brought on by the failure of the Church-sponsored bank during the nationwide financial panic of 1837. At that time, rather than conservatively concentrating his forces, the Prophet had sent many Church leaders on missions throughout the East. He had also commissioned the apostles Heber C. Kimball and Orson Hyde and others to inaugurate overseas missionary work by preaching in England for a year. There they had good initial success, building a number of branches with a total membership of over fifteen hundred and leaving an ongoing mission in the hands of Joseph Fielding, Willard Richards, and William Clayton. But though conversions continued, losses from membership had kept the total strength about the same, and the impetus provided by the arrival of members of the Twelve in 1840 was dramatic. Again the Prophet had responded to persecution, this time the near extermination of the Saints in Missouri, with radical courage, sending his strongest group of supporters abroad to build the kingdom rather than clutching them close. Such inspired daring did indeed save the Church—by doubling its membership in one year; by starting the continuous flow of faithful and in many cases skilled converts who would help build Nauvoo and create the Zion in the mountains; and by testing, training, and unifying the group of missionaries (apostles and others) who would have to resolve the great crisis of leadership at Joseph Smith's death and would then provide four of the Church's presidents, those who would govern it to the dawn of the twentieth century.

Wilford Woodruff, whose success in England is best known, was constantly amazed at what the Lord was using him and his colleagues to do. At the end of his mission, while visiting the places he hàd entered as a stranger only twelve months before but where there were now fifteen hundred baptized converts, all ready to go to Zion, he reflected: "I have never seen so many Saints receive the work of God in so short a time and so many ordained Elders, Priests, etc., as on this occasion, and what adds much joy and consolation to my mind . . . is that (with very few exceptions) the officers and members universally have maintained their integrity, kept the faith, and are faithfully passing through many trials for Christ's sake."[4] Brigham Young's own summary on parting is, characteristically, somewhat reserved and general:

> It was with a heart full of thanksgiving and gratitude to God, my heavenly Father, that I reflected upon his dealings with me and my

brethren of the Twelve during the past year of my life, which was spent in England. It truly seemed a miracle to look upon the contrast between our landing and departing from Liverpool. We landed in the spring of 1840, as strangers in a strange land and penniless, but through the mercy of God we have gained many friends, established Churches in almost every noted town and city in the kingdom of Great Britain, baptized between seven and eight thousand, printed 5,000 Books of Mormon, 3,000 Hymn Books, 2,500 volumes of the *Millennial Star*, and 50,000 tracts, and emigrated to Zion 1,000 souls, established a permanent shipping agency, which will be a great blessing to the Saints, and have left sown in the hearts of many thousands the seeds of eternal truth, which will bring forth fruit to the honor and glory of God, and yet we have lacked nothing to eat, drink or wear: in all things I acknowledge the hand of God.[5]

But in addition to these public achievements, Brigham made of his English mission an intense experience of personal development. We have a more concentrated insight into his inner feelings and growth during this period than any other because from it comes over half of his surviving holograph writings: two diaries and fifteen letters.[6] These writings from his own hand, which have been neglected by his biographers, reveal at the beginning stages of the mission a sensitive, somewhat droll and self-deprecating and in some ways still relatively young and inexperienced man in his late thirties. They go on to help reveal his development as a self-confident executive planner and doer and a mature spiritual leader capable of meeting the coming challenges of his forties in Nauvoo and on the plains west.

The mission to England began with two dramatic departures more characteristic of the earlier Brigham, the rashly faithful disciple of Joseph who would dare anything for the Lord and his Prophet. When what was apparently the last of the Saints publicly left Far West on April 20, 1839, both they and the Church's enemies were convinced no one would return. But Brigham Young was already preparing to do just that, along with Orson Pratt and John Taylor, the available members of the Twelve (Parley P. Pratt was still in prison, John Page was somewhere on the road with the refugees, and Heber C. Kimball was waiting in hiding in Far West). The three apostles first named had met in Quincy and considered other leaders' arguments that in the Saints' persecuted condition the Lord would not require the Quorum of the Twelve to fulfill to the letter his year-old instructions about leaving for their missions to England from Far West.[7] It would be remarkable enough to go on such missions at all, given their present straits. The others agreed with Brigham, however, that "the Lord God had spoken and it was our duty to obey and leave the event in his hands and he would protect us."[8] Brigham Young's characteristic forcefulness is revealed in his own account of how he brought one member of the Quorum along with them after they had started back into Missouri:

> We met brother John E. Page and his family on a sideling hill, with his load turned bottom-side upwards: among other things, he had upset a barrel of soft soap, and he was elbow deep in the soap, scooping it up with his hands. I told him I wanted him to go to Far West with us. He replied, he did not see that he could, as he had his family to take to Quincy. I told him his family would get along well enough, and I desired him to go up with us. He asked how much time I would give him to get ready. I answered, five minutes. We assisted in loading his wagon, he drove down the hill and camped, and returned with us.[9]

Meeting at the temple site at Far West extremely early on the morning of the day designated, April 26, the five apostles (Brigham Young, Heber C. Kimball, Orson Pratt, John E. Page, and John Taylor) ordained Wilford Woodruff and George A. Smith (both previously nominated by the First Presidency and sustained by the Church), thus providing a bare minimum quorum of seven apostles present, directed the laying of a token stone for the foundation of the temple, and "took their leave . . . agreeable to the revelation."[10] At real peril to their lives, nineteen men and women, who had not yet escaped Missouri and thus were in hiding, had gathered so the seven apostles could literally, as directed by revelation, "take leave of my saints in the city of Far West."

The apostles returned to Illinois (taking the last group of refugees with them), assisted in settling the scattered Saints on the future site of Nauvoo, and spent the summer getting ready for their missions—preparing physically as much as their destitute condition would allow and spiritually through meetings with the Prophet. A particularly memorable gathering was held at Brigham Young's house on July 2, though he recorded only that "brother Joseph taught many important glorious principles calculated to benefit and bless [us] on [our] missions."[11] As usual, Wilford Woodruff provided much more detail: President Smith blessed each missionary and his wife individually ("If we were faithful," Woodruff wrote, "we had the promise of again returning to the bosom of our families and being blessed on our missions and having many souls as seals of our ministry") and then gave counsel which Elder Woodruff recorded carefully and which all the apostles, on the evidence of their actions and journal reflections in England, took literally as the guide for their work. Given their past troubles with dissension and apostasy, it was advice much more relevant to their welfare than the practical instructions on funding their trip or organizing their work that some might have expected:

> Then Joseph arose and presented some precious things of the king-dom unto us in the power of the Holy Ghost, yea precious principles that ought to be engraven upon our hearts and practiced in our lives. . . . Ever keep in exercise the principles of mercy and be ready to forgive our brother on the first intimations of repentance and asking forgiveness and should we even forgive our enemy before they ask it our heavenly father would be equally as merciful unto us. And also we ought to be willing to repent of and confess all of our own sins and keep nothing back, and let the Twelve be humble and not be exalted and beware of pride and not seek to excell one above another. But act for each other's good and honorably make mention of each other's name in our prayers before the Lord and before our fellow men, and not backbite and devour our brother.[12]

When the apostles tried to leave in August, the malaria that infested the low, swampy ground where they had settled along the Mississippi had disabled nearly everyone, and it seemed to them that dark powers struggled to hold them back. John Taylor was among the first to leave (on August 8), since he was then relatively well, though on his journey he became extremely ill and had to be left behind for a while. His wife, Leonora, wrote him on September 9:

> This has been a distressed place since you left, with Sickness. Allmost evry individual in evry Family sick . . . we were expecting Joseph [their baby] would die but the Lord spard my dear Child in answer to Prayer. Mary Anne is well and I keep upon my Feet *grunting about*. . . .
>
> Brother Young Family are all sick, him and all. The[y] could not get a drop of watter. I feched them several Pails.[13]

Brigham Young's own description of his departure, a few days after Sister Taylor's letter, is simple, quite restrained—as his daughter later said of it, "like his own character, devoid of high lights or grewsome details":[14]

> September 14, 1839.—I started from Montrose on my mission to England. My health was so poor I was unable to go thirty rods to the river without assistance.

After I had crossed the river I got Israel Barlow to carry me on his horse, behind, to Heber C. Kimball's, where I remained sick till the 18th. I left my wife sick, with a babe only ten days old, and all my children sick and unable to wait upon each other.[15]

In his journal Heber C. Kimball added, concerning Brigham's family, "Not one soul of them was able to go to the well for a pail of water, and they were without a second suit to their backs, for the mob in Missouri had taken all they had."[16]

Brigham himself, as he left home, was wearing a cap made out of a pair of old pantaloons and took along a quilt because he had no overcoat until some Saints in New York made him one. He commented that he thus "had not much of a ministerial appearance."[17] But though deathly ill for a time (he was literally carried from place to place as he and a few companions were shuttled by the Saints across Illinois), he gradually recovered strength and began to have experiences commensurate with his calling—even though he lacked the "appearance." It is difficult now, in modern comfort, to quite imagine men and women such as these, who surely loved each other and their families as well as we do, but who were willing to part under such conditions and travel alone into huge struggles continents away or remain alone in certain poverty and suffering. Even their equally devoted descendants today would find such circumstances good reason for at least a delay. It is clear from the journals and letters that what, at least in part, sustained them was a clear conviction that they were indeed engaged in a work for the Lord of worldwide, even cosmic, significance, anticipated from ancient times and bound to succeed as a central part of God's fulfillment and ending of human history, and thus a work bound to be ferociously opposed by the forces of evil, which then must be ferociously thrust aside.

They were also sustained by continual evidence that the Lord was directly sustaining them. Brigham, for instance, found that $13.50 given them by the Saints and kept in his trunk became like the Old Testament widow's cruse of oil and barrel of meal that were continually replenished; drawn from again and again, it provided eighty-seven dollars' worth of fares and meals as they traveled by stage across Indiana and Ohio to Kirtland. There they found John Taylor, nearly recovered from his illness, and joined him in preaching to the Saints remaining in that city. (Brigham bluntly notes, "There was some division of sentiment among the brethren in Kirtland, many of whom lacked the energy to move to Missouri last season, and some lacked the disposition."[18])

Finally, the apostles gathered at the Kirtland Temple on Sunday in a ceremony that reveals the increasingly important spiritual dimension of Brigham Young's leadership:

> I preached in the forenoon, brother Taylor in the afternoon. In the evening I anointed brother Taylor in the house of the Lord. . . . Brother Kimball opened the meeting by prayer; I then anointed brother Taylor with pure sweet oil, and pronounced such blessings as the Spirit gave utterance. Brother Taylor then arose and prayed for himself. Brother Turley, one of the Seventies, was anointed by D. S. Miles, one of the Presidents of Seventies, which was sealed by loud shouts of hosanna; then their feet were washed and the meeting closed.[19]

Brigham's growing confidence in the power of the Lord available to him, combined with humble recognition of his own roughness as an instrument and his need for polishing, is revealed again in his entry, written while crossing Lake Erie:

> The lake was so rough that no boat came into port until the 26th, when we went on board the steamboat Columbus. . . . The wind rose about one o'clock in the morning. I went upon deck and felt impressed in spirit to pray to the Father, in the name of Jesus, for a forgiveness of my sins, and then I felt to command the winds to cease, and let us go safe on our journey. The winds abated, and I felt to give the glory and honor and praise to that God who rules all things.[20]

Brigham's characteristics as a frontiersman from Jacksonian America, previously engaged mainly in farming, carpentry and other hand crafts to make his family's way, and only slowly being refined by his responsibilities, are also revealed in his writings about this journey. Especially apparent are his physical and moral toughness and his rather dry sense of humor. Crossing Illinois the missionaries had put up at the home of a fellow Mormon named Draper, who happened to notice a bottle of tonic bitters carried by George A. Smith and exclaimed, "You are a pretty set of Apostles, to be carrying a bottle of whiskey with you." Brigham brusquely notes: "We explained to him what it was; this appeased his righteous soul, so that he consented to have us stay over night."[21] The next night Brigham and Heber stayed at the home of another member, a Dr. Modisett, who went over to see the others, who were very sick.

> The doctor expressed great sympathy for them when he returned to his house—relating over the poverty of brother Stowe and the

brethren's ill health, he shed many tears, but he did not have quite sympathy enough to buy them a chicken or give them a shilling, though he was worth some four or five hundred thousand dollars.

While jumping onto a ferryboat in New York, Brigham slipped and fell full against an iron ring on the deck, severely dislocating his shoulder. He matter-of-factly records:

> I asked brother Hedlock to roll me over on my back, which he did; I directed brothers Kimball and Hedlock to lay hold of my body, and brother Pratt to take hold of my hand and pull, putting his right foot against my side, while I guided the bone with my right hand back to its place. The brethren wound my handkerchief round my shoulder and helped me up. When I came to a fire I fainted, and was not able to dress myself for several days.[22]

Brigham says of the voyage across the Atlantic: "I was sick nearly all the way and confined to my berth. . . . When I landed on the shore I gave a loud shout of hosannah."[23] When he arrived in England he was so emaciated by illness that his own cousin, Willard Richards (who had remained there since coming with Heber Kimball in 1837), did not recognize him.

The apostles Taylor and Woodruff had sailed first, arriving in Liverpool on January 12, 1840. Then, after a brief conference with Richards and the other brethren who had remained in charge of the mission, they had separated. In Wilford Woodruff's words it was decided that "Elders John Taylor and Joseph Fielding go to Liverpool [where Taylor had relatives] . . . and Elders W. Woodruff and Theodore Turley go to the Potter[ie]s and there inquire the mind of the Lord upon the importance of going to Birmingham. And that Elder W. Richards have the privilege of going whare the spirit direct him."[24] As John Taylor wrote, they "were rejoiced to see the order and amity that prevailed in the Church"[25] and decided not to interfere or make any changes until the rest of the apostles joined them.

But that would take nearly three months, and in the meantime Elder Woodruff had reason to become very anxious for the apostles' arrival. As they arrived, all the apostles had remarkable experiences and significant success almost immediately, but Elder Woodruff was led into an unusually dramatic situation. After laboring only a few weeks in the set of five towns that make up the "Potteries," famed for the manufacturing of English china and crockery, he recorded in his journal that "The Lord warned me to go to the South."[26] (Elder Turley, working separately from Wood-

ruff, was jailed in Stafford from March 16 to May 9.) Elder
Woodruff had met and stayed a few times in the home of William
Benbow, a member of the small LDS branch at Hanley; and it was
to the home of William's brother John, a relatively well-to-do
farmer near Castle Froome in Herefordshire, that the Spirit led him.
John Benbow and his family "accepted the testimony" within a few
days and provided Elder Woodruff access to the United Brethren, a
well-organized group of Primitive Methodists in the area who were
well prepared by their own searching and beliefs to receive the
gospel message. A month later 150 had been baptized, including 48
lay preachers (who were immediately ready to resume preaching,
though under their new convictions), and 200 others were ready
for baptism. Elder Woodruff was overwhelmed by the rapidity of
conversion and by the administrative and physical problems it
posed. "I cannot do the work alone," he wrote Willard Richards on
March 31.[27] On April 3, he added, "It has put me at times to my
wits end to know what to do with so many places of preaching and
preachers," and he expressed his yearning for the rest of the
apostles to come from America.[28]

A few days later the others did arrive, and Brigham Young
immediately took stock of the progress in Liverpool under John
Taylor and called Willard Richards and Wilford Woodruff to
Preston, the traditional Church center in Lancashire, for Quorum
meetings and general conference. At the first meeting Willard (who
had been appointed in July 1838 by revelation, D&C 118) was
ordained an apostle, bringing their strength to eight, and Brigham
Young was confirmed by unanimous vote as "Standing President of
the Twelve."[29]

The eight apostles were an exceedingly diverse as well as able
group of men—culturally, intellectually, and in their skills and
interests; but during their year in England under Brigham's close
leadership and association they came to work more and more in
unity with each other and with the First Presidency in America. It
is important to explore that diversity of perspective and talents
briefly; these men's experiences in England help us envision and
understand what was happening at the same time to Brother Brigham, and it is one of the most significant and neglected evidences
of Joseph Smith's and Brigham Young's similar greatness that they
attracted and kept the respect and loyalty of such a group of men.

The apostles were all young men, and most came from work-
ing-class backgrounds which made them deeply sympathetic to the
plight of the English lower classes during this time of great eco-

nomic stress in England's "hungry forties." Heber C. Kimball, Brigham's closest friend since well before they joined the Church together, was (next to Brigham) the most senior of the group at age thirty-eight. Like Brigham, Heber was blunt, harshly honest at times, usually given to rather laconic reports of his own activities and observations, but still often reaching to a colorful originality of insight and expression that Brigham loved and imitated. (One instance is Elder Kimball's description of the emigration process the apostles inaugurated, from a letter to the First Presidency, May 25, 1840: "We have witnessed the flowing of the Saints towards Zion; the stream has begun, and we expect to see it continue running until it shall have drained the salt, or the light, from Babylon, when we hope to shout hosanna home."[30])

Twenty-two-year-old George A. Smith endured constant illness—including much bleeding from his lungs and a raw throat that prevented his preaching for certain periods—with a stoicism that impressed even his London companion, Heber. But he was also gifted with a perceptive sensitivity and reflective articulateness that provides his journal with well-phrased insights, sometimes border-ing on the caustic. After serving with success in the Potteries district for four months, Elder Smith spent two months—until illness, exacerbated by the smoke and fog, forced him to leave—working with Heber Kimball and Wilford Woodruff in the much less responsive London area. He gives fine descriptions of London, the noise and chaotic crowding, the sense-stunning whirl of urban life, and also the many "stupendous and beautiful structures."[31] He and the other apostles who came to London (including Brigham) visited St. Paul's Cathedral, Covent Garden, and the British Mu-seum (where Elder Smith formed an acquaintance with the keeper of Egyptian Antiquities, who took them on an extensive personal tour on a day the museum was closed[32]).

The apostles observed the "gold and silver of the rich exposed to view" on Regent Street.[33] But George A. was not overly im-pressed, reflecting that "the day is not far distant when the riches and glory of the Gentiles would flee away," and that London "which is now a Queen with 1,500,000 souls in one hundred years may be a heap of ruins"; he noted, after visiting Queen Victoria's stables and seeing twenty-four beautifully matched cream-colored horses, that "the beds they lie on are better than those which half the people in London sleep upon."[34] Heber Kimball's comment in a letter to his wife, after this visit to the queen's palace and stables was, "You would be astonished to see the stur there is made over a little queen at the same time thousands Starving to deth fore a little Bread."[35]

John Taylor, thirty-one, a native Englishman and former Methodist preacher, was, like George A., gifted with well-educated articulateness; but in addition he had a mature, refined, almost elegant (but still direct) spiritual and emotional clarity and power that is revealed in his letters to his wife and in his diary. One example is his first letter to Leonora after leaving Nauvoo, in which he relates details of the violent illnesses that had "nearly terminated [his] existence."

> One thing I do know, that there is a being who clothes the lillies of the valley and feeds the ravens and he has given me to understand that all these things shall be added and that is all I want to know. He laid me on a bed of sickness and I was satisfied. He has raised me from it again and I am thankful. He stopped me on my road and I am content. When my way is open to proceed I shall go on my way rejoicing. If he took me I felt that it would be well. He has spared me and it is better. The Lord does all things well. Bless his holy name Oh my soul and forget not all his mercies.[36]

Except for a few months of effective work in Ireland and the Isle of Man, Elder Taylor spent the year in Liverpool, building up a strong body of Saints in the city that eventually became the center for administration of the mission — as well as helping much with the emigration and printing activities there. He notes, in a letter to his wife dated January 30, 1840, of which parts are copied in his diary, the poignance of meeting for the first time with Saints in his own native land and how he was "much pleased and edified at the kindness and love manifested by the brethren and sisters and with their simple unadorned manner"; but he also notes the "peculiar feeling at seeing [a member's] wife after dinner leave the house, her husband (a shoemaker) and children to work in a factory (a practice very prevalent in this and other manufacturing towns); thus breaking up those social endearments that unite the family. It makes my heart bleed to see these things; when will the earth cease to mourn."[37]

Elder Taylor gives us the fullest accounts of response to the apostles' preaching. On Sunday, January 26, he went with Joseph Fielding to a chapel of the Aitkenites, where Fielding's brother-in-law was a preacher, and "heard a young man preach who seemed very devoted, lamented over the state of the professing Church, prayed for the blessing of the Holy Ghost and looked for the

coming Kingdom of Christ, etc., etc." Elder Taylor felt a great
desire to share "the glorious things of the Gospel" in response to
that expressed need and asked for and was given an opportunity to
address a group of the sect's "Class Leaders" and preachers after the
service. He complimented them for their correct views, based on
Bible study, of what was lacking in Christianity and their fervent
seeking of the Holy Ghost and announced dramatically that he and
his brethren were there with

> those things that you are so anxiously looking for and praying that
> you may receive (Glory to God was shouted by many present and
> great emotion manifested). That thing has taken place which is
> spoken of by John in the revelations and I saw another angel flying
> in the midst of Heaven having the everlasting gospel to preach, etc.
> (Rev. 14). . . .
> —Brethren & Friends I feel an anxious desire to deliver this testi-
> mony—I feel the word of the Lord like fire in my bones and am
> desirous to have an opportunity of proclaiming to you these bless-
> ings that you are looking for. . . . Many present rejoiced, others
> wept, some were jealous and angry.

Of a speech given the next Sunday to a congregation of three
hundred gathered at a rented hall, he reports:

> I preached from Jude upon the faith that was once delivered to the
> Saints. I spoke upon the desire that had been manifested by men in
> different ages to reform—that Luther, M[e]lanc[h]thon, Calvin,
> Wesley, Whitfield and others since them had tried to bring about the
> ancient order of things & that however laudible their attempts might
> have been they had failed. . . . that the Lord had sent us to baptize
> and called upon them to repent and be baptized in the name of Jesus
> Christ. . . . that if any wanted to be baptized they may make it
> known to us after the congregation was dismissed. There was great
> emotion in the meeting, many wept, others rejoiced and praised the
> Lord. The spirit of the Lord indeed was with us and bore testimony
> to what we said and I plainly saw that it was the power of God and
> not the wisdom of man. . . . after meeting a young man came to me
> and told me that the Lord had showed these things to him in a
> vision. He rejoiced and said that he would be baptized. A young
> woman came to me and wept and said that she knew it was the
> truth the power of God and the word of God.—Several said that
> they believe we were the Servants of God and wanted to obey [the]
> Gospel.[38]

The other members of the Twelve were having similar experiences. Orson Pratt, age twenty-eight, probably the best

educated and most characteristically intellectual of the apostles, made many converts, though on a more modest scale than the others, in Scotland. Even Orson's older brother, Parley P. Pratt, thirty-two, who devoted his main energies to publication (especially as editor of the *Millennial Star*, the new paper started under Brigham's direction), participated in the remarkable harvest of that year.

But by far the greatest response to the gospel took place in Herefordshire. After Wilford Woodruff's exciting report in their April conference, Brigham Young assigned the new apostle, Willard Richards, to assist Elder Woodruff and went there himself for a while. Wilford, thirty-two, reveals himself in his journal as a voluble, intense observer of detail and a self-conscious reflector on the meaning of things. He includes whole chapters of background history on the places he visits. He measured the buildings exhaustively (he even used a clever geometric device for measuring the height of Old Ledbury Church, which involved having George A. Smith, apparently of about the same height as he, lie on the ground at a measurable distance from the base where he could line up the top of Woodruff's head with the steeple); he read history and travel accounts (Mosheim, Reverend Joseph Wolff), both in preparation for his mission and during it; and in the midst of the pressure and excitement of his success in Herefordshire he took time out, "after having my mind prepared for a lonely walk and meditation by reading P. P. Pratt's remarks on the 'eternal duration of matter,' "[39] to report in detail his reflections on past human history and future events evoked by examining the ruins of Roman entrenchments on Malvern hill. Elsewhere he graphically describes the hell-like bleakness of the Potteries area; tells of a destitute boy of fifteen who became notorious for running barefoot behind the stage each day—over eighty miles in twelve hours—"to get a living by receiving what money the passengers saw fit to give him, about one shilling per day";[40] reports with much equanimity being pelted with stones and eggs, even during meetings and while baptizing; and retains through all an engaging, almost boyish astonishment at his own success and a joyous directness about himself, commenting often, "We had an interesting time." He even shares his dreams, many of them almost humorous since they are of catching fish, an obvious symbol of the work of the ministry. But once he reports, "I dreamed that I saw men and children killed to be eat because of the soreness of the famine."[41]

Willard Richards had remained in England as a counselor to Joseph Fielding since the first mission in 1837; he had married an Englishwoman to whom he was much devoted, so much in fact that he had been criticized severely by members of the Preston Branch for what they considered to be the excessively fancy dress of his wife and for his too solicitous attention to her—at neglect of his ministry, as they supposed—and Joseph Smith became involved in defending him.[42] He quickly became an effective member of the Quorum, being especially helpful in maintaining records and history and assisting with publications. The excellent progress report to the First Presidency, September 5, 1840, from "Brigham Young and Willard Richards," is mainly in his phrasing and is in his hand, and the essay "On Election and Reprobation," published in the February 1841 *Millennial Star* by the same coauthors, seems also in good part his work. He also participated from the very beginning with the other apostles in healing and preaching in Herefordshire, where he earned Elder Woodruff's gratitude and praise.

Elder Richards apparently was very close to Brigham Young, who addressed him as "Beloved Willard Richards," used him as his only coauthor, and, from the evidence in surviving letters, shared more openly with him than with anyone the details of his personal concerns and perspectives, feeling free to reveal both his insecurities and his attempts at humor. On June 10, 1840, in the midst of relating mission business, Brigham writes Willard, "Be carful not to lay this letter with the new testament writings, if you doe sombody will take it for a text after the [Millennium] and contend about it."[43] At the close he cautions, "Now my Dear Brother you must forgive all my noncense and over look erours," and his next letter on June 17 ends: "Excuse erours and mestakes. You must remember its from me." In the June 17 letter, Brigham moves with characteristic tender directness into that area that had earlier caused Willard trouble, apparently in response to a question about how the young man could appropriately see the wife he sorely missed —or whether he should at all:

> Now as to the other question about Jennet thus saith the scripter he that provideth not fore his own house has—but perhaps he has no house. Well has he got a famely, yes he has got a wife. Then let him see that she is taken care of and her hart comforted. But stop say som why doe you not tak care of your famely. I doe when circumstances doe not render it otherwise. There is a difference betwene 3 months jorny and a fue ours ride. Now I say to anser my own feelings com as soon as you can leve things there. This is not

by revelation nor by commandment so put it not with the anapistles of the new testement but Brigham sayes come and see your wife.[44]

These then were the gritty, complex, and diverse individuals who under Brigham Young's leadership in England forged themselves into perhaps the most dramatically effective missionary force the Mormon Church has known and into a devoted, disciplined, and mutually loyal body who were never again, even in the crises of the Nauvoo persecutions and Joseph Smith's death, troubled by the problems that plagued the Quorum in its first four years. What was Brother Brigham's contribution? The evidence is not easy to come by, but the details come together from the various writings of the apostles and from the record of their activities and achievements which were like Brigham's own or of those he was directly involved in. Perhaps most telling is that he clearly won the respect and devotion of the Quorum members, being able not only to supervise their work from afar but to fit in directly with the extremely varied style and duties of the articulate editor, Parley P. Pratt, in Manchester, the almost frantically successful and curiously perceptive evangelist, Wilford Woodruff, in Herefordshire, and yet again with Elder Woodruff and Heber C. Kimball in the challenging and relatively unrewarding work in London.

Of course, much was accomplished by Brigham's growing executive skill and sensitivity — and the self-confident forcefulness and creativity that skill made possible. At that first conference in April he had established committees for the various tasks decided on by the Twelve, placing himself on each committee; but then, rather than remaining desk-bound at headquarters in Manchester, he immediately went with Elder Woodruff to survey the remarkable harvest of converts in Herefordshire. Among many other results, this experience provided an opportunity after one month to borrow sufficient money from two members there, John Benbow's wife, Jane, and Thomas Kington, to finance the planned publishing. An intriguing evidence of the administrative care with which Brigham was working to build the apostles' unity as a quorum is a small certificate, somehow preserved from those days and now in the Young papers. It shows that upon getting the needed money President Young met with Richards and Woodruff, made the publication decisions, and had them recorded on the certificate, which was then signed by those apostles. Then on his way to Manchester, Brigham stopped in Burslem to get George A. Smith's signature before proceeding.[45]

In Manchester, Brigham moved ahead rapidly with the hymn book and the *Millennial Star* and also supervised the organization of the first company of emigrants. He held another general conference in July at which the hymns were formally approved and a very important full-time local missionary system was established by calling for volunteers (he got twenty) in the general meeting and then making assignments the next day for each volunteer to go with a Quorum member. This missionary force was to prove very effective in following up on the seminal but scattered evangelizing done by the apostles, through opening new fields, and in building a ministry that would continue after the apostles left. At the conference it was also decided to have Parley P. Pratt return to New York to get his family (apparently with the intention of having him remain in charge after the other apostles left) and to have President Young edit the newborn *Star* in his absence. Brigham records, "I was much confined to the office for several months, proofreading the Hymn Book, conducting and issuing the *Millennial Star*, Hymn Book and Book of Mormon, giving counsel to the Elders throughout the European Mission, preaching, baptizing, and confirming."[46]

Another ship of emigrants was organized to leave on September 8 and then another conference prepared for and held in October. An interesting evidence of Brigham's executive burden and manner of functioning survives in a slip of paper on which he noted preparatory memos to himself of "Bisness of the confrence on the 6 of Oct":

> Where shall the Book of Mormon be bound? What Stile shall it be bound in?
>
> How shall we dispose of it?
>
> Who Shall take charge of the Maleneal Star if P. Pratt does not come?
>
> Is it best for som of the 12 to goe home this fall and come back next Seson?
>
> What time shall the next company goe to America and how Shall they be organized to goe? . . .
>
> Who shall have authority to ordane officers in the Churches?
>
> Will the Church help Brother Richards?
>
> Who shall make or prepare the [index] to the Book of Mormon.[47]

All of these matters were resolved by the Quorum at the conference.

In October and November, Brigham continued his various administrative and publishing duties, while also he engaged in

Both samples courtesy of Church Archives
The Church of Jesus Christ of Latter-day Saints

Note in Brigham Young's handwriting showing preliminary agenda for October 6, 1840, conference in Manchester.

Note showing the young Quorum President's process of building apostolic unity in the decision-making process (publication decisions in May 1840).

preaching and baptizing in the Manchester and Preston areas. He had hired the huge Carpenter's Hall in Manchester for meetings for one year and mentions preaching there "to an attentive congregation of about 1,500"[48]; he also tells of organizing the priesthood in Manchester to gather on Sunday mornings and go out street preaching, thus providing about forty "preaching stations," both for teaching and for notifying gatherers about the regular meetings in Carpenter's Hall, a procedure that has been a regular and effective Mormon proselyting tool up to the present.

In early December, Elder Young spent two weeks with the somewhat discouraged Elders Kimball and Woodruff in London. Heber had written his wife, as a first impression back in August, that there was "so much nois that we can neither Sleep nor think,"[49] and Wilford had written in his journal, "The minds of the people here in London are taken up with everything but the things of God and righteousness." Wilford added, just before Brigham's arrival, "There is so much agoing in the city to draw the attention of the people that it almost requires a trump to be blown from heaven in order to awaken the attention of the people to the subject of the fulness of the gospel."[50]

Brigham's visit served its purpose, because after some sight-seeing he and the others preached to the largest gatherings they had yet been able to attract, several indicated a desire to be baptized, and an independent minister talked of joining the Church and bringing his congregation with him. That night Elder Woodruff recorded: "We then met at Father Corners [their first convert back in August] and communed with the Saints and had a good time. I rejoice at the prospect that appears this day for an opening for I have laboured a long time in London and the work has gone slow but now it appears like a wide opening. May the Lord roll on his work spedily I pray."[51] Brigham visited the College of Surgeons with a Dr. Copeland, who had been attending seriously to the apostles' message and was baptized the next month. Then Young returned to Manchester, stopping to preach and hold a conference in Herefordshire and another with Elder Smith in the Potteries.

Beginning in January, the apostolic mission began to draw to a close with a flurry of last-minute activities, completions, and arrangements for the future. Brigham asked advice from all the apostles about when they should leave; moved between Manchester, Preston, and Liverpool completing the printing of the Book of Mormon and getting it copyrighted; wrote letters concerning the developing emigration to the apostles and all presiding elders; or-

ganized another company of emigrant Saints; and made arrangements for the final conference in April, which turned out to be a
great organizational and spiritual triumph, a fitting completion to
the success and growth achieved in the year's work.

But integral to these administrative responsibilities and achievements are the evidences and results of Brigham's spiritual strength
and growth during the two years since his daring fulfillment of a
difficult directive from his God through his Prophet. A good
example of this combination is Brigham's organization of the emigration route from Liverpool to Nauvoo, which very quickly
became firmly established (about a thousand left in Church-sponsored companies that first year) and developed a fine reputation for
its disciplined orderliness; by the time the apostles left, shipowners
were vying for the Mormon trade.

Central factors in the effectiveness of the emigration system
were spiritual and moral dimensions introduced by two decisions:
first, the organization of each company with a leader (who was also
often clerk and historian to the company) and counselors (each in
charge of a certain number of the emigrants), all of whom were
chosen by the Twelve or by other presiding Church leaders and
"set apart to their respective duties by the laying on of hands";
second, Young's initial insistence, approved by the Twelve, that
only those members be involved in Church emigration who received "recommends" and "that we recommend no one to go to
America that has money, without assisting the poor according to
our counsel from time to time."[52] Here, of course, lay the seeds of
the Perpetual Emigrating Fund, which later took thousands of
destitute Saints from Europe and the eastern United States to Utah
in the faith that they would reimburse the fund after getting into a
situation where they could themselves produce something; but the
basic Mormon principle of mutual responsibility put into operation
in this practical way by Brigham bore immediate fruit. For example,
when Jane Benbow, who had lent Brigham money for the Church's
publications, and her husband emigrated in September 1840, they
relinquished all claims to the money in favor of others who would
emigrate to America the next season.[53]

One crucial difference between an executive genius and a
prophetic leader is the ability not only to produce followers who
are willing disciples—even martyrs—but to produce other prophets as well. Brigham became that kind of prophetic leader as he
developed during those two years of preparation and service in
England the kind of qualities that come with confirmation from the

Lord of spiritual success. He gained the unique confidence that results from daring and successful ventures in faith across a spectrum of supremely important life activities. And that confidence in turn empowered even more successful ventures and brought Brigham Young the crucial, liberating acceptance by himself of his own worth as a servant of God and acceptance by others of him in that role. Immediately after that initial conference, when President Young went to Herefordshire with Elder Wilford Woodruff, he did not just check things out and help improve the organization, as any good administrator would, but he joined fully in the preaching, with all its risks and rewards. Elder Woodruff records:

> May 14. I walked to Ledbury with Elder Young, from thence to Keysent Street and preached but amid much disturbance and as the meeting was about breaking up the congregation was besmeared with rotten eggs. . . .
>
> June 3rd. . . . A notable miracle was wrought by faith and the power of God in the person of Sister Mary Pitt at Dymok. She had been confined 6 years to her bed, with the spine which mostly deprived her of the use of her feet and ancles. And had not walked for 11 years, ownly with the use of crutches. Elders Young, Richards, and Woodruff lade hands upon her and rebuked her infirmity and her ancle bones received strength and she now walks without the aid of crutch or staff.

Brigham also participated in the delicate matter of transforming the main body of United Brethren, including its organized branches, area conference, meetinghouses, and preachers, into a fully Mormon organization. It was not until after Brigham left Herefordshire to return to Manchester that a conference of preachers and members of the Bran Green and Gadsfield Elm Branch of the United Brethren was convened at the Gadsfield Elm Chapel by Thomas Kington, formerly superintendent of the United Brethren but now a Mormon elder, who then moved that the meeting "be hereafter known by the name of the Bran Green and Gadsfield Elm Conference of the Church of Jesus Christ of Latter Day Saints."[54] But while Brigham Young was still there with Elder Woodruff, on May 18, he had helped prepare for the organization change by assisting in a tactful transformation of one fine United Brethren custom into a Mormon one: "Elder Kington made a feast for the Saints, which had been a custom among the United Brethren. But as they now were all receiving the fulness of the gospel they had become saints. The Saints began to collect at 2 o'clock. . . . We truly had an interesting time. Elder Young addressed the

Saints clothed with the power of God. And then asked a blessing upon the food prepared. We then sat down to the table and eat and drank with nearly 100 Saints possessing glad hearts and cheerful countenances."[55]

At the July conference Elder Young not only inaugurated an extensive, continuing missionary force for the British Mission but gave the Saints, including the apostles, a sense of his prophetic vision by calling and ordaining a member of the British Army who was on his way to the East Indies to carry the gospel there as a missionary and by appointing seventeen-year-old William J. Barrett of Burslem to preach the gospel in the new British colony in South Australia. And when he later began the street preaching in Manchester, Brother Brigham didn't just send the elders out, but, as he records the experience himself, on one Sunday in November, "went to the Priesthood meeting in the morning and felt impressed to tell the brethren to go home. The police, who had been instructed to arrest all street preachers that morning [because of Methodist complaints against the Mormons], took up about twenty, who all proved to be Methodists. When the magistrate learned they were not 'Mormons' they were dismissed."[56]

Such inspired pastoral leadership was not only felt and appreciated by the others of the Twelve but was increasingly participated in by them; their journals indicate a growing sense that they really were apostles, of the same kind and having the same power as Christ's original Twelve, and led by one with the stature of Peter, the first chief apostle. Heber C. Kimball, blunt and practical like Brigham, participated increasingly in miracles, speaking in tongues, responding to impressions of the Spirit that led to successful contacts for preaching, taking on the idiom of the New Testament to describe events that were truly biblical. ("On the 6 of May in this place a large number came together from different parts. It was a Pentecost to the Saints."[57])

George A. Smith turned increasingly from wry sarcasm and pointed social criticism to record miraculous healings of the sick ("I have been called to administer many times when I was sick myself, and yet, such was their faith, in the ordinance of laying on of hands, that they were healed through faith and obedience to the commandments of Jesus Christ"[58]). And he also began to participate in the Pentecostal spirit: "For the last twenty days I have been so busy with preaching, baptizing, confirming, and teaching the people that I had not time to journalize any; and have seldom gone to bed before 2 o'clock in the morning, as people were constantly in my room enquiring about the work of the Lord."[59]

Wilford Woodruff, the curious, voluble, self-astonishing apostle who had reaped the greatest harvest, made journal entries that give us perhaps the best sense we have of the pastoral role the apostles came to play and the poignance of their parting:

> 21 Sept, 1840 [after a conference at Froome Hill in Herefordshire] After standing upon my feet 8 hours in conference, conversing much of the time, ordaining about 30, confirming some, healing many that wer sick, shaking hands with about 400 Saints. walking 2 miles and Preaching 4 hours in the Chimney Corner, I then lay down and dreamed of ketching fish.
>
> March 15, 1841 [after his last conference at Gadsfield Elm Chapel in Herefordshire] The Saints universally feel that the Judgments of God are near in this land and are anxious to gather with the Saints in Nauvoo as soon as possible. But many are vary poor and see no door open as yet, and some are placed in all the perplexing circumstances that possibly can be and are flocking around me by scores at a time and asking council what to do. As soon as meeting closed multitudes crouded around me, many hands were presented on evry side to bid me farewell, many calling for me to bless them before I leave them, others crying out do lay hands on me and heal me before you go. Br. Woodruff I am turned out of Doors for my religion. What shall I do.
>
> . . . Many parted with me with tears in their eyes. Many of the Brethren and Sisters followed me to Turkey Hall whare I spent the night, and filled the house until a late hour Begging council and instruction at my hand.[60]

But finally the parting had to be made, and the closing scenes were an appropriate climax to the year's work, with Brigham Young playing the appropriate central role. Orson Hyde arrived in England in late March on his way to dedicate Palestine for the gathering of the Jews, so the Quorum gathered nine strong (with Parley Pratt back from New York). At the council meeting of the Twelve, held on April 2, 1841, Brigham Young formally expressed appreciation "to meet once more in council after a long separation, and having passed through many sore and grievous trials"[61]; recorded the copyright he had now obtained for the publishing of the Book of Mormon and transferred title for any financial profits to Joseph Smith; placed the Hymn Book and the *Star* in the hands of Elder Pratt and wrote a letter to the Saints in England delineating carefully the administrative organization, with Elder Pratt at the head, and the emigration procedures to be followed; set a date for the apostles to leave England; and voted to continue their business as part of the general conference.

That last conference was the impressive one already partially described, with Elders Woodruff and Smith administering the sacrament to the large congregation, all nine of the apostles bearing testimony in turn, and Elder Hyde speaking on the "Gathering of Israel," in which they all realized he was himself playing an important, long-prophesied part. The apostles publicly reviewed the achievements of the past year, evidence of which was both before and within them, and enjoyed what Woodruff called "perfect union and harmony."

In these scenes Brigham Young was the commanding figure and is referred to for the first time by Wilford Woodruff simply as "The President."[62] Brigham discoursed on the office of patriarch and nominated and ordained a second patriarch for England (he had chosen the first in that initial conference a year before); he presided while a huge, richly ornamented cake, sent to the apostles from New York by one of the members, was exhibited, blessed, and served to the congregation of over seven hundred (the official minutes record, "During the distribution several appropriate hymns were sung, and a powerful and general feeling of delight universally pervaded the meeting"[63]); he led the Twelve as, in the words of Wilford Woodruff, they "lade hands upon the head of Elder Orson Hyde and Blessd Him in the name of the Lord, as he had been set apart by the first Presidency to take a mission to the Holy Land, the City of Jerrusalem whare Jesus Dwelt, for the purpose of laying the foundation of a great work in that land. . . . Much of the Spirit of God rested upon us"; and at the end of the last conference meeting, the minutes tell us, "Brigham Young and William Miller then sang the hymn 'Adieu, my dear brethren,' etc., and President Young blessed the congregation and dismissed them."[64] A week later, just before they were to set sail, Brigham conducted the apostles, with perfect aplomb, to be honored guests at a tea party given by a large gathering of Saints in the Music Hall at Liverpool. Elder Woodruff writes:

> The Saints have rented this hall for their meetings. It will seat about 2000. This is the first time I hav visited Liverpool since I first landed. It gave me peculiar feelings to sit down with 200 Saints in this place thinking that when we first landed [there] was not one in the city but ourselves.[65]

The historian James B. Allen has written, apropos Brigham Young, "A man becomes a leader not only because of his ability to organize, persuade, and direct activities of others with diverse attitudes and abilities, but also because of his devotion to the unifying ideals of the particular group involved."[66] Certainly a central key to Brother Brigham's success and growth on his mission to England was his fidelity to Joseph the Prophet and the principles and ideals he taught as "Mormonism." Shortly after arriving in England, in fact on the date of the first general conference, April 16, 1840, Brigham wrote to Joseph, in his own hand and distinctive idiom, enclosing the minutes of the conference and the Twelve's council meetings, giving the rationale for the decisions that had been made about publishing a hymn book, and then imploring:

> If you see anything in or about the whole affair, that is not right, I ask, in the name of the Lord Jesus Christ, that you would make known unto us the mind of the Lord, and His will concerning us. I believe that I am as willing to do the will of the Lord, and take counsel of my brethren, and be a servant of the Church, as ever I was in my life. . . .
>
> I request one favor of you, that is, a letter from you, that I may hear from my friends. I trust that I will remain your friend through life and in eternity.[67]

Three weeks later Elder Young wrote again:

> Through the mercy of our heavenly Father, I am alive and in pretty good health; better than I should have been, had I remained in America. I trust that you and family are well, and I ask my heavenly Father that we may live forever; but not to be chased about by mobs, but live to enjoy each other's society in peace. . . . It is better for me to be here, because the Lord has called me to this great work, but it is hard for me to be parted from my old friends whom I have proved to be willing to lay down their lives for each other. . . .
>
> . . . I want to ask some questions. Shall we print the Book of Mormon in this country immediately? They are calling for it from every quarter. . . . Is the Book of Doctrine and Covenants to be printed just as it is now, to go to the nations of the earth; and shall we give it to them as quickly as we can? . . . Will the Twelve have to be together to do business as a quorum? Or shall they do business in the name of the Church? Why I ask this is for my own satisfaction; if the Lord has a word for us, for one I am willing to receive it.[68]

He goes on to describe the exciting response of people in England ("simple testimony is enough for them") and their extreme poverty; he asks how to best emigrate those who are beginning to want to go but have no means and whether to ordain seventies to the ministry while in England.

Brigham Young was sincerely seeking counsel, which clearly he followed when he received it, but he was not immobilized by the long mail delays. Joseph Smith sent a response to the above letter with Lorenzo Snow (who left Nauvoo on July 19 to join the missionaries in England), "which gave the Twelve permission to publish the Book of Mormon, Doctrine and Covenants, and hymnbook, but not to ordain any into the quorum of Seventies; and likewise some general instructions."[69] But in the meantime Brigham had organized and sent one emigrant company, published the hymn book, and was well on his way with the Book of Mormon. On September 5 he and Willard Richards wrote their long, strikingly insightful and articulate report to the First Presidency, particularly emphasizing and detailing their impression of Britain's economic and social conditions and the failure of histories to report properly, and of most people to understand deeply or care about, the life of the common people, which they then describe at length; but again the main theme is the desire to get counsel from the Prophet, and to follow it:

> According to council we have gathered from different parts of England and Scotland a company of Brethren and Sisters who are now in Liverpool ready to sail for America on Monday next. Most of them are very poor; those who have money have given most of it to help those who had need. As this was not sufficient; *we*, seeing the poverty and distress of some families, *have made* use of *our own credit*, among the brethren to carry them along with the rest. . . .
>
> We desire to ask you have we done right? Or is it a right principle, for us to act upon, to involve ourselves, to help the poor Saints to Zion? . . .
>
> Shall we gather up all the Saints we can and come over with them next Spring?
>
> Have we done right in Printing a hymn book?
>
> Are we doing right in Printing the Book of Mormon? . . .
>
> We want council and wisdom and any thing that is good. Our motto is *go ahead*. Go ahead — and ahead. We are determined to go — until we have conquered every foe. So come life or come death we'll go ahead, but tell us if we are going wrong and we will right it.[70]

Joseph responded October 19, 1840, with an equally long, articulate and loving letter, speaking directly to the Quorum's concern to be in harmony with him:

I can assure you, that from the information I have received, I feel satisfied that you have not been remiss in your duty; but that your diligence and faithfulness have been such as must secure you the smiles of that God whose servant you are, and also the good will of the Saints throughout the world.

The spread of the Gospel throughout England is certainly pleasing; the contemplation of which cannot but afford feelings of no ordinary kind, in the bosom of those who have borne the heat and burden of the day.[71]

Joseph gives approval of the hymn book (which he had received) and of their going ahead with publishing the Book of Mormon and (if they wish) the Doctrine and Covenants, and he manifests his growing confidence in the Twelve by explicitly granting them the freedom their obedience had earned and that they had already begun to use:

There are many things of much importance, on which you ask counsel, but which I think you will be perfectly able to decide upon, as you are more conversant with the peculiar circumstances than I am; and I feel great confidence in your united wisdom; therefore, you will excuse me for not entering into detail. If I should see any-thing that is wrong, I would take the privilege of making known my mind to you, and pointing out the evil.

Brigham Young wrote back on December 5 and again on December 30, mainly giving details of his visit to the rather down-hearted apostles in London, and reported:

The prospect for the spread of the Gospel brightened up while we were there. Our feelings were very clear and decisive that Elder Kimball had better stay with Elder Woodruff. I was much interested while there with my brethren. I pray the Lord to roll on His work in that great city. I feel much for the people in that place! yea my feelings are exquisite, for why, God knows; but I believe it is for the glory of God, and the good of souls.[72]

The winding-up actions of the Quorum, reported especially in their final epistle to the Church members in Britain, were directly responsive to Joseph's counsel and well exemplify the unity and effectiveness the apostles had achieved, in good part through their increasing fidelity to him as their Prophet.[73] Joseph Smith was ex-tremely well pleased with the accomplishments implied in that epistle — both the great work that had been achieved and that which still lay before the British Saints — and he responded quickly and dramatically to the proven quality and solidarity of the Twelve and the demonstrated devotion and ability of the Quorum's president. A few days after Brigham's return from England the Prophet visited him in his home and conveyed a revelation to him:

> Dear and well-beloved brother, Brigham Young, verily thus saith the Lord unto you: My servant Brigham, it is no more required at your hand to leave your family as in times past, for your offering is acceptable to me. I have seen your labor and toil in journeyings for my name. I therefore command you to send my word abroad, and take especial care of your family from this time, henceforth and forever. Amen.[74]

And a month later, on August 16, 1841, at a special conference of the Church presided over by President Young, Joseph Smith made the momentous announcement "that the time had come when the Twelve should be called upon to stand in their place next to the First Presidency, and attend to the settling of emigrants and the business of the Church at the stakes."[75] Accordingly, the Twelve were established in their proper governing role over all the Church, and Brother Brigham was unknowingly embarked on the course which would lead beyond Carthage and would make him the Church's second prophet and president and its leader to the west.

But for now he could only be grateful for a relatively stationary and peaceful ministry. On April 25, 1841, on the ship coming home, he tells us, "I felt as though I could not endure menny such voiges as I had indured for 2 years . . . and ware it not for the power of God and his tendere mercy I should despare."[76] The single entry for 1842 in the two diaries covering this period is:

> January 18th . . . This Evening I am with my wife alone by my fire side for the first time for years; we enjoi it and feele to prase the Lord.[77]

Brigham And Joseph

Just before Brigham Young died he was removed from his canopy bed and placed before an open window where he could get better air. His twenty-seven-year-old daughter, Zina, who was among the numerous family members present, recounts that "he seemed to partially revive, and opening his eyes, he gazed upward, exclaiming: 'Joseph! Joseph! Joseph!' . . . This name was the last word he uttered."[1]

There is no question about Brother Brigham's lifelong preoccupation with Joseph Smith, the man who had won his love and loyalty and had given him the means to transform his life—and whom he reluctantly, but masterfully, succeeded as President of The Church of Jesus Christ of Latter-day Saints. But there remain some difficult questions about the nature of that preoccupation, and there is a constant danger, it seems to me, that the answers will tend toward one of two serious errors: Some are tempted to see Joseph Smith as the great master prophet, the creative, inspired, visionary genius, and Brigham Young as merely a disciple, the practical doer who carried out the martyr's uncompleted plans with a kind of plodding grit. On the other hand, some think of Brigham as the tough administrator and powerful leader of men who made workable some of the visions of Joseph, the impractical dreamer. Both mistakes derive from the common notion that the two, though in some ways complementary, were essentially different men, as expressed in appraisals such as this: "Joseph was . . . a dreamer, a planner, a mystic; Brigham was to become a man of practical actions, a statesman, decisive, vigorous and determined."[2]

An overwhelming impression that emerges from a careful study of the writings and activities of both men is that all of those adjectives could be applied, almost with equal appropriateness, to either one. I am convinced that what united them and paved the way for Brigham Young to fill Joseph Smith's place, not only at the head of the Church but in the hearts of the Mormon people, was

not their differences, however complementary, but their fundamental similarities. I also feel certain that for us to understand the
quality of Brigham's absolute loyalty, even unto death, and his
complex sense of depending on but developing from the foundation laid by Joseph, would require some understanding of President
Young's conviction that, whether or not he himself was a great
man, he was the one appointed by God to follow Joseph as the
prophet in charge of the kingdom.

The effects on Brigham of his first meeting with Joseph in
1832, and the subsequent close association of the two, were certainly profound, but again can be misunderstood. Some have
thought the rather unemotional Brigham was swept off his feet by
the imaginative, passionate, articulate young prophet. But Brigham
himself said about his feelings after baptism and *before* he met
Joseph: "I wanted to thunder and roar out the Gospel to the
nations. It burned in my bones like fire pent up . . . nothing would
satisfy me but to cry abroad in the world, what the Lord was doing
in the latter days."[3] It is quite clear that what touched Brigham was
not mere charisma, but the conviction, born of the Holy Ghost
even before their first meeting, that Joseph was a *prophet*, in fact, *the*
spokesman for God in this dispensation of time, and that the Mormon teachings were not only good, or reasonable, but uniquely *true*
unto salvation:

> I did not embrace Mormonism because I hoped it was true, but
> because I knew it was that principle that would save all the human
> family that would obey it. Joseph Smith lived and died a prophet,
> and sealed his testimony with his blood. . . .
>
> Joseph Smith has laid the foundation of the kingdom of God in
> the last days; others will rear the superstructure. . . .
>
> . . . I know that he was called of God, and this I know by the
> revelation of Jesus Christ to me, and by the testimony of the Holy
> Ghost. Had I not so learned this truth, I should never have been
> what is called a "Mormon," neither should I have been here to-day.[4]

It is clear that Brigham's feelings about the Prophet were not
merely personal; they were inseparably connected to his compel-
ling and never-wavering conviction of Joseph's divine calling. And
the haunting, driving force of his life's work, particularly after
taking upon himself the mantle of Joseph in 1844, was the desire
and determination to be true to that calling — rather than merely to
Joseph the man.

Brigham responded to elements in Joseph that were intrinsic to himself, and he also avidly learned from the Prophet because of his profound trust in Joseph's calling; aware that Joseph was not super-human or infallible but a man he could genuinely identify with and try to be like with some hope of success, he also understood how that calling from God made Joseph different:

> Though I admitted in my feelings and knew all the time that Joseph was a human being and subject to err, still it was none of my busi-ness to look after his faults.
>
>   . . . It was not for me to question whether Joseph was dictated by the Lord at all times and under all circumstances or not. I never had the feeling for one moment, to believe that any man or set of men or beings upon the face of the whole earth had anything to do with him, for he was superior to them all, and held keys of salvation over them. Had I not thoroughly understood this and believed it, I much doubt whether I should ever have embraced what is called "Mor-monism." . . .
>
>   It was not my prerogative to call him in question with regard to any act of his life. He was God's servant, and not mine. . . . That was my faith, and it is my faith still.[5]

As we have seen, Brigham's loyalty to Joseph and ability to learn from him were demonstrated very early. He stayed that first winter of 1833 in Kirtland working at odd jobs for other members, and the next summer he participated in the famous Zion's Camp march to aid the Saints in Missouri; all through his life he was to look back on those times as especially dear to him for the privilege it brought of being close to the Prophet and learning from him day by day. The organization of the camp, by tens, then fifties, and then hundreds, impressed Brigham as prophetically inspired and effective, and he used the plan four years later in evacuating thou-sands from Missouri into Illinois, and then again in England when he devised the system for emigrating shiploads of Saints to America. (And, of course, it was the basic plan used by Brigham Young in the great exodus across the plains to Utah, an organiza-tion he is often given credit for but which had its beginning with Joseph and Zion's Camp.)

But the learning was by no means merely practical. William C. Staines records, in his journal of the exodus from Nauvoo, an account of a speech Brother Brigham gave one evening while visit-ing Staines's camp in Iowa:

> Spoke of the time when the brute creation would be perfectly docile and harmless. It would be brought about by our faith and patience.

That we should not kill the rattlesnakes but should cultivate the spirit of peace with them. Saw two of them in his travels — told them to move out of the way and they did — that Br. Joseph taught this when the camp went to Missouri 13 years ago. As long as the brute creation sees anything to harm them, so long the enmity will exist.[6]

President Young later had this to say about his opportunities to learn from Joseph:

In the days of the Prophet Joseph, such moments were more precious to me than all the wealth of the world. No matter how great my poverty — if I had to borrow meal to feed my wife and children, I never let an opportunity pass of learning what the Prophet had to impart.[7]

Only two years after being called as an apostle, Brigham's loyalty was given what he later called his one severe test. After the failure of the Kirtland Anti-Banking Society in 1837 many members apostatized, including members of the Quorum; in fact, Joseph was to lament, only Heber C. Kimball and Brigham, among the original Quorum, did not ever "lift their heel against me."[8] The reason Brigham Young remained true, he later recalled, was that after a momentary doubt ("not concerning religious matters . . . but . . . in relation to [Joseph's] financiering"), he recognized his mistaken priorities and repented: "During this siege of darkness I stood close by Joseph, and, with all the wisdom and power God bestowed upon me, put forth my utmost energies to sustain the servant of God and unite the Quorums of the Church."[9] Brigham's loyalty had developed an emotional, almost physical quality that is perhaps uniquely characteristic: Concerning a time when he once offered to cowhide a man who came into Kirtland claiming Joseph had been "cut off" and he was to take the Prophet's place, he later commented, "When I saw a man stand in the path before the Prophet to dictate him, I felt like hurling him out of the way, and branding him as a fool."[10]

Brigham again and again demonstrated to Joseph not only tenacious loyalty but the courage and competence and spiritual power to succeed in increasingly difficult crises and assignments — not only to succeed by some general human standard of success but to measure up to Joseph's prophetic vision. He got the Saints out of Missouri by putting the Church leaders and members under covenant that they would share their resources until all, no matter how poor or weak, could leave, and by returning many times himself to bring others out; he returned to Far West with the other apostles, in mortal danger, to fulfill to the letter Joseph's revelation requiring them to take leave from the Saints at the temple site for their missions in Great Britain; and he led the apostles in Britain to a degree of success that more than fulfilled the Prophet's high expectations, winning not only his gratitude and admiration but increased administrative freedom and confidence during the mission and a new role for the Twelve when they returned.

Brigham Young was later (in defense of the right of the Twelve to govern the Church) to quote the reference in the Doctrine and Covenants that places the Quorum of the Twelve "equal in authority and power" to the First Presidency;[11] but it was when the Church President, in August 1841, went beyond that revelation and earlier practice by giving the Twelve new assignments, "the settling of the emigrants and the business of the church at the stakes," and commissioning them "to bear off the Kingdom in all the world," that the process was set in motion that directly prepared Brigham to be Joseph's eventual successor and the Saints to accept him as such. That fall and the next year the Prophet met in council more and more frequently with the Twelve. By 1843 this often took place without the other members of the First Presidency, since Sidney Rigdon was in Pittsburgh and Hyrum Smith was on other assignments. Meanwhile, Joseph delegated to the Twelve an increasing amount of ecclesiastical and economic responsibility and power: Early in 1842 he assigned them to help in the disappointingly slow ingathering of Saints to build up Nauvoo that he had called for, and Brigham and Heber were, along with others, much occupied in the spring and fall with missions to exhort members to respond to the Prophet's call. Much of the responsibility for assigning and supervising missionaries, as well as those responsible for emigration, was delegated to the Twelve in 1842. They were also given the task of recruiting a force of 380 elders and participating with them in traveling through the eastern United States to counter the perverted views on polygamy and attacks on Joseph being broadcast by the apostate John C. Bennett. In April 1843 Joseph Smith bypassed the established committees and appointed the Twelve to gather funds for the temple and sell shares in the Nauvoo House, and the apostles spent much of the remainder of the year, again led by Elder Young and Elder Kimball, traveling on this assignment.

In the meantime the Prophet involved the Twelve in taking over for the Church the private printing establishment of the *Times and Seasons;* moved beyond earlier statements that the Twelve were not to be involved in local Church affairs by assigning them jurisdiction in the trial for membership of Benjamin Winchester in Philadelphia; and had them participate in the complex and successful economic process of aiding Saints from the eastern United States to gather to Nauvoo by transferring their property to the Hotchkiss Syndicate in the East to pay off the Church debt for the Nauvoo lands and then giving them some of that land when they arrived. Finally, in 1844, the Twelve played a primary role in organizing and then participating with the elders who traveled in the spring and summer of 1844 campaigning for Joseph Smith for President of the United States and preaching both his political views and the restored gospel—which is why they were away from Nauvoo when he was killed on June 27.

In all of this development of the power and prestige of the Quorum, Brigham Young played a central role, both as leader and participant (being away himself for extended periods on various assignments). As a result, Joseph's confidence in and dependence on him constantly increased. Brigham became generally known as "President Young" and seems to have gradually become more close in counsel to Joseph; he was the one to take the Church President's place when he had to be in hiding and was in every practical sense the second in command (except for Hyrum's role as close advisor and defender on spiritual and doctrinal matters). As early as the summer of 1842 there are entries in Brigham's "Manuscript History" such as the following:

June 29   Rode out with the Prophet, and looked at lands the Church had for disposal.

Jul 31   Attended Council with the Prophet and others.

In the month of July I attended Councils, waited upon the immigrants; and as President Joseph Smith kept concealed from his enemies, I had continual calls from the brethren for counsel, which occupied much of my time.[12]

Joseph and Brigham's relationship was not merely ecclesiastical. When Brigham returned from his ingathering mission in the fall of 1842, he was struck with a terrible illness that nearly killed him; Joseph administered to him, prophesied that he would live, and then personally cared for him, sitting with him for hours and carefully instructing and supervising his attendants for many days during the crisis period. President Young said much later, concerning this time, "I used to think, while Joseph was living, that his life compared well with the history of the Saviour."[13] This was on a public occasion, which tends to encourage exaggeration, but in a private letter in 1853 he wrote:

> In 1833 I moved to Ohio where I became acquainted with Joseph Smith Jr., and remained familiarly acquainted with him in private councils, and in his public walk and acts until the day of his death, and I can truly say, that I invariably found him to be all that any people could require a true prophet to be, and that a better man could not be, though he had his weaknesses; and what man has ever lived upon this earth who had none?[14]

Brigham did not go on to specify those weaknesses, and he certainly gave no hint about them while Joseph was alive, speaking often during the Nauvoo period in praise of the Prophet and in definition and defense of Joseph's calling:

> Who is the author of this work and gathering? Joseph Smith, the Prophet, as an instrument in the hands of God, is the author of it. He is the greatest man on earth. No other man, at this age of the world, has power to assemble such a great people from all the nations of the earth, with all their varied dispositions, and so assimilate and cement them together that they become subject to rule and order. This the Prophet Joseph is doing. He has already gathered a great people who willingly subject themselves to his counsel, because they know it is righteous.[15]

There are interesting indications, however, that by this time the Quorum President was beginning to think not only of the Prophet but the Twelve when he talked about deference to Church leadership. Note what he said in a speech in August 1843, one week after the one quoted above:

> A man or woman may ask of God, and get a witness and testimony from God concerning any work or messenger that is sent unto them; but if a person ask for a thing that does not concern him, inquiring concerning the duty of a Presiding Elder, what the Prophet *or the Twelve* ought to do, etc., he will not get an answer.[16]

Brother Brigham was, however, perfectly clear about the relation of the Twelve to the Prophet:

> The Twelve may get a revelation in any part of the world concerning the building up of the Kingdom, as they have to establish it in all parts of the world . . . but not to lead the Church — that belongs to the head of the Church.[17]

And again, late in that same year, 1843, on another occasion when Joseph's absence seems to have left Brigham automatically in charge:

> I attended prayer-meeting in the Assembly Room. President Joseph Smith being absent. I presided and instructed the brethren upon the necessity of following our file leader, and our Savior, in all his laws and commandments, without asking any questions why they were so.[18]

Joseph Smith had won Brigham Young's perfect loyalty, but here again part of the reason may well have been the value Joseph himself placed on loyalty. Important also was the Prophet's tender, openhearted ability to give love to and express confidence in others. From his cell in Liberty Jail, Missouri, Joseph wrote his wife Emma, "Never give up an old tried friend, who has waded through all manner of toil, for your sake, and throw him away because fools may tell you he has some faults."[19] And perhaps even more revealing of his ingenuously forthright tenderness and its effect on others is the following from George A. Smith's diary, where he reports a conversation with Joseph in which George A. had characterized W. W. Phelps's editorial abilities with exactness and wit:

> Joseph laughed heartily and said I had the thing just right. . . . At the close of our conversation, Joseph wrapped his arms around me and presed me to his bosom and said, "George A., I love you as I do my own life." I felt so affected I could hardly speak.[20]

Brigham was also deeply affected by that quality in Joseph, which both echoed and encouraged a similar quality in himself—what Joseph had characterized, in a letter from Liberty Jail in 1839, as "gentleness and meekness . . . love unfeigned . . . faithfulness . . . stronger than the cords of death."[21]

Brigham did not learn of Joseph's death until almost three weeks after it happened, although he later remembered that on the day of the martyrdom, while sitting in the depot in Boston, waiting for the train to Salem, he had "felt a heavy depression of spirit, and so melancholy [he] could not converse with any degree of pleasure."[22] He saw newspaper accounts of the assassination on July 9 but discounted them because of the current sensationalism about Mormonism; but on the sixteenth, while in Petersboro, New Hampshire, he heard a letter from Nauvoo read which gave details of the murder of Joseph and Hyrum. He roused himself from absolute despair, decided on a course of action, and returned to Boston the next day to take the other apostles back to Nauvoo. Wilford Woodruff describes the scene that took place when Brigham arrived in Boston:

> Elder Brigham Young arrived in Boston this morning. I walked with him to 57 Temple Street, and called upon Sister Vose. Brother Young took the bed and gave vent to his feelings in tears. I took the big chair, and veiled my face, and for the first time gave vent to my grief and mourning for the Prophet.[23]

Nearly a month later, shortly after the dramatic meeting where Brigham and the rest of the Quorum of the Twelve were authorized to lead the Church in Joseph's place, he wrote to his daughter in Massachusetts:

> It has ben a time of mourning. The day that Joseph and Hyrum ware brought from Carthage to Nauvoo it was judged by menny boath in and out of the church that there was more than 5 barels of tears shead. I cannot bare to think enny thing a bout it.[24]

Brigham had developed the ability to grieve deeply at this great personal loss, but he had also learned from Joseph how to cope with crushing new situations and to move ahead with courage. He recovered quickly from the fear felt by many that the Church's religious authority had died with its Prophet.

> The first thing which I thought of was, whether Joseph had taken the keys of the kingdom with him from the earth; brother Orson Pratt sat on my left; we were both leaning back on our chairs. Bringing my hand down on my knee, I said the keys of the kingdom are right here with the Church.[25]

That seems to have been Brigham's "moment of truth," because, although suffering deeply with grief and immediately beset by major problems, from that time he acted with remarkable single-mindedness and effectiveness to shepherd the stunned Church and unite it under the authority of the Twelve.

There were already strong forces working in the Quorum's favor, and, despite the bewilderment of most of the Saints, there was apparently a strong presumption of the appropriateness of Brigham Young's leadership. Brigham Young's letter to his daughter Vilate on August 11, quoted from earlier, gives us a direct and fresh impression of how he and the Twelve were received when they returned to Nauvoo on August 6.

The Brethren ware over joyed to see us come home, for they ware littel children without a Father, and they felt so you may be sure. All things are now reviving up agan. The Brethren prayed with all faith for us to return. . . . I have ben in Councel all most all the time sence I arived here. But this much I can say, the spirit of Joseph is here, though we cannot enjoy their persons. Through the grate anxiety of the Church there was a confrence held last thursday [August 8]. The power of the Preasthood was explained and the order there of, on which the hol Church lifted up there voises and hands for the twelve to moove forward and organize the Church and lead it as Joseph lead it, which is our indespencable duty to due. We shall organize the church as soon as posable.

All things were, in fact, "reviving up again," but the process had not been quite as smooth as would seem from this letter; it was successful mainly because "the spirit of Joseph" did indeed manifest itself in Brigham in remarkable, to many witnesses miraculous, ways.

The returning apostles immediately found that Sidney Rigdon, the only remaining official member of the First Presidency (William Law had apostatized and plotted against Joseph), had returned from Pittsburgh, where he had gone a year earlier when a rift developed between him and the Prophet. Rigdon claimed the right to act as a "guardian" of the Church for Joseph on the basis of a vision he said he had received on the day of the Prophet's death. The President of the Quorum acted swiftly to unify the leaders, and then the members, against this and other claims that threatened the Church with disintegration. The next morning Brigham met with all the apostles at the home of John Taylor, who was still recovering from his terrible wounds received at Carthage, and in the afternoon he had a council meeting of all Church leaders at the Seventies' Hall, where he called on Sidney Rigdon to explain his vision. Elder Rigdon, whose claim, on the basis of official ecclesiastical policy (actually, *lack* of it), was certainly credible—though almost absurd in terms of his performance or status over the previous two years—made his case in quite personal, almost ambitious terms:

> It was shown to me that this church must be built up to Joseph, and that all blessings we receive must come through him. I have been ordained a spokesman to Joseph, and I must come to Nauvoo and see that the church is governed in a proper manner. Joseph sustains the same relationship to this church as he has always done. No man can be the successor of Joseph.

. . . I have been consecrated a spokesman to Joseph, and I was commanded to speak for him.[26]

Brigham Young responded, at this council meeting of leaders, with characteristic forcefulness but at the same time with impersonal, almost self-effacing, bowing to the will of God:

I do not care who leads the church . . . ; but one thing I must know, and that is what God says about it. I have the keys and the means of obtaining the mind of God on the subject. . . .

Joseph conferred upon our heads all the keys and powers belonging to the Apostleship which he himself held before he was taken away, and no man or set of men can get between Joseph and the Twelve in this world or in the world to come.

How often has Joseph said to the Twelve, "I have laid the foundation and you must build thereon, for upon your shoulders the kingdom rests."

The Twelve, as a quorum, will not be permitted to tarry here long; they will go abroad and bear off the kingdom to the nations of the earth, and baptize the people faster than mobs can kill them off. I would like, were it my privilege, to take my valise and travel and preach till we had a people gathered who would be true.

My private feelings would be to let the affairs of men and women alone, only go and preach and baptize them into the kingdom of God; yet, whatever duty God places upon me, in his strength I intend to fulfill it.[27]

President Young, having given the leaders something to think about, called for the whole Church to gather the following Tuesday (which would have been August 13) at 10:00 A.M. to resolve matters, but the very next morning (Thursday), Wilford Woodruff records: "in consequence of some excitement among the people and a disposition by some spirits to try to divide the Church, it was thought best to attend to the business of the Church in the afternoon that was to be attended to on Tuesday. The Twelve spent their time in the fore part of the day at the office and in the afternoon met at the Grove."[28] In his holograph diary for the period Brigham Young recorded his feelings with a directness of emotion that the hurried phrasing and phonetic spelling helps us share:

This day is long to be remembered by me. It is the first time I have met with the Church at Nauvoo since Brs. Joseph and Hyrum was killed — and the aucasion on which the church was [called] somewhat painful to me. Br. Rigdon had come from Pitsburg. . . . I perseved a spirit to hurry business, to get . . . a Presadecy over the Church,

Priesthood or no Priesthood right or rong, and this grieved my heart. Now Joseph is gon it seemd as though menny wanted to draw off a party and be leders. But this cannot be. The Church must be one or they are not the Lord's; the saints looked as though they had lost a frend that was able and wiling to counsel them in all things; in this time of sorrow . . . I arose and spoke to the people. My heart was swolen with compasion towards them and by the power of the Holy Ghost, even the spirit of the Prophets I was enabled to comfert the harts of the Saints. . . . I lade before them the order of the Church and the Power of the Priesthood. After a long and laboras talk of a bout two hours in the open air with the wind blowing, the Church was of one hart and one mind. They wanted the Twelve to lead the Church as Br. Joseph had done in his day.[29]

At that Thursday meeting Sidney Rigdon presented his claims, and then Brigham Young, in describing the central role the Twelve had played since 1835, affirmed in the strongest terms what most of his hearers already knew in their bones, many having been converted through the apostles' work in England and having seen them for three years become more and more involved in Joseph's confidence and in his work. He also made indirect references to the rift that had developed between Joseph Smith and Sidney Rigdon (of which the latter's absence since April 1843 was an obvious evidence) and to the instability of him and other possible leaders compared to Brigham ("Here is Brigham, have his knees ever faltered? Have his lips ever quivered? Did he flinch before the bullets in Missouri?"); and he again roused their fears of the consequences of not following established, experienced leaders like the Twelve ("If you want any other man to lead you, take him, and we will go our way to build up the kingdom in all the world"). He played on their guilt for the Prophet's death, but in a way that served at the same time to offer relief for their feelings through loyalty to the Twelve in building up the kingdom:

> You did not know who you had amongst you. . . . He loved you unto death — you did not know it until after his death; he has now sealed his testimony with his blood. If the Twelve had been here, we would not have seen him given up — he should not have been given up. He was in your midst but you did not know him; he has been taken away for the people are not worthy of him. . . . I swear to you I will not be given up. There is much to be done. . . . as for myself I am determined to build up the Kingdom of God. . . .[30]

At the same time he defused possible resentment on the part of the Saints that the articulate counselor to Joseph the Prophet was being cast off:

Perhaps some think that our beloved Brother Rigdon would not be honored, would not be looked to as a friend, but if he does right, and remains faithful, he will not act against our council nor we against his, but act together, and we shall be one. . . .

. . . all this does not lessen the character of President Rigdon; let him magnify his calling, and Joseph will want him beyond the vail.

At this point, Amasa Lyman arose. He was in an interesting dual position because he had been chosen an apostle by Joseph during a short time when Orson Pratt was suspended, in 1842, and then placed by Joseph in the First Presidency (though never formally sustained by the Church) when Orson was reinstated; but he spoke strongly in favor of the Twelve to lead the Church, as other apostles had done earlier in the day. Rigdon was apparently overwhelmed by the obvious effect of the preceding speeches on the audience and, as Wilford Woodruff tersely records, "called upon W. W. Phelps to speak in his behalf as he could not speak." Rigdon may have thought that Phelps, not an apostle, favored him, but his choice of speakers was bad. Phelps said: "I believe enough has been said to prepare the minds of the people to act. . . . If you want to do right, uphold the Twelve." After a few supportive remarks by Parley P. Pratt, Brigham Young put matters to a vote; he first proposed that all respond, by quorums, to the question, "Do you want Brother Rigdon to stand forward as your leader, your guide, your spokesman?" But Brother Rigdon, apparently seeing the audience's will and wanting to avoid a clear rejection, requested that Brigham put the other option first: "Does the church want, and is it their only desire to sustain the Twelve as the First Presidency of the Church? . . . All that are in favor of this, in all the congregation of the Saints, manifest it by holding up the right hand." The minutes record that there was a universal vote — and no negative votes when those of "contrary mind" were called to manifest it.

The result was perfectly logical and predictable, given the development of the Twelve in the previous five years, but it had by no means been assured when the Twelve returned to Nauvoo two days before and found a growing uncertainty that could have soon destroyed the Church. President Young's decisive actions and speeches on the seventh and eighth, and his effective deploying of the support of the Twelve, constituted a *tour de force* and began to reveal new dimensions and a new voice. But he was still Brigham. His speeches make clear both his absolute conviction that the Twelve should lead the Church and his willingness to use every device possible to convince a bewildered people of that truth; they show both his genuine reluctance to try to fill Joseph's shoes ("I do not know whether my enemies will take my life or not, and I do not care, for I want to be with the man I love") and his brilliant marshalling of enthusiasm to support him in that very task ("Brother Joseph the Prophet has laid the foundation for a great work and we will build upon it. . . . There is an almighty foundation laid, and we can build a kingdom such as there never was in the world"[31]).

Many who were present later remembered seeing in Brigham Young that day a new appearance and hearing from him a new voice, but one that was also very familiar — that of the Prophet Joseph. For them the "mantle of Joseph" was given directly, miraculously, to Brigham. George Laub recorded (in his journal which was not written until early 1846) that when President Young spoke, "his Voice was the Voice of Brother Joseph and his face appeared as Joseph's face,"[32] and Wilford Woodruff recounted, long after, "Just as quick as Brigham Young rose in that assembly, his face was that of Joseph Smith."[33] The earliest contemporary account that survives, though it is less specific, is from the journal of William Burton in May 1845: "But [Joseph's and Hyrum's] places were filled by others much better than I once supposed they could have been, the spirit of Joseph appeared to rest upon Brigham."[34] But an account from nearly seventy-five years later, a reminiscence by aged Bishop George Romney at a stake conference in Utah on June 22, 1919, gives perhaps a sense of what the experience came to mean for the average member of the Church like himself:

> They were children as it were; and when the man of God, as the people knew him, was taken away they did not know what would become of them. That was the condition we were in — sorrow and anguish for the loss of that man. I said the people were all children. But they knew the shepherd's voice. Sidney Rigdon and others said, "I am the man, I am the man" but it did not take. The sheep knew better. And when the Twelve returned from the east, I shall never forget in this world or in the world to come the scene as Brigham Young arose after Sidney Rigdon had used up an hour and a half delivering an eloquent discourse. When Brigham got up the mantle of Joseph Smith fell upon him. It was Joseph's voice; it was Joseph's appearance, and I testify to you, if I never again do so on this earth, in the presence of God and angels, that this is verily the truth. This is true — that the mantle of Joseph did fall upon Brigham Young and the people knew it.[35]

I believe the old man's testimony. But there is no way to recover with certainty the sights and sounds of that day, and we are
as yet without the historian's best tool, an eyewitness account
recorded soon after. What we *can* be certain of is the spiritual and
emotional void created in the Saints by the death of Joseph Smith
the Prophet, the literal mouthpiece of God on the earth and one
whom they loved as "Brother Joseph"; we can be certain that they
wanted a legitimate successor, one approved of by Joseph and one
like him. It is clear that Brigham's actions and speeches on his
return to Nauvoo carried a new sense of authority (he began his
crucial speech on August 8, "For the first time in my life, for the
first time in your lives, . . . without a Prophet at our head, do I step
forth to act in my calling in connection with the Quorum of the
Twelve, as Apostles of Jesus Christ, . . . who are ordained and
anointed to bear off the keys of the kingdom of God in all the
world"). And of course the miraculous transfiguration may have
been perceived only by those with eyes to see and ears to hear —
and mainly by the ones even among those who *needed* as well as
were open to receive additional witness.

However that may be, we can be absolutely certain of one
thing: Whatever the Saints remembered of the miraculous was
confirmed in the following months by the *reality* of President
Young's leadership as he did in fact become a Joseph — a manifestly
inspired prophet — to his people. He lost no time at all in asserting
himself: On the first page of the manuscript "History of Brigham
Young," which begins with the day after the August 8 meetings,
President Young records how that day he met with the Twelve and
eleven others at his house and proceeded, with what seems remarkable assurance, not just to preserve but to *develop* the kingdom
on the Prophet Joseph's foundation:

> I proposed righting up the Quorums of the Priesthood, giving to
> each one its place. I remarked that Joseph's presence had measurably
> superceded the necessity of carrying out a perfect organization of the
> several quorums.[36]

In that first meeting the leaders accordingly discussed organization
of the seventies, appointed the senior bishops to act as trustees of
the general financial concerns of the Church, and asked for reports
to be prepared by various committees such as the Nauvoo House
Committee.

Some selected entries from Brigham Young's holograph diary
for this period give perhaps the best indication of how his activities
and sense of assurance developed over the next few months:

On Sunday [August] the 18, I preached to the Saints in the morning. I had good liberty and by the help of the Lord I was enable to satisfy the Bretherin and unite them together so they . . . will finish the Temple.

Sept. 20, 1844 Went to the temple, called at Sister Evans, seald hir up to hir husban Horres; hir oldest son stood as proxy. Laid hands on Sister Durly; the Lord is with me continuly.

Sunday morning 22. . . . I preached to the congragation of the Saints, had a good time. Told the Saints some new things. . . .

Friday, [January] 24th 1845. Brs. H.C. Kimball and N.H. Whitney was at my house; we washed and anointed and praid, had a good time. I inquaired of the Lord whether we should stay here and finish the templ. The ansure was we should.[37]

Indeed they did finish the temple, doing as much in the next eighteen months as had been done the previous three years. And here perhaps we can see a quality in Brigham that distinguished him from Joseph—not mere practicality, because Joseph had that too in a special way, but a willingness, even a compulsion, to organize and *do*, to take Joseph's plans and visions and drive people, even goad them, to get the plans actualized. Joseph had other priorities that sometimes interfered with strict efficiency, even in the realization of his own dreams, but Brigham moved directly ahead, in a way that clearly developed from the Prophet's training but was just as surely his own style and a preparation for his leadership on the trek west and in Utah.

An instructive example is recorded in a set of minutes (located in the LDS Church Archives) which reports a meeting of the quorum of the high priests at the Masonic Hall in Nauvoo, January 6, 1845. As part of the further development of the organization of the priesthood quorums that President Young had indicated was necessary now that Joseph was gone, the high priests had been placed in charge of eighty-five districts encompassing the United States; this meeting was called to consider building a hall for the quorum, perhaps on the precedent of the Seventies' Hall that Joseph had proposed and Brigham had pushed through during the previous fall. After several proposals, including one for a very large building, President Young, according to the scribe, commented on the "great strength in the High Priests quorum, an almighty strength. The Seventies were frightened when he proposed to them to build a little one story hall that would cost a few hundred dollars, but the High Priests can build a large hall without difficulty." On this expansive note Brigham called for a vote of those "in favor of having such a hall built and are willing to do something for it themselves, and not merely look on and see their brethren build it" and of course got an enthusiastic unanimous vote. He then suggested, calling the president of the quorum, George Miller (whom he first praised as "an Architect"), to corroborate his judgment, that the building that had been proposed would cost at least fifteen thousand dollars. When all nodded proud agreement, he took immediate advantage of the enthusiastic, acquiescent mood he had built. He pointed out that up to one year before there had been no public hall in Nauvoo where a congregation could convene, except the small room in Joseph Smith's store, and reminded them that the Seventies' Hall had been delayed a season because it had not been completed by the previous winter. It was similarly likely that something would happen to the high priests' plans so that there would still be no place for them to meet well over a year in the future. Then he applied the clincher:

> Now if you will go and finish off the *upper story of the Temple* [underlining by the scribe] you will have a place in which you can receive your washings and anointings and endowments. Would it not cost less to do this, than to build a hall from the start? (Yes, Yes, from all parts of the congregation.) Well then, go to work and finish off that upper room, and then you can get your endowment, and your priesthood.[38]

The scribe matter-of-factly concludes, "On taking the question, President Young's proposition, to finish the upper room of the Temple, was unanimously accepted."

Brigham Young was certainly developing his own inimitable style of leadership as his inner sense of rightful authority grew and was reflected back by the response of the Saints. He used his voice and example in ways that were picturesque, abrasive (though acceptably so to most), marvelously motivating to almost everyone, and at times tenderly spiritual. He said to the Saints in Nauvoo as he began his Presidency, "I have traveled these many years, in the midst of poverty and tribulation, and that, too, with blood in my shoes, month after month, to sustain and preach this Gospel and build up this Kingdom,"[39] and they knew he spoke the truth and were moved to follow his example. When persecution from the surrounding settlers began to develop again in the spring of 1845, with threats that the Mormons would be driven out and with trumped-up charges against President Young and others, he rose before the gathered Saints and thundered, "I swear by the God of heaven that we will not spend money in feeing lawyers. All the lawsuits that have been got up against the saints, have been hatched up to fee lawyers, tavernkeepers, etc. I would rather have a six-shooter than all the lawyers in Illinois."[40]

Brigham Young recorded in his history for Sunday, November 20, 1845, that while he was meeting with a large group of Church leaders in the attic story of the temple, "the doorkeeper reported that there were two officers waiting at the foot of the stairs for me. I told the brethren that I could bear to tarry here where it was warm as long as they could stay in the cold waiting for me."[41] And just before Christmas, when a U.S. marshal came to the temple to arrest Brigham and others, the Mormons put Brigham's cap and a cloak on William Miller. When Miller went down and began to get into Brigham's carriage, he was arrested and taken off and not recognized until he arrived at Carthage. President Young's people responded with enthusiastic delight to such sallies and escapades — especially this last one, which they and he remembered as the "Bogus Brigham" escape;[42] they laughed and were encouraged to face their great tasks and dangers.

The dangers were serious and increasing, particularly after a renewal of mob violence broke out in September of 1845, and it became clear that the Saints would have to completely leave Nauvoo (rather than merely establishing new colonies in the West, as the leaders apparently had been considering since Joseph Smith suggested it in early 1844). But for the first year of Brigham's stewardship his leadership brought great progress, and peace enveloped Nauvoo, which Brigham redesignated "The City of Joseph."

Brigham Young described, in a letter to Wilford Woodruff in England on June 27, 1845, the progress of Nauvoo and the Saints during the past year:

> It being one year this day since the massacre of our beloved brethren Joseph and Hyrum, we have concluded to spend the day in conversation, counsel and prayer. . . . We have met from time to time to offer up our prayers and thanksgivings before the Lord for the salvation and peace of the saints, and that the Lord would enable us to finish the Temple and the Nauvoo House that the brethren might obtain their endowments, for this we have supplicated by night and by day, and hitherto we have been prospered in a manner beyond our most sanguine expectations. . . . The most perfect union, peace and good feeling has invariably prevailed in our midst and still continues. It seems like a foretaste of celestial enjoyment and Millennial glory. . . .

The brethren are clearing the ground round the Temple, and we expect to have the Tabernacle reared, so as to be ready to meet in this fall.

. . . There are many good buildings erecting in different parts of the city, there is not much sickness in the place, and there never was a more prosperous time, in general, amongst the saints, since the work commenced. Nauvoo, or, more properly, the "City of Joseph," looks like a paradise. All the lots and land, which have heretofore been vacant and unoccupied, were enclosed in the spring, and planted with grain and vegetables, which makes it look more like a garden of gardens than a city; . . . Many strangers are pouring in to view the Temple and the city. They express their astonishment and surprise to see the rapid progress of the Temple, and the beauty and grandeur of Mormon looks.[43]

This may now be seen as the deceptive calm before the storm that broke just two months later, and it should not be taken to suggest that Brigham Young did not have serious problems and some failures — a few of his own making. His verbally vivid, somewhat hotheaded forthrightness, probably intrinsic to his own particular mode of successful leadership, was costly. Even in the miraculously successful meeting on August 8, 1844, Brigham had overstepped his bounds and had to back up. The manuscript record of his speech that day shows that he lumped Sidney Rigdon, Amasa Lyman, and William Law together (all had been in some sense counselors to Joseph and therefore possible pretenders to leadership, but Law was also a betrayer) in a number of thinly veiled derogations ("Now if you want Sidney Rigdon, Amasa Lyman, or Law to lead you, or any body else, you are welcome to them, but I tell you in the name of the Lord, that no man can put another between the Twelve and the prophet Joseph"). Shortly after this statement Amasa Lyman broke in and began to speak quite defensively (and according to the minutes, Brother Brigham apologized):

I do not rise to Electioneer. I am gratified with the open, frank, and plain exposition of President Young . . . I never did conceive that [my relationship with Joseph] gave me a precedence to go before the Twelve. I do not make exception to anything he has said except my name being coupled with William Law. President Rigdon feels the same (Pres. Young asked pardon for it, and it was granted).[44]

Elder Lyman's name was subsequently crossed out — probably by President Young — from all such references throughout the scribe's record of the President's speech, and it does not appear in the printed versions. But resentments cannot be crossed out. Though the minutes of the meeting record a unanimous vote for the Twelve, by the end of August various dissident groups were forming—some leaving Nauvoo—and people were being excommunicated for refusing to follow the Twelve's direction.

Most prominent among those excommunicated was Rigdon; despite the President's call, at the end of the August 8 meeting, for the people to vote to "uphold [Brother Rigdon] in the place he occupies by the prayer of faith and let him be one with us and we with him," the disappointed counselor to Joseph had not been reconciled. One possible cause may have been that Brigham Young, in that same final speech, had assigned him to return to Pittsburgh rather than indicating that Rigdon would be truly welcomed into the ruling councils in Nauvoo: "He has been sent away by Brother Joseph to build up a kingdom; let him keep the instructions and calling; let him raise up a mighty kingdom in Pittsburgh, and we will lift up his hands to Almighty God."[45] Of course, Rigdon had rebelled against plural marriage and other new revelations given in Nauvoo, and it is unlikely that Brigham could have held him there or used him any more than Joseph did.

Brother Brigham was always rather unforgiving of what he thought was disloyalty, as well as somewhat suspicious of smoothly articulate, well-trained, but "impractical" intellectuals, and Rigdon seemed to him sufficiently guilty on both counts. President Young records in his holograph diary, September 1, 1844 (a few days before Rigdon was excommunicated for refusing to follow the Twelve), that he went to the meeting ground to hear Rigdon preach: "His discorce was compelecated and some what scattered. He said he had all things shone to him from this time. . . . There was grate things to take place but he did not tell what the saints should due to save themselves."[46]

Brigham knew what the Saints needed to do to save themselves, and though he certainly had some visions himself, he was impatient with abstract visionaries who did not seem to know concretely what must be done. He was quick and tough and unforgiving with those who seemed to know and yet would not do, and he lost a number of splinter groups and individuals and constantly strained his relationships with some of those who served closely with him. The President himself may have finally felt that the pressure of his unprecedented responsibilities was causing him to push his people too hard, because on August 17, 1845, he records:

> This morning I dreamed I saw brother Joseph Smith and as I was going about my business he says brother Brigham don't be in a hurry — this was repeated the second and third time, when it came in a degree of sharpness.[47]

But Brother Brigham's people, in the large majority, respected and, I am increasingly convinced, loved him. Few could fail to respond to the tender spirit revealed in this letter to Lucy Mack Smith, who had apparently complained about not receiving a carriage the Twelve had promised to provide her:

> My Dear aged mother Smith, for so I feele to caul you, my mother in the gospel, and the mother of my Dear Brother Joseph, the prophet and seer.
>
> . . . The caredge is not yet done. When it is you shall relize all that you have had promised to you. . . . I beg of you not to have enny unplesent feelings on the subject. It is nothing but a comon caredge that is perishable and will soon be decayed, and so shall our earthly tabernacles, and I pray the all mighty God our hevenly Father to help us to so live and walk before him that we may be [accepted] of him. All that I have is at your command to make you happy the little time you have to live with us. I shall caul and see you as soon as I can convenently.
>
> May the Lord Bles and comfort your hart. I am your son and frend as ever. P. S. The carriage will be sent to you this evening for you to use.[48]

And who could not appreciate and share in the mood of joy and satisfaction that, despite the mobs and the sure knowledge the Saints must leave the next spring, enveloped the October 1845 general conference (the first one held in three years, since Joseph Smith had stopped them pending completion of the temple), when part of the temple was dedicated and Brother Brigham was moved to relax into one of his somewhat rare expressions of gently self-deprecating humor:

> When we first (again) preached in the grove, I charged the brethren not to let their cattle get into the gardens of the widows and the sick; and if the widows shot them, I would stand between them and harm, and someone, on the Friday following shot my only cow.[49]

That genial mood was caused mainly, it would seem, by Brigham's happiness about the near completion of the temple, and his feelings about the temple seem to be a crucial key to the complex dimensions of the character of this "practical" man who responded to the visions of Joseph — and his own. In a speech on

August 18, 1844, apparently necessitated by the continuing division and unrest among the Saints despite the resolution of the problem of succession ten days before, Brigham Young bluntly warned them, "If you leave this place for fear of the mob, before God tells you to go, you will have no place of rest." He rallied them with his own determined vision: "We want to build the Temple in this place, if we have to build it as the Jews built the walls of the Temple in Jerusalem, with a sword in one hand and the trowel in the other."[50] This might have seemed merely practical counsel at a time when the Church still had the hope of being able to stay in Nauvoo. (He says in the same speech, "Sow, plant, build, and put your plowshares into the prairies: one plowshare will do more to drive off the mob than two guns.") But a year later, when mob action had started again and it was becoming amply clear to all the Saints that they would have to leave to maintain peace, President Young's vision remains:

> Sept. 16, 1845 . . . I proposed to the council that we seek peace for the present by agreeing with the mob to leave in the spring, which was agreed to. I decided to put all the carpenters to work on the Temple, and all others to getting in the families and grain, etc.
>
> Sept. 19, 1845 [to the men of a posse gathered to protect the Saints from the mobs] . . . Let all other work be stopped (except the Temple, but let the hands continue on it, if they have to carry the sword in one hand while they work with the other) and devote our time to our protection and safety.[51]

If this persistence in finishing the temple, at great cost in scarce resources and time when they were also preparing to leave it (it was given its final dedication as a completed building in secret the next April by a few members of the Quorum after Brigham and most of the Saints had left), even maintaining the effort when they were under mortal attack (when Brigham spoke to the posse on September 19, people had already been killed on both sides)—if this can be called "practical" it is the same kind of practicality that motivated Brigham when he led the Twelve back into enemy territory in Missouri in 1839 to fulfill the Lord's command.

It is easy to misunderstand Brigham's "practicality." He unquestionably had a certain vigorous decisiveness and quick forcefulness that made him different from Joseph; but, very much like Joseph (and, of course, partly through Joseph's influence and his own loyalty to Joseph), he also had a sense of the value of the symbolic, of the dramatic, of spiritual values more important than

simple efficiency and quantitative results. Going to Far West at risk
of their lives and finishing the temple only to leave it to the mob
were indeed practical—because it was psychologically and spiritually necessary, for both Brigham and the Saints, to keep faith
with Joseph the Prophet, to complete his vision and fulfill his
prophecies, the commands of God given through him.

In the case of the temple it was more important even than
being better prepared physically for the trek west that the Saints
receive the spiritual strength and vision available from the ceremonies in the house of the Lord. It was there that they could, in
the "endowment," be symbolically washed and made clean from
the stains of this world and of their own lives, could go from their
rough frontier homes to look upon their finest craftsmanship and
be taught the religious history of the world in a way that dramatically encouraged them with a vision of their personal place in that
history and imaged for them the possibilities of gentleness,
progress, and perfection. There they could make sobering covenants of consecration and obedience that would so prepare them
that, through the achievement of a unique level of group cooperation, they would not only survive but make the desert
blossom. And there, in sacred ordinances and in sealings of marriages for time and eternity, they could be taught devotion to
family and fidelity to each other; they could be included in bringing salvation to the great family of God's children, living and dead,
and being eternally united to them.

All in all, it was in the temple that the people of Nauvoo
could receive the greatest possible influx of idealism to work its
slow transformation on the clay of their lives. It is one measure of
how important this was to their leader that he spent enormous
amounts of time nearly every day and many nights all through that
winter, until the sudden departure in February, officiating in the
ceremonies in the temple. It is an indication of the complex nature
of Brigham Young's famous practicality that during the winter,
while six thousand of the Saints were carefully organized and out-
fitted for the first wagon companies, the top floor of the temple
was finished and about the same number of Saints received the
endowment and sealing ordinances. Such "practicality"—that took
into account the full range of human needs and aspirations—was
akin to Joseph's own.

Joseph and Brigham were similar in another way that must not
be forgotten. It is perhaps best revealed in their most unreserved

expressions, their personal letters to their wives, and has been well characterized by the historian Richard Bushman in some comments on Joseph Smith:

> Joseph . . . is not like other individuals (notably, revolutionaries, legislators or religious leaders) who become so absorbed in their public life that their private life is neglected, who seem to have little left for the people who are closest to them, but concentrate instead on the public occasion, the public cause, the good of the people, the fight against evil, etc. That was not true of Joseph. Though he was so engaged, he still drew back to his family and there obtained his deepest satisfactions.[52]

Joseph's concerns and emotions are easily seen in his letter to Emma on November 12, 1838, just after being placed in Liberty Jail:

> I received your letter, which I read over and over again; it was a sweet morsel to me. Oh God, grant that I may have the privilege of seeing once more my lovely Family, in the enjoyment of the sweets of liberty and social life, to press them to my bosom and kiss their lovely cheeks would fill my heart with unspeakable gratitude. . . . Tell little Joseph, he must be a good boy. Father loves him with a perfect love; he is the Eldest — must not hurt those that are smaller than him, but comfort them. . . . Julia is a lovely little girl; love her also. She is a promising child; tell her Father wants her to remember him and be a good girl. . . . Oh, my affectionate Emma, I want you to remember that I am a true and faithful friend, to you and the children, forever. My heart is entwined around you forever and ever.[53]

Compare Brigham's words to his wife Mary Ann, written on June 12, 1844, while traveling to the East on his last mission for Joseph:

> My beloved wife, while I am wating for a boat to goe to Buffalo, I improve a fue moments in wrighting to you. . . . This is a plesent evening on the Lake but I feele lonesom, O that I had you with me this somer I think I should be happy. Well I am now because I am in my cauling and doing my duty, but older I grow the more I desire to stay to my own home insted of traveling. . . .
>
> . . . How I want to see you and [the children]. Kiss them for me and kiss Luny twice or mor. Tel hir it is for me. Give my love to all the famely. . . .
>
> I do feel to Bless you in the name of the Lord.
>
> You must excuse all mistakes.[54]

But though both of them were gentle with family and friends, Brigham was given, much more than Joseph, to the picturesque forthrightness in speech that we think of as characteristic of the nineteenth century frontier. And of course, despite their very similar humility and tenderness and their focus on and delight in their wives and children and friendships, regardless of the costs and cares of their public lives, they were profoundly different from each other in some major ways.

Perhaps the greatest difference between Brigham Young and Joseph Smith has been well characterized by LDS historian Leonard J. Arrington, who describes Joseph as a "universalist" and Brigham as a "particularist": Joseph was not only interested in "Mormonism" in the narrow sense, but participated in national politics, read widely and attended lectures, studied Hebrew, German, and Egyptian, and spoke and wrote on an incredibly wide range of topics. He attracted to him an amazing variety of talented people, many of whom he immediately put in leadership positions where their diverse talents could be used. He was curious and searching and rejoiced that the restored gospel embraced all truth, putting that claim into practice by reaching out—to books, to other faiths, to all the membership—for new ideas, asking the Lord about the truth of philosophies and practices he encountered and receiving a constant flow of revelations in response. He enthusiastically sent the Twelve and other missionaries to the American Indians, to Canada, Europe, Russia, the East Indies, the Pacific Islands (even one to dedicate Jerusalem for the regathering of the Jews), for the gospel was for everyone—and in fact its optimistic message of restoration and exaltation was eagerly received by many and the Church grew almost explosively in many places.

Joseph's universalism exacted an inevitable price: The Prophet appointed diversely talented men to positions of trust who later turned out to be weak or disloyal or worse, as in the cases of John C. Bennett and William Law—whose betrayals may well have cost him his life. There was a rich diversity in the philosophies of early Latter-day Saint intellectuals, with a corresponding ferment in discussion of doctrines and a pragmatic and rather sporadic development of Church government that were unsettling to some—even, at the time of crisis after Joseph's death, splintering to the Church. Though he was sometimes criticized for his pragmatic, somewhat disorganized ways, Joseph successfully lived with these inevitable costs of the nonexclusive universalism and growth he valued and, as Arrington rightly says, "that is why Mormonism did not become a sect, as did all of Mormonism's contemporary movements."[55] But, as Arrington also notes, there is need for the particularist as well:

> I suppose it is inevitable, after such a surge of expansion and rather chaotic growth, that there follow a phase of consolidation, of financial reckoning, of coming to grips with practical problems, of the strengthening of organizational procedures and of the clarification of doctrine. This is where the particularist is both necessary and productive. Thus the Lord saw fit to sanction the election of the dynamic but methodical Brigham as successor to the brilliantly creative, but somewhat erratic Joseph.

Brigham the particularist certainly did those "necessary" things and did them with his own kind of brilliance. But among his most interesting and attractive qualities was that he also had in him, or had learned from Joseph, the universalist vision that people are ultimately more important than plan or program, and, like Joseph, he could care for and value people despite their weakness. For instance, Brigham had a nearly lifelong feud with Orson Pratt, which was probably rooted in Brigham's inability to forget or completely forgive Orson's occasional lack of perfect loyalty and submission to Joseph. Their most severe confrontation came over differences in doctrinal interpretation, which in 1860 reached the point of seeming to President Young to threaten his authority as the prophet and led him to require Orson to publicly recant.

But despite such serious differences, it is recorded in President Young's office journal that merely a few days after requiring Orson's recantation, in April 1860, he called him in to "inquire into his pecuniary circumstances," and finding that Orson's family was destitute, Brigham provided him with some supplies and then helped Orson get some teaching jobs and his son get work. In October, Heber C. Kimball came in to the President's office with a report that some people were "trying to ride down Br. O. Pratt [probably because of his recantation]; but it would not do, [for] Br. Pratt was a man of unusual firmness." He added that President Young had remarked, "If Bro. Orson was chopped up in inch pieces each piece would cry out Mormonism was true."[56] And Brigham clearly appreciated Pratt's intellectual and rhetorical abilities because he chose him to represent the Church in answering the celebrated challenge of the chaplain of the U.S. Congress, Dr. John P. Newman, to debate the biblical authority for polygamy in the Salt Lake Tabernacle in 1870—a debate in which Elder Pratt triumphed with what Newman found to be astounding erudition and style.

Brigham Young and Joseph Smith also had both similarities and differences in their handling of this world's goods. For instance, Brigham could, as he did in a sermon in 1852, cogently portray "why Joseph was not a successful merchant":

> Joseph goes to New York and buys 20,000 dollars' worth of goods, comes into Kirtland and commences to trade. In comes one of the brethren, "Brother Joseph, let me have a frock pattern for my wife." What if Joseph says, "No, I cannot without the money." The consequence would be, "He is no Prophet," says James. Pretty soon Thomas walks in. "Brother Joseph, will you trust me for a pair of boots?" "No, I cannot let them go without the money." "Well," says Thomas, "Brother Joseph is no Prophet; I have found *that* out, and I am glad of it." After a while, in comes Bill and sister Susan. Says Bill, "Brother Joseph, I want a shawl, I have not got the money, but I wish you to trust me a week or a fortnight." Well, Brother Joseph thinks the others have gone and apostatized, and he don't know but these goods will make the whole Church do the same, so he lets Bill have a shawl. Bill walks off with it and meets a brother, "Well," says he, "what do you think of Brother Joseph?" "O he is a first-rate man, and I fully believe he is a Prophet. See here, he has trusted me this shawl." Richard says, "I think I will go down and see if he won't trust me some." In walks Richard. "Brother Joseph, I want to trade about 20 dollars." "Well," says Joseph, "these goods will make the people apostatize; so over they go, they are of less value than the people."[57]

Brigham was in some ways a better merchant than Joseph, but his very ability to create this sketch, with its humorous tone of grudging admiration, reveals his basic sympathy with Joseph's attitude (the basic intent of this speech was to curb pioneer selfishness in using the timber resources). As we shall see, there is a profound sense in which the exodus he led west was, like Moses' leading of the children of Israel through the desert for forty years, not so much an escape as a means of teaching them to live higher moral and spiritual laws, and his famous colonization of the Great Basin was not so much an economic and political achievement (in which it was not at all a complete success) as an intentional and spectacularly successful process for making converts into Saints.

Brigham Young knew well what the central purpose of the gospel was and where he had learned it:

> I feel like shouting hallejujah, all the time, when I think that I ever knew Joseph Smith, the Prophet whom the Lord raised up and ordained, and to whom He gave keys and power to build up the kingdom of God on earth and sustain it. These keys are committed

to this people, and we have power to continue the work that Joseph commenced, until everything is prepared for the coming of the Son of Man. This is the business of the Latter-day Saints, and it is all the business that we have on hand.[58]

Even though Brigham had loved Nauvoo as the "City of Joseph," when he left it with the first pioneer group on February 15, 1846, he set his face to the West and the unfinished business of the Saints without reluctance. On March 9 he wrote to his brother Joseph Young from the "Camp of Israel" fifty-five miles west of the city:

> I feele as though Nauvoo will be filed with all maner of abomnations and it is no place for the saints and the spiret whispers to me the Brethrin had better get away as fast as they can. . . . Due not think, Brother Joseph, I hate to leve my house and home. No! Far from that. I am so fred from bondedge at this time that Nauvoo looks like a prison to me. It looks plesent ahead but dark to look back.[59]

His apprenticeship to Joseph was over; he could speak in what was truly his own voice and in the confidence that he was accepted and acceptable in his role as leader of the LDS people; this is from a letter, written to Charles C. Rich from Winter Quarters the next January 4, urging him to prepare for the journey west with the vanguard:

> Our Council met at Christmas and decided to send on a Pioneer company as early as possible, with plows, seeds, grain, etc. and make preparations for eatables at the foot of the mountains on this side and when the grass starts we will follow, as many as can go. Your name is among the number and we want you to go with us. . . . Gird up your loins, Brother Rich, put on your armor, cheer up your heart, and being filled with Almighty faith, prepare for the battle as fast as possible. If you are sick be made well. If you are weak, be made strong. Shake yourself like a mighty man; make the forest echo to the sound of your voice and the prairies move at your presence.[60]

Courtesy of Church Archives
The Church of Jesus Christ of Latter-day Saints

*The young President of the Quorum, about 1843 (age 42); from a
daguerrotype understood to have been taken in Nauvoo and presented
to Clara Decker Young.*

Courtesy of Church Archives
The Church of Jesus Christ of Latter-day Saints

The leader of the trek west, about 1847 (age 46).

Courtesy of Church Archives
The Church of Jesus Christ of Latter-day Saints

*President of the Church and governor of the Territory of Utah; under-
stood to have been taken on his fiftieth birthday, June 1, 1851.*

Courtesy of Church Archives
The Church of Jesus Christ of Latter-day Saints

At the time of the handcart tragedy and the "Reformation," about 1855-56 (age 54-55).

Courtesy of Church Archives
The Church of Jesus Christ of Latter-day Saints

At the conclusion of the "Utah War," July 1858 (Age 57); taken in the Beehive House by Marsena Cannon upon return from "the Move" south.

Courtesy of Utah State Historical Society

*Governing a prospering territory (though no longer governor), about 1861
(age 60); taken with the studio prop of C. R. Savage which appears in
many other photographs of the time.*

Courtesy of Church Archives
The Church of Jesus Christ of Latter-day Saints

During the Civil War, but peace in Utah, about 1864 (age 63).

Courtesy of Church Archives
The Church of Jesus Christ of Latter-day Saints

The five Young brothers (l. to r.) Lorenzo, Brigham, Phineas, Joseph, and John, about 1871 (Brigham was 70).

Both photographs courtesy of Church Archives
The Church of Jesus Christ of Latter-day Saints

Two different moods in the United Order period, about 1874 (age 73).

Courtesy of Church Archives
The Church of Jesus Christ of Latter-day Saints

The aged prophet beginning the last year of his life, in 1876 (age 75).

Courtesy of Church Archives
The Church of Jesus Christ of Latter-day Saints

The last photograph, after the St. George Temple was dedicated and just before his death, summer of 1877 (age 76).

Brigham As Moses: The Iowa Crossing
4

On February 26, 1847, Brigham Young wrote a letter from Winter Quarters to Jesse C. Little, president of the eastern Church area, in Boston:

> I expect to start for the mountains before you arrive, as it is necessary for a pioneer company to be on the way as early as possible to insure crops ahead, and I know of no better way than for me to go with the company, and if the brethren love me as I do them, they will not be long behind. I feel like a father with a great family of children around me, in a winter storm, and I am looking with calmness, confidence and patience, for the clouds to break and the sun to shine, so that I can run out and plant and sow and gather in the corn and wheat and say, Children, come home, winter is approaching again and I have homes and wood and flour and meal and meat and potatoes and squashes and onions and cabbages and all things in abundance, and I am ready to kill the fatted calf and make a joyful feast to all who will come and partake.[1]

One year before, Brigham could not have spoken with such fatherly assurance and optimistic biblical imagery. But during that year he had gone through a trial with his people in which he had learned to be a Moses and they had come to accept him as one. Brother Brigham had come to love them with a new compassion, even though, like Moses, he had learned that his purpose was not merely to lead his people in an escape from bondage and persecution, but to build them into a unified, self-reliant, spiritually powerful people. In that more significant task the greatest enemy was not the government or the mobbers — the Gentiles — but the covenant people themselves.

As ancient Israel camped near Sinai and prepared for its journey to the promised land, Moses spoke for the Lord: "Now therefore, if ye will obey my voice indeed, and keep my covenant, then ye shall be a peculiar treasure unto me above all people: for all the earth is mine. And ye shall be unto me a kingdom of priests, and an holy nation."[2] On October 8, 1845, just two weeks after

Brigham and the Twelve, in the face of a sharp renewal of mob activity, had committed the Church to leave Nauvoo the following spring, they wrote to the Church in the name of the Lord:

> The exodus of the nation of the only true Israel from these United States to a far distant region of the west, where bigotry, intolerance and insatiable oppression lose their power over them — forms a new epoch. . . .
>
> . . . We therefore invite the saints abroad generally so to arrange their affairs as to come with their families in sufficient time to receive their endowments, and aid in giving the last finish to the House of the Lord previous to the great emigration of the church in the spring. . . . Wake up, wake up, dear brethren, we exhort you, from the Mississippi to the Atlantic, and from Canada to Florida, to the present glorious emergency in which the God of heaven has placed you to prove your faith by your works.[3]

Brigham, of course, did not then realize the magnitude of what lay before him. But he had already been through enough persecution and hardship in Ohio and Missouri to have a good idea. It took a remarkable person to conceive of that impending emergency as "glorious," to announce to a people already battered by persecution that "a crisis of extraordinary and thrilling interests has arrived" and ask them "to consider well . . . the various and momentous bearings of this great movement, and hear what the spirit saith unto you by this our epistle."

Speaking at the October 1845 conference, when the situation was being discussed with the Nauvoo Saints just before that epistle from the Twelve to the whole Church was drafted, the apostle Amasa Lyman had recognized in succinct terms both the emergency and its gloriousness:

> Perhaps in the congregation before me there is every variety of feeling, which can be found on the face of the earth: yet we find their feelings undergoing a change, and that this people are approximating to a *Oneness*. . . . When they first heard the gospel, they hailed and cherished it with joy; and they have come up here to receive additional instruction: yet perhaps, they have made but a limited calculation of how far they would have to go, in obedience and sacrifices, and to how much persecution and suffering they would be subject that they might come up out of the fire as gold seven times tried. . . .
>
> . . . Some persons suppose that when they had once lost their all, they had suffered enough: . . . They have to get rich, and be made poor, about twenty times over, before they will become straight. I

expect the rich will have to be made poor until the poor are made rich; and then there will be nobody poor.[4]

Elder Lyman had hit on the central issue in the trying out of the Saints: Could they move beyond their perfectly natural instincts for material comfort, away from selfishness? Or, more precisely, *what* could so move them? The apostles knew the answer. One of the first speakers in the conference was Parley P. Pratt: "In our natural state, ask yourselves if you could be brought to endure and enjoy a celestial law, without an experience of the kind we have passed through for the last fifteen years?"[5] And George A. Smith, with characteristic wit, followed immediately with the observation "that a revelation was given in Missouri in regard to the saints consecrating their property which was not understood at the time; but they were soon brought to their understanding, for the Lord in his providence caused it all to be consecrated, for they were compelled to leave it." Then Elder Smith continued in a serious extension of that point:

> Here is one principle in which [the Lord] wants this whole people to unite. When we were to leave Missouri the saints entered into a covenant not to cease their exertions until every saint who wished to go was removed, which was done.
>
> We are better off now than we were then, and he wants to see the same principle carried out now, that every man will give all to help to take the poor; and every honest industrious member who wants to go. He wants to see this influence extend from the west to the east sea.[6]

Brigham Young had learned not to let such a perfect moment for leadership action pass, and he immediately "moved that we take all the saints with us, to the extent of our ability, that is, our influence and property," which motion was "seconded by Elder Kimball, and carried unanimously." He then said:

> If you will be faithful to your covenant, I will now prophesy that the great God will shower down means upon this people, to accomplish it [the resolution] to the very letter. I thank God that the time has come so much sooner than I expected, that that scripture is being fulfilled, "My people shall be willing in the day of my power"; and I almost feel to thank our friends abroad for hastening it on now.[7]

On the second day of the conference Heber C. Kimball picked up the same theme in one of his greatest sermons:

I am glad the time of our exodus is come; I have looked for it for years. . . . We are now about coming to the Apostolic religion; i.e., you will sell all, and come and lay it down at the Apostles' feet. But it has taken a good scourging for fifteen years to bring us to this. There may be individuals who will look at their pretty houses and gardens and say, "it is hard to leave them"; but I tell you, when we start, you will put on your knapsacks, and follow after us. . . .

We want to take you to a land, where a white man's foot never trod, nor a lion's whelps, nor the devil's; and there we can enjoy it, with no one to molest and make us afraid; and we will bid all the nations welcome, whether Pagans, Catholics, or Protestants. We are not accounted as white people, and we don't want to live among them. I had rather live with the buffalo in the wilderness; and I mean to go if the Lord will let me, and spare my life. Let us become passive as clay in the hands of the potter; if we don't we will be cut from the wheel and thrown back in the mill again.[8]

Images were important in forming the self-consciousness of this people in preparation — Elder Lyman's "gold seven times tried" and his and Elder Pratt's metaphor of a nursery of thousands of small fruit trees that "as they expand towards maturity . . . must needs be transplanted, in order to have room to grow." But especially powerful for Brigham Young was that image which Heber Kimball (the man closest to him and whose speech most moved him) took directly as a parable from his own early vocation: "passive as clay in the hands of the potter." Brigham, who may well have worked with Heber at his wheel and kiln back in Mendon, New York, repeated and developed the image as a means to understand and communicate what was happening to him and the Saints, and by the time they had completed the great exodus to Utah it had come to be an image for his own roles as President of the Church and Great Basin colonizer. He said that the incoming population, the immigrants from Europe and the East, were "like the potter's clay which brother Kimball uses for a figure," people who "have got to be ground over and worked on the table, until they are made perfectly pliable, and in readiness to be put on the wheel, to be turned into vessels of honor."[9]

The overarching allegory, of course, one which each of the other images pointed to and which grew in power as almost each day brought confirming events — whether miracles, suffering, or chastening — was that of the children of Israel. The Church had long identified with ancient Israel, the chosen people, for essentially theological reasons: Latter-day Saints accepted a unified picture of the world's religious history which made themselves not only spiritual descendants of Christ's former-day followers, but also heirs of the covenant and blessings of Abraham because of God's restoration, through them to the modern world, of the ancient order of salvation. When President Young addressed the whole Church in that epistle on October 9, 1845, speaking of "the exodus of the nation of the only true Israel from these United States," the identification began to be literal. When he met with Church leaders in the temple the following January 24, "for the purpose of arranging the business affairs of the Church prior to our exit from this place," he assured them, "my faith is that God will rule the elements . . . and the Lord will fight our battles, as in the days of Moses."[10] He never accepted the title of Moses for himself, but he lived the allegory: When he crossed the Mississippi from Nauvoo on February 15, 1846, he traveled on four miles to the bluffs and "would not go on until all the teams were up," himself down in the mud pushing, and then proceeded to the first encampment at Sugar Creek where others had been waiting; the next day, after going off up the valley with two of the apostles to pray, he organized the encampment to move out, and when, the following day, he assembled all to explain the plans and arose in a wagon and cried with a loud voice, "Attention! the whole camp of Israel," they were beginning to know who they were and who he was.

What strikes me most forcibly in reading the journals and letters of those who were part of that great trek to a promised land is that they identified imaginatively not only with the ancient pattern of Israel's deliverance in its positive aspects and faith-confirming parallels, but also with the process of development through trial, error, and repentance that kept Israel in the desert for forty years: They rejoiced in the freezing over of the Mississippi late in February so that many could cross with greater ease and safety as if through the Red Sea. The descent on October 9, 1846, of flocks of exhausted migrating quail into the hands of the starving refugees from Nauvoo caused them to praise God "that what was showered down upon the children of Israel was manifested to them in their persecution."[11] And when they found in their promised land a freshwater lake, much like the sea of Galilee, sending its water along a broad river to a larger salt sea, it was simply obvious that Heber Kimball should name that river the Jordan.

But it is also clear that Brigham, like Moses, learned quickly that his greatest problem was not the modern-day Egyptians, but the human weaknesses and ignorance of himself and his people whom God was trying to redeem. In the exasperatingly slow

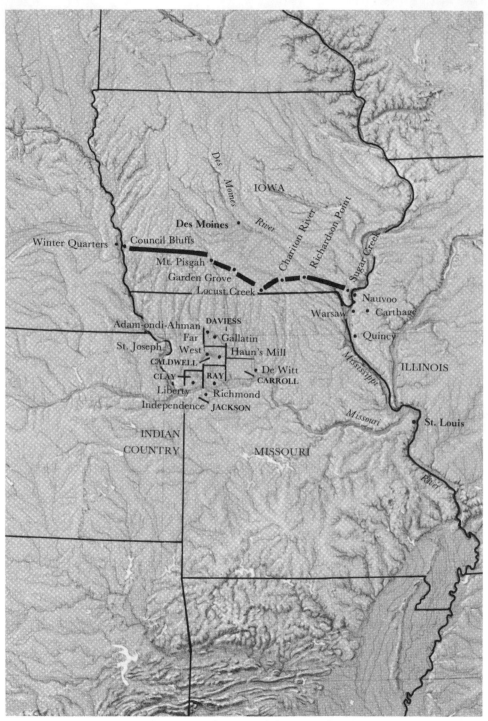

Missouri settlements and the Iowa trek.

struggle across the mud of Iowa, Brigham had to overcome the delays caused by his people's fear and even unwillingness to follow counsel and also by his own overinvolvement in details of work and organization; during the nine-month stay at Winter Quarters he railed often at "those who lied and stole and followed Israel" and said he "would prefer traveling over the mountains with the Twelve only than to be accompanied with . . . those who continued to commit iniquity";[12] during the pioneer trek the next spring he reached the point of calling that company of rather rambunctious young men to severe repentance on penalty of his refusing to lead them further;[13] and when they reached the valley, many, beginning with the leaders and including Brother Brigham, felt it perfectly appropriate to cleanse themselves of the many mistakes of the past and begin again with a rebaptism in the waters flowing into the Jordan.

Still, these modern children of Israel, like their ancient prototype, were not only Brigham's greatest opposition and source of suffering; they were the source of his joy and his purpose for being. Together they became a remarkable people as they managed to succeed in the incredible migration, and their story is best told in their own diaries and journals. To establish perspective it should be remembered that, despite the martyrdom of Joseph and Hyrum, the Mormons did not want or plan to leave Nauvoo, and when the exodus became necessary their hasty departure caused great suffering and eventually much death. To symbolize the intention to stay, Brigham had added to his own house in the fall of 1844, and in February 1845 he had gone with one hundred of the Church leaders to dedicate the site of a dam to be built across the Mississippi in connection with a huge power and navigation project (including a canal around the Des Moines rapids).[14] That project might have made Nauvoo a major American industrial city, and the plan undoubtedly aroused anxieties and jealousies and fed the appetite for persecution which soon developed.

After the open mob attacks the following September (1845) and the commitment to leave, every effort was made for preparation, but the task was enormous. It was made more difficult by the greed of neighbors who held back from paying even the much deflated, forced sale prices for homes, shops, farms, and goods and then acted to force a precipitous departure by the Saints so they could obtain many things for nothing. With such factors operating, when Brigham suddenly decided to leave ahead of time the next February the exodus was unique in American experience. Choosing to abandon their beautiful, developing city and seek a refuge in the wilderness rather than engage in civil war, over ten thousand people prepared to move almost en masse as an act of religious faith. Most were, compared to other westering emigrants, relatively poor, even destitute; many were recent converts from the lower classes in Europe, and even the ones who had begun to build some material security in Nauvoo had received only a fraction of value for their property. They started out to the West without a certain destination and with no professional guides and were in fact the only such group who went without anyone along who had been that way before.[15] They placed their trust in Brigham and the other leaders, who gathered all available information and maps on the West and consulted mountain men along the way, but who finally trusted in turn that through divine aid they would, in the words of a song composed and sung along the way, "find a place which God for us prepared, far away, in the West."

William Clayton composed that song on April 15, 1846, while sitting on a wagon tongue with his feet in the mud of Iowa, only halfway across the state after two months of traveling. Excerpts from his diary of that day are revealing of him, of the unusual nature of his people, and of Brother Brigham:

> This morning Ellen Kimball came to me and wishes me much joy. She said Diantha [his wife whom he had left in Nauvoo while he served as clerk of the first pioneer camp] has a son. . . . Spent the day chiefly reading. In the afternoon President Young came over and found fault about our wagons, etc. In the evening the band played and after we dismissed . . . retired to my tent to have a social christening. . . . We had a very pleasant time playing and singing until about twelve o'clock and drank health to my son. . . . Henry Terry's horses are missing and have been hunted today but not found. This morning I composed a new song — "All is well" ["Come, Come, Ye Saints"]. . . . In the evening I asked the President if he would not suffer me to send for Diantha. He consented and said we would send when we got to Grand River.[16]

William Clayton was a meticulous, educated English convert who loved books; he was a fine musician and had a flair for observing, even rhapsodizing over, the new forms of nature they were moving into. He had small hands, and he liked to dress rather elegantly. What was this man doing standing guard, rounding up cattle, supervising six wagons of Church goods and records, often pitching tents in severe rain and struggling to right them again after they were blown down in severe wind? Like many others without any previous experience, he was learning from a relatively few who had grown up on the frontier to be a pioneer — and, like the others, was succeeding. His journal entry reveals another unusual aspect of the Mormon migration: It was one of the very few which contained large numbers of women and children and had to deal with the many special difficulties — slower travel, childbirth, childhood diseases, additional accidents, the need for larger groups to provide protection — that families posed as compared with the usual company of young male adventurers. Of course, realizing this, Brigham tried at first to restrict the vanguard company in Iowa to well-provisioned men only, and after failing in that and seeing much suffering and delay as a consequence, he *made certain* that they traveled essentially that way the next year in the lead group to Utah.

In Clayton's journal entry we can also see evidence of the loving anxiety Brother Brigham felt as he tried to cope with the great mass of people stampeding much faster than he had planned into the wilderness. At any rate it wasn't at all easy, but people like Clayton, though inexperienced and having to learn mainly by their mistakes how to pioneer, brought an amazing range of skills and interests and a somewhat naive blitheness of spirit that epitomizes the unique nature of this migration. In Brigham's sharing of that spirit, though he was also experienced and soberly effective as a frontiersman, there is something that strongly draws us to him, as it obviously did a wide range of people in his own time.

Those who crossed the Mississippi in early and middle February before the river froze over and later after it had melted again had a difficult, dangerous time maneuvering the flatboats loaded with wagons through the cold and wind and ice floes. As they gathered at the first camp on Sugar Creek, the cold which eventually froze the river, getting to twenty below zero some nights, caused those who were waiting for Brigham and others much suffering. But life went on — in her journal, Eliza R. Snow records that nine babies were born one night — and when Brigham arrived they began under his encouragement to organize to move: "I told the brethren they were the best set of fellows in the world, still there was a great chance for improvement. I blessed them in the name of the Lord."[17]

Brigham returned to Nauvoo for a few days to bring others on, and when he got back they were soon joined by Clayton and Pitt's band, which Clayton had been part of in England and, as one of his last acts in Nauvoo, had at Brigham's direction helped outfit with instruments. The band was immediately called on to play for the Saints camped there in primitive conditions, and it played every night while they were at Sugar Creek, with Peter Hansen soloing on the violin. When they moved on to Reed's Creek, the camp (which had swelled to five hundred wagons and about five thousand people) was visited by curious settlers from nearby Farmington, who were so impressed by the band they insisted on a concert for them in town. The band got a free dinner and stayed late (Brigham finally sending out a patrol for them because of his continuing unease about gentile intentions). These musicians became an important source of revenue as they were asked for a series of paid concerts further on in Kesoagua and then other places.

But it was a struggle for everyone to provide fodder for the livestock (since grass was not yet available) as well as keep themselves fed, especially as an increasing number were running out of supplies, having left Nauvoo without adequate preparation in their anxiety to be with the leaders. Those, like Brigham, who had brought eighteen months' provisions as planned, shared with the others and were soon destitute themselves, and everyone had to start finding alternatives. Corn was purchased for whatever work the nearby settlers would accept — cutting rails, building houses, transporting goods (especially furs along the Missouri River later on), giving concerts, but the little money in private and Church treasuries was being used up and people began to trade what few expendables they had brought. Clayton, for instance, tells of packing up precious china he had brought from England to send off with trading parties traveling out from the route (even south into Missouri) to find grain.

In these dark days in Iowa the seriousness with which most of the Saints took their mutual assistance covenant certainly saved many lives. Clayton records that some of Hosea Stout's guards joined his small company and admitted having no food: "I dealt out some of my own flour and bacon to them, determined to comfort them some if I could and not willing to see anyone in our company suffer while I have anything left."[18] But such sharing, of course, finally brought everyone to nearly desperate straits. Clayton's journal reports that by May 22 he was out of everything but a little corn and had begun to consider sending away some of the Church teamsters, whom he had been supporting along with his large family. Then he heard that men he had sent trying to trade for food were returning with meal and bacon: "This was joyful news to me and I felt my heart much relieved."

Hosea Stout was a quite different man—tough, temperamental, an experienced outdoorsman, and deeply loyal to Brigham. He had been captain of the police in Nauvoo and was given similar authority over the camp guards en route and the police at Winter Quarters. His record gives us otherwise unavailable insight into the disciplinary problems of this imperfect people being chastened. It also gives us some account of Brigham's authoritarian side, tempered by his growing wisdom, mercy, and ability to attract and love and use effectively a variety of people—from Stout himself, who stood guard in the night, flogged fornicators, and disciplined thieves, to Orson Pratt, who took longitude, latitude and altitude readings en route and spent his time at Winter Quarters "studying the polarization of light."

It is Stout who tells of food and cattle feed being wasted at first through too much being taken from the commissaries, and of Brigham chastising those responsible and then organizing a reporting system to stop the practice.[19] Like Clayton, Stout complained of Brigham's habit of changing orders and plans as he adjusted to the developing chaos in Iowa; but, also like that very different Englishman, he remained loyal to the President, adjusted to the changes and, despite his own precarious situation and lack of supplies, shared to the last with others:

> June the 20th 1846. This morning I went some three miles to Henry Mours [Mowers] camp to see Br. S. Wixom to try and get some meal, for hunger began to grin hard around us. But I got none and was now entirely out and knew not where the next meal would come from, so my wife went to preparing our dinner, which might be properly called our "ultimatum." . . . Just as it was ready Elder Henry G. Sherwood rode up very hungry. I invited them to stop . . . and take dinner, to which they readily consented, little thinking that they were going to help make away with all I had and then leave me in this wild and desolate place to risk the kind hand of Providence for the next. We had a joyful time and plenty to eat but none left.[20]

A few days later Stout was able to obtain food and continue on the last leg of the journey along the Indian trail toward Council Bluffs, but the worst had not yet come:

> June the 28th . . . I awoke very early this morning and immediately discovered my child to be dying. . . . He gradually and slowly de-

clined untill forty minutes after seven when its spirit took its leave
of its body without any apparent pain but seemed to go to sleep.

. . . Discouraged, desolate and such frequent disappointments as
had lately been my lot and no reason to expect any thing better in
future could now only occupy my mind and the mind of my wife,
the bereaved mother. We had now only one child a daughter left
and that was born on the road and what was its fate. Was it to be
laid by the way side also?[21]

No, it wasn't, but many others were to be, including a wife and
newborn child of Stout's at Winter Quarters; and many already
had been "laid by the way side" in the exodus, including two sons
who had died in Stout's arms, one of "whooping cough and black
canker" on May 8 at Garden Grove. Stout reports one man dying
because he simply "wore out" on the road and tells of a number of
accidents in which children fell under wagon wheels and were
killed and women (one was his wife whom he barely saved) caught
their dresses in the wheels and were pulled under.

This was what it was like in the trek across Iowa. But as
Brigham Young improved the organization of all the companies by
late in April and then established permanent colonies at Garden
Grove and Mount Pisgah for raising crops to be harvested by the
following groups, he moved along the trail to the Missouri River
with new confidence. After arriving at Council Bluffs on June 14,
establishing a ferry, and beginning to work out arrangements with
the Indian agency and the Omaha Indians there, Brigham still
hoped to get a vanguard off to the mountains that summer. Stout,
who was a few days behind, struggling with his own griefs and
hunger, reports an emissary passing him going back to Mount
Pisgah, the second permanent settlement, to raise four hundred
volunteers for the first pioneer company. But then Stout reports
another emissary passing him, one who came from the East with
word that "there were some officers of the United States Army at
Pisgah with a requisition from the President of the United States,
on us for 500 soldiers to march to Santa Fe against Mexico and
from thence to California and there to be discharged and their arms
given in at the expiration of one year. . . . We were very indignant
at this requisition and only looked on it as a plot laid to bring
trouble on us as people."[22] Brother Brigham, who had been seeking
some kind of federal help, though this offer came as a surprise, was
able, despite the negative feelings among his followers, to use his
accumulated power with the Saints to raise in a few days five
hundred volunteers to march off under Captain James Allen. The

character of the gentile visitors helped; even Stout was impressed with Allen's unassuming demeanor as he explained his mission — and then was convinced, along with others, by Thomas Kane, who had become sympathetic with the Mormon plight, had helped arrange for the recruitment of the Battalion, and had come from Washington to assure them that the government offer was well-intentioned.[23]

By this time Stout had managed to catch up with Brigham:

> [President Young] inquired into and I related to him my situation and the suffering that I had passed through. . . . He borrowed 109 pounds of flour for me . . . and said if I could borrow any thing that I needed he would see it paid. . . . My prospects for living seemed to brighten for he acted like a friend that was willing to help in time of need.[24]

Gradually Brigham Young had given up hope of sending even a small group west that season. Looking on the resources provided by the Battalion pay and clothing allowance as a Godsend, he began to marshal resources for a long winter layover on both sides of the Missouri. Kane remained with the Mormon encampment for over two months because he became terribly ill with malaria; he was carefully ministered to, became a steadfast friend to Brigham, and provided effective service to the Church over many years. In his own account of a farewell ball for the Mormon Battalion he gives some insight into the remarkably good spirits the people maintained despite the reality of their situation and their feelings as an exiled people:

> Light hearts, lithe figures, and light feet had it their own way from an early hour till after the sun had dipped behind the sharp sky line of the Omaha hills. Silence was then called, and a well cultivated mezzo-soprano voice, belonging to a young lady with fair face and dark eyes, gave with quartette accompaniment a little song, the notes of which I have been unsuccessful in repeated efforts to obtain since, — a version of the text, touching to all early wanderers:
> "By the waters of Babylon we sat down and wept."
> "We wept when we remembered Zion."[25]

Kane aided in obtaining permission from the government for the Mormons to winter on Indian lands and even build settlements and plant crops until all had successfully emigrated. Brigham Young had bargained for these things with Captain Allen in the first discussion about the Battalion, and Allen had made assurances that actually exceeded his authority. But Kane's advice to the

Mormon leaders as they wrote President Polk, and his own letters to various officials, made the permission certain and provided Brigham with the resting place he needed in which to consolidate, prepare, and plan for the great journey west. After hearing Kane's encouragement to settle in the Great Basin rather than in Oregon or on the California coast, Brigham wrote in his letter to Polk on August 9 that he intended to seek a "location west of the Rocky Mountains, and within the basin of the Great Salt Lake or Bear river valley."[26]

This final decision of the Saints' destination had a long history. Just as the Mormons had for some time thought of themselves as in some sense the modern "children of Israel," so they for many years had thought of themselves as in some sense destined to go west. But just as the full meaning of that identification had to be learned through a literal exodus and long chastening, so also the specific nature of their trek and its particular destination and purpose had to be learned gradually through trial and change. The Book of Mormon, published in 1830 and the chief tool of conversion for the early Saints, had included a quotation by an ancient American prophet of Isaiah's prophecy: "And it shall come to pass in the last days, when the mountain of the Lord's house shall be established in the top of the mountains, and shall be exalted above the hills, and all nations shall flow unto it."[27] This statement of destiny was re-phrased and repeated many times in the revelations given in the following years to Joseph Smith:

> But before the great day of the Lord shall come, Jacob shall flourish in the wilderness, and the Lamanites shall blossom as the rose.
>
> Zion shall flourish upon the hills and rejoice upon the mountains, and shall be assembled together unto the place which I have appointed.[28]

Brigham might have remembered a blessing given to his brother Lorenzo in 1834 by Hyrum Smith which predicted that Lorenzo would go with the body of the Saints to the valleys of the mountains.[29] And according to a report made by Anson Call and others after the trek to Utah, and added to Joseph's history, there was an even more specific prediction made by Joseph Smith on August 6, 1842:

> I prophesied that the Saints would continue to suffer much affliction and would be driven to the Rocky Mountains, many would apostatize, others would be put to death by our persecutors or lose their

lives in consequence of exposure or disease, and some of you will live to go and assist in making settlements and build cities and see the Saints become a mighty people in the midst of the Rocky Mountains.[30]

Brigham had not been present when that prophecy was made, but he knew of the Prophet's thinking, because he recorded in his own history, for February 21, 1844, "Brother Joseph directed the Twelve to select an exploring company to go to California [which then included present-day Utah] to select a location for the settlement of the Saints." He was also certainly aware that Joseph had sent Orson Pratt and John E. Page to Washington in March of 1844 with a plea for federal assistance in an immigration to either Texas or Oregon, a plea which was rejected, although a number of congressmen favored assisting in a move to Oregon because the fever of what became known as "manifest destiny" was waxing hot and they wanted to strengthen the hand of the United States in that area disputed with England. Brigham also knew that Joseph had made an appeal to the British government for help in a move to Vancouver Island — which was likewise turned down.

Vancouver Island must have been a serious possibility for the Saints' relocation, because when Brigham met in late September 1845 with General J. J. Hardin, Stephen Douglas, and others of an appointed mediation committee sent by Governor Ford, he reported that "General Hardin said he would do all in his power by counsel, etc., to help us, and approved of our proposed location at Vancouver's Island. . . . Judge Douglas said Vancouver's Island was claimed by the United States, and he felt sure there would be no objection to its settlement, or to the settlement of Oregon."[31] And he added to the October 9 Epistle to the Church, "There are said to be many good locations for settlements on the Pacific, especially at Vancouver's Island near the mouth of the Columbia." But either things were not yet clearly decided or Brigham was intentionally trying to disguise his intentions from potential enemies, because he later had his scribe record in his private history for September 9, 1845, that the "General Council [Council of Fifty] met. Resolved that a company of 1500 men be selected to go to Great Salt Lake valley and that a committee of five be appointed to gather information relative to emigration."[32]

Brigham Young was perhaps both somewhat uncertain and very prudent. It seems likely that, despite a very strong inclination, he was not finally certain of the exact location for the promised Zion until he looked down on the Salt Lake Valley from a pass high in the Wasatch peaks eight miles to the east and was given a vision of its future fertility and peace that accorded with an earlier vision of the promised place. Though crops were even then being planted by the advance group in the valley, he could still have moved on the next year if he had become convinced that was right.

Brother Brigham was both pragmatically flexible and politically skillful in this matter of destination—just as he was in responding to problems like the year's delay in his plans caused by disobedience to his counsel, and to opportunities like the sudden willingness of the previously unresponsive government to help through recruiting the Mormon Battalion. He displayed the highly unusual ability to assess a developing situation, make a firm rational decision (even though it might go counter to all his previous intentions), adjust his feelings to the results, and proceed with inspiring energy to the event. This quality is clear in the decision, in September 1845, to abandon Nauvoo entirely, although up to that point it seems that both people and leaders had been confident they would be able to stay in their beloved city and were only considering other locations as *additional* colonizing sites. It was again manifest in February 1846, when Brigham suddenly decided, on the basis of new information, to begin the exodus in the dead of winter even though the mob leaders had assured amnesty until later when grass and water would be available. In these decisions he was able to set his face "like flint" to the West, away from past comforts and affections. But in the long process of preparing and directing the gigantic migration he displayed what seems a contradictory, but for him was a complementary, quality of energetic teachableness—adjustability, willingness to fail, and the ability to regroup and try again in a new way.

The winter of 1845-46 had been a time of intense preparation for the Saints—physical preparation as the city was turned into a giant wagon-building shop and provisions were stocked, and spiritual preparation as the temple was completed, endowments received, and family sealings performed. Brother Brigham took the lead in both of these general preparations but was also intensely engaged in the process of determining where to go and by what timetable. He reports that on December 20 he and a few of the Twelve "heard F.D. Richards read *Fremont's Journal*, giving an account of his travels to California."[33] John C. Fremont, who was fast becoming the most famous western explorer, and his recently published journal and maps were a major influence in what seems to be Brigham's increasing focus on "Upper California"—which then included both the fertile San Joaquin Valley and the valleys draining into the Great Salt Lake. On December 27 there was a meeting in which "the visit of the marshal [the one who was foiled in his attempt to arrest Brigham] and the immigration to California were the prominent topics. Elder Parley P. Pratt read from Hastings' account of California."[34] (Hastings was the explorer who blazed and promoted the "Hastings Cutoff," which shortened the trail to California by two hundred miles and which was the route Brigham eventually followed from Ft. Bridger to the Salt Lake Valley.) On December 31, President Young and Heber C. Kimball "examined maps with reference to selecting a location for the saints west of the Rocky Mountains, and reading various works written by travelers in those regions."[35]

By this time it is clear that the destination was west of the mountains, probably "upper California" and therefore the Great Salt Lake, and a month later the Church's leader had decided to leave at once. He had received a letter on January 29, 1846, from Samuel Brannan in New York, who was preparing, with Brigham's counsel, to take a shipload of Saints around Cape Horn to California. Brannan reported that he had learned from Amos Kendall, the former Postmaster General with whom he had been negotiating some kind of help for the Church, that the "government intended to intercept our movements by stationing strong forces in our way, to take from us all fire arms on the pretense that we were going to join another nation."[36] On January 4, Brigham had seen a letter to the local county sheriff from Governor Ford hinting that the regular army might soon get involved in attempts to make arrests in Nauvoo; later he recorded his feelings of that day: "We will run no risk of being murdered by them as our leaders have been."[37] Ford later admitted in his own history that this had been a pure fabrication to get the Mormons to leave earlier than agreed upon, and it seems clear from later actions that Amos Kendall was also lying to try to frighten the Mormons into accepting a scheme intended to enrich himself. But these letters only added to Brigham's nervousness about genuine attempts to arrest him and other leaders on charges of counterfeiting and to what seems an inspired sense that the time was right, possibly because the people were at a psychological, if not a physical, peak of readiness.

Another crucial factor in the early departure from Nauvoo was Brother Brigham's fundamental abhorrence of violence. This may sound strange, considering the myth that the sensationalist Eastern press built up around him later in Utah and which has persisted as a rumor even among his own people — of an all-powerful authority who had the means and the will to dispose of his enemies, Mormon or non-Mormon, by secret assassination. And it seems to contradict his aggressive rhetoric in reaction to murder and persecution ("[Joseph] should not have been given up; I swear to you I will not be given up"; "I would rather have a good six-shooter than all the lawyers in Illinois"; "Give them the cold lead"[38]). But though this strong public language was effective in rousing the Saints to group solidarity behind him, and though it expressed his own true feeling of extreme offense at their violated rights, in every case this expressed urge to violence was followed by reasoned and carefully passive response.

In fact, it seems quite clear that he hated bloodshed — it repelled him at the very core of his being — and he was willing to take major risks and make huge sacrifices to avoid it. As soon as men were killed in the attempt to protect Nauvoo against the renewal of mob action in September 1845, he called back the posse and agreed to leave in the spring. The rather hasty decision to leave in February, earlier than had been agreed upon, even though he knew he and his people thus faced greater hardships, was largely based on evidence that if they remained additional warfare was inevitable. Brother Brigham reports a dream during that flight from Nauvoo that gives his true feeling about violence:

> I was pursued by a beast which threatened my life, and I fled into a house for safety, the beast following me appeared to change into a human being which I attempted to shoot with a seven shooter, to save my own life but it would not go off, then to bluff off the person I drew my small six shooter which went off contrary to my expectations, the ball passed through the brain of the individual, soon as the blood started the man came to his senses and was sorry for what he had done. I felt so bad because I had shot a man, that I awoke and was thankful that it was but a dream.[39]

On February 2, 1846, the brethren in council "agreed that it was imperatively necessary to start as soon as possible." Brigham told them to procure boats and have families ready to leave "within four hours" notice. He then "met with the captains of hundreds and fifties and laid my counsel before them, to which they all consented, and dispersed to carry it into execution." Late that night, after visiting the grave of Willard Richards's wife with Willard and Heber, he, with those two men, "made inquiries of the

Lord as to our circumstances and the circumstances of the Saints and received satisfactory answers. Retired about 1 a.m."[40]

That next year of flight must have been the most difficult of Brigham Young's life, at least in the anxiety of enormous responsibility; the constant frustrations of obstacle, hardship, thwarted plans; and the pain of his own personal growth. There were some fine moments of miraculous assistance and joyful hope and sense of achievement, but the black mud of Iowa and the black scurvy of Winter Quarters—and through it all his overshadowing awareness of fifteen thousand people strung out over five hundred miles in a dangerous wilderness, all depending on him—darkened his life. What pulled him through and eventually made the tragedies of Iowa and Winter Quarters into a great triumph of spiritual strengthening for him and the Church was his sense of purpose and his insistence, increasingly consistent in detail as he learned from his experience, that all actions and decisions must accord with that purpose even when they violated his practical judgment and thwarted his own plans.

But the next day after the February 2 decisions, despite President Young's announcement that there would be no more administration of the temple ordinances, many gathered at the temple, anxious to receive their individual endowments and marriage sealings. Brigham told the Saints that if they delayed longer their way would be hedged up and their enemies would intercept them, that they would build more temples elsewhere, and that he was going to get his wagons and be off—and he walked away from the temple. But when he checked later, the temple was still "filled to overflowing," and so, "looking upon the multitude and knowing their anxiety . . . we continued at work diligently in the house of the Lord." That day they performed ordinances for about three hundred people, and then over five hundred on each of the next few days. Brigham appointed Joseph Young to preside in Nauvoo and to organize groups of elders to meet and pray each night in the temple for the people in their exodus and the Twelve who would lead them (a practice that continued—noted carefully in his journal—until the last group was expelled). He then tried to get away the following week, since a few families had left on February 4 and others were following to the first camp on Sugar Creek. But he didn't make it until February 15, and when he reached Sugar Creek he explained to those who had been there up to two weeks camping in the snow that he had had to wait on others and "if all had come on according to counsel, I should have been here sooner, if I had come without a shirt to my back."[41]

This was not the last delay. Weather and human cussedness combined in such a way that it took four months to cross Iowa's three hundred miles. By comparison, the next year it took the "Pioneer Company" only three months to cover the remaining thousand miles to the Salt Lake Valley. Of course, that later pioneering caravan was designed for speed, being composed essentially of young men carefully provisioned and organized, with adequate animals. This is what Brigham had planned for the whole trek, including Iowa—a trailblazing company, made up of most of the apostles and a select group, to hurry on ahead and find a gathering place and get in crops to support those following. His plans broke against human and physical reality, despite the energy with which he threw himself at the obstacles—working all day with the others building bridges and pushing wagons through mud; organizing, reorganizing, planning and praying far into the night; rushing up and down the long line of struggling groups to encourage and cajole, chastise and shame, punish and praise—all in a desperate effort to save them all and at the same time learn and teach what it was all for. That latter task he undoubtedly accomplished, despite—perhaps even because of—the delays and failures. The epic journey he led the next year to the mountains, praised ever since as the most successful immigration into the West, owed its success to the struggles, the price paid in Iowa, where Brigham learned to be the Moses his people needed—and when they learned to respond to him as such.

Not only the basic skills of emigrating but also the pattern for building and colonizing in Utah were learned in Iowa and Winter Quarters. The first problem was organization, for as soon as the exodus seemed certain the plan carefully developed in the fall of 1845 was destroyed by the many families that left Nauvoo by themselves (and unprepared) in fear of mobs or troops; others later returned in fear of cold and hunger or to try to sell property or to get the rest of their families. Even well-organized companies were scattered by the bad roads and the need of some to go off to work or buy provisions. Brigham, struggling to keep things together with his own strength, soon faced the same problem that confronted Moses after the successful crossing of the Red Sea: Diarists in the companies—Willard Richards, William Clayton, Hosea Stout—all record Brigham's incredible involvement in detail; in Richards's words, his "acting the part of a father to everybody" as he moved constantly back and forth trying to aid and comfort. Although some of this was certainly necessary to provide reassurance, specific blessings, and decisions for a traumatically dislocated and endangered people, Stout, who was in charge of the guards, gives us a hint of how things got out of hand when he notes that on March 15 he reprimanded his men severely for "continually running to Pres. B. Young for advice and council about matters which had already been laid down."[42] Brigham himself revealed what was happening when he wrote on March 9, to Joseph Young, "There is so much talking to me that I cannot wright and I due not know what I wright and you must read it wright though it may not be writen only scratched";[43] and again on March 15 to his wife Harriet Cook, "There were so meney talking to me I cannot wright."[44] The drain on him was so terrible that on May 3, in addressing a congregation at Garden Grove, President Young said: "I am reduced in flesh so that my coat that would scarce meet around me last winter now laps over twelve inches. It is with much ado that I can keep from lying down and sleeping to wait the resurrection."[45]

When the old patriarch Jethro, Moses' father-in-law, visited the Camp of Israel and saw him spending all day handling the press of miscellaneous details from all kinds of people, he said to Moses: "Thou wilt surely wear away, both thou, and this people that is with thee," and recommended that he choose good men and place them over the people "to be rulers of thousands, and rulers of hundreds, rulers of fifties, and rulers of tens. . . . They shall bear the burden with thee."[46] This is exactly the organization that had been set up while the Saints were still in Nauvoo; but the organization had fallen apart, and Brigham's first concern was to regroup, which he did partially at Sugar Creek and again at Richardson's Point Camp in early March; but the full, careful reorganization took place on March 27 at Shoal Creek, near the Chariton River.

This did not solve all the problems, by any means. The immediate cause for Brigham's uncharacteristic complaint on May 3 was a perennial problem—the people needed to trust the leaders enough to follow their counsel not only when it was inspiring but when it was difficult:

> When the removal westward was in contemplation at Nauvoo, had the brethren submitted to our counsel and brought their teams and means to me and authorized me to do as the Spirit and wisdom of the Lord directed with them, then we could have outfitted a company of men that were not encumbered with large families and sent them over the mountains to put in crops and build houses, and the residue could have gathered. . . . none would be found crying for

bread, or none destitute for clothing, but all would be provided for as designed by the Almighty. But instead of taking this course, the Saints have crowded on us all the while, and have completely tied our hands by importuning, saying do not leave us behind. . . . They are afraid to let us go on and leave them behind; forgetting that they have covenanted to help the poor away at the sacrifice of all their Property.

. . . I know that the same cause caused Joseph to lose his life, and unless this people are more united in spirit and cease to pray against Counsel, it will bring me down to my grave.[47]

Orson Pratt, with a touch of stern humor, said later at Winter Quarters "that the reason why the Twelve had changed their counsel so often was, because the people did not abide the best counsel, which was given by the spirit of God."[48]

Brother Brigham's counsel, and the counsel of those of the Twelve with him, whom he always consulted carefully before making major decisions, did change, and it seems crucial to understand the process by which he learned to make and cope with those changes. That process is very hard to analyze, especially since the official history kept by Willard Richards, though written for Brigham in the first person and later approved by him, does not reveal the inner man as well as a personal diary might have. But I sense a great change in Brigham during those Iowa months, not a reversal or a sudden acquisition of entirely new qualities but a trial of the soul that matured him and carved out new dimensions of feeling and insight that prepared him for the tasks ahead, tasks which were enormously different and more difficult than his successful uniting of the Church after Joseph's death. It was as if he had to learn, after some miraculous, unexpected successes in Nauvoo (created in good part through his own rapidly developing energy and charismatic powers of motivation), that he had limits, and that his people did too. There in the mud of Iowa, Brigham developed in important ways, and though he certainly always retained his strict toughness and his impatience with weakness and disloyalty, he never lost the humility and humane flexibility he gained there.

Again, a great deal of Brigham's tension paralleled that felt by Moses when he found himself caught between his people's disobedience to the Lord's clear directions and his compassion for them. This sometimes put Moses in the position of asking, "Wherefore hast thou afflicted thy servant and wherefore have I not found favour in thy sight, that thou layest the burden of all this people upon me?"[49] but also pleading, "Yet now, if thou wilt forgive their sin—; and if not, blot me, I pray thee, out of thy book which thou hast written."[50] Elder Pratt's appeal that the counsel of the leaders was given by the Spirit of God was not a bullying overstatement; under Brigham's direction the leaders made much effort to obtain that Spirit and clearly believed it came to them. President Young's journal record is confirmed by many others that despite (actually because of) the harrowing demands of the exodus, he took great pains to keep close to the God of Israel—by careful observance of the Sabbath (no travel, trading, working, hunting, except in dire emergency); by taking the Twelve and others off away from the camps at frequent intervals for formal prayer and worship services; and, of course, by constantly seeking prophetic guidance.

I cannot agree with Nels Anderson's witty but flippant stereotype, while comparing Brigham to Joseph, that "one suspects, after reviewing his record, that [Brigham] acted first and prayed afterward." Anderson is more correct in suggesting that when Brigham "emerged from his chamber of prayer, it was to give instructions and not to read a new revelation."[51] When the original plan to send a select, fast-traveling pioneer company ahead was continually delayed, Brigham kept trying different ways to make it work. On April 18 he records that he met with the captains of hundreds, fifties, and tens to select persons to go on trading expeditions to surrounding settlers and also to find men to

> outfit themselves for the mountains, and they can get ready immediate. The rest of the company go to Grand river where they can locate themselves for the season, and the borrowed teams that are going back to Nauvoo—go on to help the families on to the location. These are the whisperings of the Spirit to me. . . . I stated that unless the hands of the Twelve could be untied it would be impossible for them to go over the mountains.[52]

Three weeks later, after nine straight days of rain at their first permanent settlement at Garden Grove, with wagons being abandoned in the mud and nearby mills unable to grind, Brigham wrote (for the Council of the Twelve) to those who had been out trading in surrounding communities for food and fodder to join them immediately:

> It will be better to sacrifice a few wagons, horses and beds to sustain us while we are putting in crops . . . than it would be to omit planting and then have to sacrifice one-half or all of our property to keep us alive next winter. . . .

. . . Do for the best but hasten to help us with the crops, for on this depends the salvation of this people temporally and spiritually. Such are the whisperings of the spirit to me.[53]

But a month later on June 7, as they began to move out along the Indian trail through western Iowa towards Council Bluffs on the Missouri River, Brigham recorded that he "told the saints they were hedging up their own way by the course they were pursuing. . . . I can safely prophesy that we will not cross the mountains this season, and that is what many of the brethren wish, they would rather go to hell than be left behind."[54]

Circumstances changed again when Brigham arrived at Council Bluffs. Only a few days before he was to be approached by Captain James Allen of the army with the requisition for the Mormon Battalion that changed his plans dramatically, Brigham (apparently much influenced by Fremont's enthusiasm for the Great Salt Lake area) was talking about sending a fast, hand-picked group on to the mountains in thirty-five days to plant crops, and he proposed to the Council sending such a company "from this to Bear River Valley in the Great Basin, without families forthwith."[55] And even after many potential members of such a company were taken into the Battalion he still hoped to send on a vanguard and asked for volunteers on July 20. But on August 1, President Young sent a letter with supplies on to Bishop George Miller (who had taken his company far ahead and was returning to check plans), telling Miller's company to winter on Grand Island in the North Platte since it was too late to try to cross the mountains.

Bishop Miller had been a continual problem from the very first, independently ranging ahead of the group—as did Parley P. Pratt for a while. Brigham Young's irritability from his desperate efforts to get the initial chaos into some order led him to have Clayton write these two adventurers on March 23 that "if they did not wait or return to organize, the camp would organize without and they be disfellowshipped."[56] Elder Pratt records in his autobiography that when they returned,

> The President then reproved and chastened us severely for several things, among which was our drawing off from the council and main body of the camp and going ahead. He said there was manifestly a spirit of dissension and of insubordination manifested in our movements. I could not realize this at the time, and protested that in my own heart, so far as I was concerned, I had no such motive; . . . yet I thank God for this timely chastisement; I profited by it, and it caused me to be more watchful and careful ever after.[57]

Brigham was strong medicine for the Saints, and some could not take the medicine as well as Parley Pratt could—including Bishop Miller, who continued to go his own way, apostatizing the following spring and going off with some followers to Texas when he couldn't convince Brigham to go there instead of west. But Brigham was also developing into a remarkable healer to the Saints who were responsive, not only to his own people and to the Omaha Indians who were their neighbors at Winter Quarters (and whom, under his leadership, the Saints built houses for, tended when wounded, and taught agriculture to), but also to many of the non-Mormons they came in contact with, especially, of course, Thomas L. Kane, a member of a prominent Pennsylvania family that had been sympathetically reading about the Mormons.

Brigham Young's unique relationship with Thomas Kane deserves further attention. Returning from Council Bluffs to Washington in September 1846, with various letters and affidavits intended to insure the good relations being built with the government, Kane wrote Brigham, whose family had just nursed Kane from near death back to health:

> I am getting to believe more and more every day as my strength returns that I am spared by God for the labor of doing you justice; but, if I am deceived, comfort yourself and your people, with the knowledge that my sickness in your midst has touched the chords of noble feeling in a brave heart.[58]

He went on to assure Brigham that if he died on the way home his papers were in order, so his father could do the Saints good service, even if he couldn't in person. This friendship came about through a series of events that reveal much about Brigham Young's attractiveness as a human being and also his Moses-like steadfastness to purpose but responsiveness to changing opportunities.

Hearing in December 1845 of President Polk's proposal to Congress that a line of forts and blockhouses be built along the Oregon Trail to aid and encourage settlement there, Brigham had written the Secretary of War asking that the Saints be given the commission, arguing "we would build them cheaper, than in any otherwise could be done, as we expect to emigrate West of the mountains next season."[59] Then, in a clear statement of his basic religious pragmatism, Brigham wrote to Jesse C. Little, on January 26, 1846, assigning him supervision of the Church in the East and instructing him to approach the nation's leaders in Washington for aid:

If our government shall offer any facilities for emigrating to the western coast, embrace those facilities, if possible. As a wise and faithful man, take every honorable advantage of the times you can. Be thou a savior and deliverer of that people, and let *virtue, integrity,* and *truth* be your motto—salvation and glory the prize for which you contend.[60]

On May 13, at a conference of the Church in Philadelphia, Jesse Little met young Thomas Kane, who gave him a letter of introduction to Vice-president George Dallas. That same day, however, Congress declared war on Mexico, and when Elder Little arrived in Washington a week later President Polk was much involved in the ensuing excitement, but a proper setting existed for some response to the Mormon requests.

A series of interviews with the president were arranged in which it was finally suggested the assistance take the form of enlistment of a thousand Mormon soldiers to march under General Kearny to secure California from Mexico—and an additional thousand to go by sea. By June 5, Polk had consulted with his cabinet and gave approval, but only for five hundred soldiers—by land, apparently because of the opposition of anti-Mormon Senator Thomas H. Benton of Missouri, who questioned the Church's loyalty and convinced the president that Mormons should constitute no more than one-third of Kearny's forces.

President Young later became convinced that Benton even conceived of this as a *test* of loyalty that the Mormons would surely fail by refusing to enlist and that Benton intended to get sufficient forces in Missouri immediately after such refusal and to use the excuse thus provided to attack and disperse the whole body of Saints. Even though Brigham, with convincing enthusiasm, led the Saints to fulfill what he called the "requisition," this is why it became the Mormon view that the Battalion was a great imposition on a persecuted people who responded with sacrificial patriotism. Only a year later Thomas Bullock reported that Brother Brigham, apparently having learned in the meantime of Benton's plot, in an early speech in the valley "damned Prest. Polk for his tyranny in drafting out 500 men to form a Battalion, in order that the women and children might perish on the Prairies—in case he refused their enlisting, Missouri was ready with 3,000 men, to have swept the Saints out of existence."[61] And two days after that, in an emotional welcoming ceremony for Battalion members just arrived from California, he stated that, because of Benton's dangerous intentions, "the Battalion saved the people by going into the army."

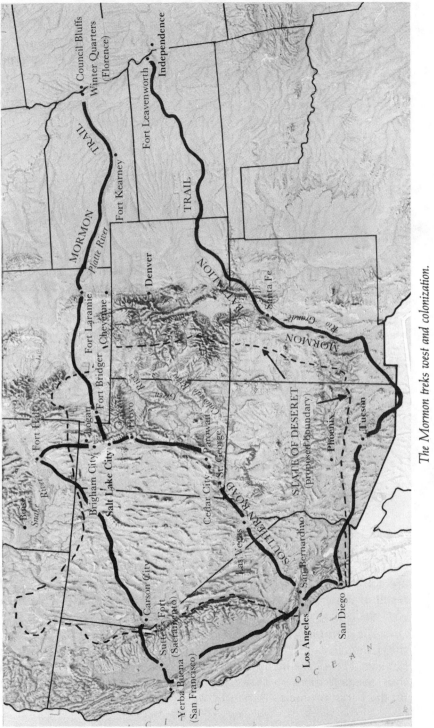

The Mormon treks west and colonization.

There is evidence that Brigham Young was correct in thinking that some kind of dirty work was afoot. An intriguing letter from Thomas Kane, July 11, 1850, hints that he had by then learned some details of the plot ("some of the persons besides the President who were willing to see you driven by force out upon the wilderness"), which he had kept confidential "for obvious reasons" but would write for the Church to have from his executors if he died.[62] If such a document exists its whereabouts are not known. But at the time, the important thing was that the Battalion provided an opportunity which did indeed benefit the Saints, and Brigham, after very little deliberation, embraced it and moved effectively to reverse the fear and resentment of his people against the government.

Whatever the truth about the Mormon Battalion "opportunity," it was as a Moses that Brigham responded to it and used it to prepare the Mormons for the greater challenges and opportunities to come further west. At a recruitment meeting soon after Kane's arrival, President Young suggested that one important reason why it was imperative to raise the five hundred volunteers was his conviction that the "requisition" was one more test, provided by the Lord, to *try* the Saints as well as help protect them:

> My experience has taught me that it is best to do the things that are necessary and keep my mind exercised in relation to the future. *I have learned to do the things necessary independent of my feelings, and at the expense of everything near and dear to me.* Many have been called upon to forsake the society of friends, wives and children and you will all be brought into a situation to learn the same lesson.
>
> . . . We want to conform to the requisition made upon us, and we will do nothing else, till we have accomplished this thing.
>
> . . . I say, it is right; and who cares for sacrificing our comfort for a few years.[63]

At that meeting Colonel Kane spoke only briefly, because of his sickness, and Orson Hyde followed: "Although you may think you are going to be led to the field of battle, my opinion is, that it will result in your obtaining peacable possession of a home, and he who sent quails may send us means of deliverance."

The companies were filled, officers chosen by Brigham and the Council, and "bishops" chosen to care for the volunteers' families. (This care included helping families with quantity buying, thus assisting them to make the best use of the money sent them by the battalion men.) A band concert was given for Captain Allen and the troops, and they were sent off with some of Brigham's good advice ("A Private soldier is as honorable as an officer, if he behaves as well"), a blessing, and a prophetic promise from President Young that was literally fulfilled: "Assured the brethren that they would have no fighting to do; told them, we should go into the Great Basin which is the place to build Temples."

Brigham As Moses: Into The Desert   5

Winter was approaching, with well over ten thousand camped along the five hundred miles between Nauvoo and Grand Island. Brigham Young organized a high council for the main encampment on the Missouri (later two for the two sides of the river) and charged them immediately with establishing schools "for the education of children during the coming winter." Apostles were dispatched to England to quash an improper emigration scheme and strengthen the Church there, which was continuing to provide lifeblood to the main body of Saints. Then Brigham became immersed in building towns for a "winter quarters." Again he took direct physical command of the work and got heavily involved in details, scouting out the best site across the river and upstream and then moving closer to the river for better cattle feed on the rushes, and, as always, giving much specific counsel: "I proposed that each company prepare a yard for cattle, build a necessary [Brother Brigham's euphemism for outhouse], keep their yard clean, draw wood, cut it short and burn it in chimneys made of turf, and have the road outside of the encampment; keep hay in the cattle yard and keep up a nightwatch."[1]

One of President Young's continuing major concerns was what appears at first a Levitical involvement in law and order:

> I said, that this Council which we have organized would act as a city and high council and decide matters of difference between the members of the church. Some had already transgressed and should be brought to justice—that I was not so much afraid of going into the wilderness alone, as to let offenders go unpunished.[2]

And he did not. Hosea Stout, as head of the police, on September 4 had some unchaste young men whipped. Stout comments that this was "the first step taken since we were in the wilderness to enforce obedience to the Law of God."[3] President Young defended the police when there was some public outcry, mainly by parents of the young men, against the punishment: "Some boys have been whipped in camp, and it is right. I did not know of it till after it was done. If we allow young men to come in here and set up their own plans, three years will not roll around before we will have cutting of throats here."[4] On January 2, 1847, Stout writes, "I have heard of no report of adultery in this place since the affair last fall . . . so effectual was the punishment."[5]

President Young clamped down on everything from the improper tying up of dogs to drunkenness. But Brigham was not obsessed with mere order — or even safety. The records of his sermons indicate that his main concern from the first was directed at developing a self-governing people. On August 20, 1846: "I said that I intended to propose to the various councils of this Church to have some way devised to instruct this people, concerning the organization of the human system, and how to take care of it."[6] August 30: "I made a few concluding remarks on the necessity of the saints obtaining experience to be prepared to govern." September 13: "A people must become acquainted thoroughly with law before they can abide it, and the time has come when we must have law and order in our midst. . . . We have the law of liberty and the Gospel and the more light and liberty and greater privileges the stricter the law." And on December 20, anticipating by ten years the 1856 "Reformation" in Utah, he preached of the need of the Saints to struggle to rise out of the mud of the trail and reshape the clay of their lives: "I instructed the Bishops to hold meetings where the Saints might assemble, confess their sins, pray with and for each other, humble themselves before the Lord and commence a reformation that all might exercise themselves in the principles of righteousness."

But everything was not this serious. On August 12: "Brother Richards, Lee and I walked south on the green and saw the young people dance about half an hour." And on September 13: "The Presidency attended singing school." On October 5: "I visited the sick. Finished stoning my well, which was thirty-two feet deep." And on December 29, 1846, with the Saints having settled in as best they could for the winter:

> About seven p.m., brothers Smithies, Hutchins, Duzette, and Clayton joined us and played on their instruments and the brethren danced.
>
> Dr. Richards measured forty-three inches round the breast, I measured forty-one inches.
>
> . . . I felt to thank the lord for the privilege of praising Him in the song and dance. I spoke in tongues and conversed with Elder Kimball in an unknown tongue.

Nevertheless, much was accomplished, and Brother Brigham showed he had gained both toughness and self-confidence and a certain mildness and patience from the trial by fire that past spring. Within six weeks a city of four hundred log houses and four hundred tents had been built at Winter Quarters, and by December, when President Young wrote Orson Spencer in England, there were seven hundred log houses, and twenty-two wards organized effectively under bishops. Brigham got the women busy making willow baskets for trading in Missouri, and he took charge of planning and building a water-powered gristmill to save on the cost of meal and flour. And all the time he planned for the trek west.

On December 18 the President reports that he "Asked the Quorum what their feelings were towards me; when all present expressed the best of feelings and their approval of my course." The Council wrote the apostles in England on January 7, "Our President doesn't stick [balk] at anything that tends to advance the gathering of Israel, or promote the cause of Zion in these last days; he sleeps with one eye open and one foot out of bed." But as had happened once before when he became this frenetic, harsh in discipline and tough in pushing his people, Brigham dreamed of Joseph giving him a kind of rebuke. In February Hosea Stout tells of Brigham relating to the high council that he saw Joseph sitting in a room:

> I took him by the hand and kissed him on both cheeks, and wanted to know, why we could not be together as we once was. He said that it was all right, that we should not be together yet. . . . Do you be sure and tell the brethren that it is all important for them to keep the spirit of the Lord, To keep the quiet spirit of Jesus.[7]

It was a mild winter, but six hundred died—including one of Brigham's wives, Mary Pierce, of "consumption," on March 17. (Thomas Kane thought the deaths were because the persecutions and exposure of the forced evacuation of Nauvoo made them susceptible to the scurvy, malaria, tuberculosis and other diseases of the Missouri bottoms.) Remarkably good spirits and high hopes persisted, however, and by January the seventies were having dances in the large Council House built in December and a huge party was arranged by the bishops—at Brother Brigham's suggestion—for the "benefit and entertainment of the poor" in their wards. President Young spoke at this function, which was called the "Silver Grey Picnic":

> I told them that this meeting was for the purpose of showing to the world that this people can be made what God designed them.

Nothing will infringe more upon the traditions of some men than to dance. . . .

For some weeks past I could not wake up at any time of the night but I heard the axes at work. Some were building for the destitute and the widow; and now my feelings are, dance all night, if you desire to do so, for there is no harm in it. . . . I enjoin upon the Bishops that they gather the widow, the poor and the fatherless together and remember them in the festivities of Israel. . . .

. . . It was indeed an interesting and novel sight, to behold the old men and women, some nearly an hundred years old, dancing like ancient Israel.[8]

On January 29, Stout wrote: "This was a fine clear warm day. No wind hardly. The snow soft. A man could take comfort in life. Everything seemed to smile."[9] Stout had been cheered in part by the announcement a few days earlier of what is Brigham Young's only canonized revelation, "The Word and Will of the Lord," which outlined the plan for migration to the West and, according to Stout, was "a source of much joy and gratification" to the people.

This revelation is preserved as section 136 of the Doctrine and Covenants. It reviews the instructions for the Camp of Israel in their journeyings to the West, the organization by hundreds, fifties, and tens, and the promise to keep the commandments of God, especially the central covenant of consecration and mutual care:

Let each company bear an equal proportion, according to the dividend of their property, in taking the poor, the widows, the fatherless, and the families of those who have gone into the army, that the cries of the widow and the fatherless come not up into the ears of the Lord against this people. Let each company prepare houses, and fields for raising grain, for those who are to remain behind this season.[10]

The revelation contains much practical advice, as well as an invitation to that saving blitheness the Saints had enjoyed throughout their exile:

If thou art merry, praise the Lord with singing, with music, with dancing, and with a prayer of praise and thanksgiving.

If thou art sorrowful, call on the Lord thy God with supplication, that your souls may be joyful.

Fear not thine enemies, for they are in mine hands and I will do my pleasure with them.[11]

By March 22, 1847, final plans were announced for the Twelve to lead a select company of 144 pioneers, two men to a wagon, west to "locate a Stake of Zion" and then return to take their families the next year, with a few large companies of families to follow that summer by July 1. Lorenzo Young's sick wife, Harriet, pleaded to be taken along to "save her life" and so two of her small children and two other women were also included, one an older daughter, Clara, who was married to Brigham. On April 5, Heber Kimball moved the first group of wagons out toward a rendezvous on the Elkhorn River twenty miles away, but President Young stayed to conduct the general conference of the Church on April 6 and then, after traveling out a few miles, returned to meet with the apostles Parley Pratt and John Taylor, who he learned had just returned from England. Elder Taylor, at Brigham's request, had brought "two Sextants, two Barometers, two artificial horizons, one circle of reflection, several Thermometers and a Telescope." The two apostles were left in charge of the Winter Quarters settlement, responsible to form the companies to come later, and on April 14 Brother Brigham started out. On the fifteenth, the company moved out together, reaching the Platte River, the main route to the West, where that night President Young "called the Pioneer camp together and addressed them on the necessity of being faithful, humble and prayerful on the journey. . . . Said we should go to bed early, rest on the Sabbath and go in such a manner as to claim the blessings of Heaven."[12]

This exodus was vastly different from the one fourteen months before, almost a lark for the mainly young, now well-trained and experienced frontiersmen. They moved out at an average rate of nearly twenty miles a day, keeping to the north bank, even though the most used trail was on the south, because Brigham Young wanted to avoid, for the companies of families to follow, possible problems from encountering non-Mormons. Brigham and Heber stood guard along with the others. They stationed mules with the guards because mules could detect intruders, and once the men drove off some Indians who were sneaking up to steal horses. William Clayton's journal captures the unusual nature of this particular western migration:

> [April] 24th. . . . Evening I walked over to Orson Pratt's wagon, and through his telescope saw Jupiter's four moons very distinctly never having seen them before.
>
> [April] 30th. . . . Brother Hanson played some on his violin and some of the brethren danced to warm themselves.

[May] 18th. . . . At seven o'clock the President called the captains of tens to his wagons and gave them a pretty severe lecture. He referred to some who had left meat on the ground and would not use it because it was not hind quarter. . . . God has given us a commandment that we should not waste meat, nor take life unless it is needful, but he can see a disposition in this camp to slaughter everything before them.[13]

When the company crossed the Platte at Fort Laramie (the halfway point), Luke Johnson, a doctor, "professionally attended several persons in the fort"; others visited the trading post and rented the ferry boat from a Mr. Bordeaux, who told them when they left that though he had been warned against the Mormons by Lilburn Boggs, their old enemy from Missouri who had just passed through, "this was the most civil and best behaved company that had ever passed the fort." Later on, when they established a ferry at the last crossing of the North Platte, the ferry was used by two Missouri companies who kept their guns and bowie knives handy; but they were so impressed with the Mormons' work, which included saving the life of a Missourian who was swept into the river, that they "put away their fears [and] were civil and kind to the brethren."[14]

Brother Brigham had other problems, however, including uncertainty about his destination. Clayton had been determining distances traveled each day, at first by estimation, then by counting wagon wheel revolutions, and finally by suggesting a set of gears — a roadometer — to give him exact measurements (Orson Pratt designed it; Appleton Harmon built it). On May 18, he examined closely his copy of John C. Fremont's map and determined that it did not agree with his scale nor Elder Pratt's latitude calculations. This map, one of the ten thousand printed by Congress along with the account Fremont and his wife wrote of his second western expedition through the Great Basin and California in 1843-44, had been sent to Brigham Young by David Atchison, a U.S. Senator from Missouri who had befriended the Mormons there in 1838. (Ironically, Thomas Hart Benton, the other senator from Missouri, was the father of Fremont's wife and the chief supporter — as the acknowledged "prophet of Manifest Destiny" — of Fremont's propagandized expeditions into various territories that Benton wanted the U.S. to acquire; but he was too set against the Mormons even to encourage them in furthering his pet project.)

Despite Fremont's achievements as a bold organizer and leader and an imaginative adventurer in tune with the westering spirit, he became notorious for his poor planning (which eventually led to tragedy for an exploring party he was leading in 1848-49), for his and his wife's romanticizing of his journeys, and, especially among mountain men, for his outright errors. For example, he showed on his map (though it was supposedly drawn from observation) that the Great Salt Lake and Utah Lake were one body of water—apparently with its north end salty and its south end fresh! And he praised north central Utah as a garden spot, fertile and well-watered. This enthusiasm may have encouraged Brigham Young toward that area, and Fremont's published reports and maps certainly were of great help to the Mormons in the trek to Utah. But later, after Brother Brigham had struggled with the sand and sagebrush in Utah, he differed somewhat from the national consensus regarding the intelligence and honesty of the immensely popular Fremont.

Even the mountain men, however, were inconsistent about the northern Utah area. A few days past Fort Laramie the pioneers met a group of French trappers "from whom we learned that Mr. [Jim] Bridger was located about 300 miles west, that the Mountaineers could ride to Salt Lake from Bridger's in two days and that the Utah country was beautiful."[15] These men had left a boat back at the crossing of the North Platte, and Brigham Young sent forty men hurrying on ahead to secure it and build a raft. Thomas Bullock reports that when the main body arrived on June 16, "Prest. Young stript himself and went to work with all his strength, assisted by the Dr. and the brethren—and made a first rate White Pine and white Cotton Wood Raft." With two good rafts and a boat, they found immigrants happy to pay one dollar per wagon to be ferried over the high water, and Brigham left a small company of men there to continue the enterprise and then ferry over the following Mormon companies.

After crossing the North Platte, the company began to move through strange new mountainous country, where Bullock commented on making snowballs for fun and Clayton on good fishing and "the romantic grandeur" of the scenery. Moving on up the Sweetwater River and through South Pass and down the Green River, they met Moses Harris on June 27, who "said the country around Salt Lake was barren and sandy, destitute of timber and vegetation except wild sage." President Young comments that the reports were all so contradictory he had to see for himself. The next day they finally met Bridger, who was on his way to Laramie but who camped overnight to talk with the Mormons. Clayton reports that he was very difficult to understand (apparently drunk), but Brigham learned that Bridger was ashamed of Fremont's map and "considered it imprudent to bring a large population into the Great Basin until it was ascertained that grain could be raised [Clayton indicates that Bridger was concerned about frost]; he said he would give one thousand dollars for a bushel of corn raised in the Basin."[16] Following Bridger's direction, Brigham turned off the Oregon Trail just past Fort Bridger and onto the quite new Hastings Cutoff toward California that passed south of the Great Salt Lake; and on July 10 the pioneers met Miles Goodyear, an Englishman with a homestead on the Weber River north of the Salt Lake Valley. Clayton recorded, "His report of the valley is more favorable than some we have heard but we have an idea he is anxious to have us make a road to his place through selfish motives."[17]

Goodyear recommended a somewhat different, more northerly route, which President Young and others explored and disapproved of. But the camp voted to follow it, and Brigham went along: "Such matters are left to the choice of the camp so that none may have room to murmur at the Twelve hereafter."[18] The next day they crossed the Bear River and were getting into present-day Utah when Brigham contracted "mountain fever" (probably Rocky Mountain spotted fever from a wood tick) and quickly became extremely ill—"nigh unto death," according to Erastus Snow. With others who were ill, he had to be left behind while an advance group went ahead under Orson Pratt; Elder Pratt was sent to find the alternate route that had been cut across the Wasatch Mountains by the Donner Party the previous year so they could avoid the narrow Weber Canyon. Finally the main group moved ahead, and Brigham may very well have thought that, like Moses, he might not be allowed to "go over into Jordan." But on July 17, after the descent down the torturous, monumentally carved Echo Canyon (whose scenery Clayton called "at once romantic and more interesting than I have ever witnessed . . . wild and melancholy," but which was so hard on Brother Brigham "he could not endure to travel farther"), Elder Kimball and others "went onto a mountain to . . . pray for President Young." The next day, a Sunday, Kimball called the camp together and proposed "that they should meet together and pray and exhort each other that the Lord may turn away sickness from our midst and from our President that we may proceed on our journey."[19] The brethren built a bowery of tree branches for the meetings that morning and again that afternoon, where "the Bishops administered the Sacrament — the brethren enjoyed a good day — near the close of the meeting Elder Kimball reported that Prest. Young was much better, that our prayers were answered, which caused all hearts to rejoice."[20] President Young was placed in Wilford Woodruff's carriage, apparently the most comfortable vehicle available, and brought behind at a slower pace, with Heber Kimball and a few others, as he recovered. On July 23, when the advance and main groups ahead of him had both entered the valley and, by Brigham's directions, had already broken and irrigated ground and planted seed, he recorded in his history:

> I ascended and crossed over the Big Mountain, when on its summit I directed Elder Woodruff . . . to turn the [carriage] half way round so that I could have a view of a portion of Salt Lake valley. The spirit of light rested upon me and hovered over the valley, and I felt that there the Saints would find protection and safety.[21]

Elder Woodruff remembered that after gazing for a time upon the vision, Brigham said: "It is enough. This is the right place. Drive on."[22]

Standing on this spot, easily accessible now on Route 65 east of Salt Lake City, it is possible to feel some of the exhilaration and fulfillment these pioneers felt after their great journey of a year and a half. It is possible to look down through granite peaks to the large golden cup of the valley, which is surrounded by those mountains yet full of light, aware that now in the valley stands a temple with spires made of that same granite and echoing the shapes of those peaks. And it is possible to sense the joy and relief and awe the pioneers must have felt as participants in the literal fulfillment of the ancient promise that the mountain of the Lord's house should be established in the tops of the mountains.

On July 23, the main group of pioneers, following the Donner Trail due west from the mouth of "Last Canyon" (now called Emigration Canyon) towards the south end of Great Salt Lake, stopped by two forks of a gentle stream (now City Creek) near a promontory, and there Elder Orson Pratt called the camp together; they "made prayer to Almighty God, returning thanks for the preservation of the Camp; . . . consecrated and dedicated the land to the Lord; and entreated his blessings on the seeds about to be planted and on our labors in this valley."[23] Then they immediately went to work, and when Brigham Young arrived the next day, July 24, he could inspect a five-acre potato farm, the beginning of a turnip patch, and grass being cut for hay. On Sunday, the twenty-fifth, after various encouraging speeches by the apostles, the President, still confined to his armchair, was brief and eloquent:

> No man can buy land here, for no one has any land to sell. But every man shall have his land measured out to him which he must cultivate in order to keep it. Besides there shall be no private ownership of the streams that come out of the canyons, nor the timber that grows on the hills. These belong to the people; all the people.[24]

By the next Wednesday, Brother Brigham was strong enough to climb the nearby peak and name it "Ensign" and to explore the valley across to the Great Salt Lake and assure the others who wanted to explore more that they had already chosen the best place to settle; he then designated the site for the temple by striking his cane to the ground, having seen the completed six-spired structure in vision. In 1853 he said that he "never looked upon that ground, but the vision of it was there. I see it as plainly as if it was in reality before me."[25]

The special mixture of the practical and visionary in Brigham Young had been fused by the fires of the great exodus into a marvelously effective leadership style, effective especially in consummating that same fusion in others. The key was selfless, co-operative, unmaterialistic service — working to "build the kingdom" (mainly the kingdom within) — but doing that through working under God's unworldly, prophetic direction in the tangible world. Images of the benefits of cooperative, religiously motivated effort stand out: Clayton, on July 12 as they took Goodyear's alternate, noted that few wagons had come this route; "the balance went the other road and many of them perished in the snow; it being late in the season and much time was lost quarreling who would improve the roads."[26]

But the Mormon Trail was unique not so much because it was efficiently, intelligently, and cooperatively made, but because it was a permanent two-way road. As Clayton's and Bullock's journals show, the pioneers constantly made new shortcuts, cut out dugways, removed stumps, constructed ferries and left crews to man them — improving the roads *after* they had passed — for those who would come later, people mainly unrelated to them by blood but tied even closer through the faith they shared and the holy covenants they had made with each other.

On August 7, at Brigham Young's recommendation, the pioneers went to the same dam they had built in the history-making implementation of irrigation, which was crucial for their survival in the desert, and began to be rebaptized, continuing the next day until there were "a total of 289 persons, who went forward, and renewed their Covenant to serve the Lord."[27] (The total, of course, includes the various groups of Mormon Battalion members, etc., which had been added to the original pioneer company of 148.) That dam symbolizes another powerful lesson the pioneers learned with and from their leaders because it reveals, in Clayton's matter-of-fact record of its construction the first day in the valley before Brother Brigham arrived, the characteristic Mormon sense of faith and works:

> At the opening [of Orson Pratt's dedicatory meeting], the brethren united in prayer and *asked the Lord to send rain on the land*, etc. The brethren immediately rigged three plows and went to plowing a little northeast of the camp; another party went with spades, etc., to make a dam on one of the creeks so as to throw the water at pleasure on the field, designing to irrigate the land *in case rain should not come sufficiently.*[28]

There are other images of the special spirit and perspective of Brigham Young's group of pioneers. On July 8 Wilford Woodruff had gone fishing in a stream near Fort Bridger, using an artificial fly for the first time since he had been in England, and caught ten times the brook trout others were taking on bait. That same day, while they were camped with the "sick detachment" from the Mormon Battalion who had joined them after wintering at Pueblo, Colorado, and while a trapper named Goodale was at the fort, a Sergeant Williams of the Battalion had seized a horse belonging to Goodale to compensate for a mule stolen from him at Pueblo by one of Goodale's men. Williams gave a receipt so Goodale could supposedly recover from his own man, and Goodale professed to be well satisfied, but he probably did so only because he felt intimidated by the large force of Mormons. The next day, as Bullock records it, "Prest. Young gave the horse back to Goodale in the neatest, quietest, prettiest way possible; for which Goodale expressed his thankfulness to 'Captn. Young.' "[29]

When he was well again and at his destination, Brigham Young stayed only one month before retracing his path back east. He led out in the public meetings which with much discussion accomplished the planning of the city, with its famous graphlike logicality, wide streets, and generous lots: "And let each man cultivate his own lot. In regard to Schools . . . the people on a block, can choose a school for themselves. Let the children be kept ... on the lots or in the houses. We will have our bathing places directly and in three years we shall not know what sickness is—all said 'Amen.' "[30] He sent out explorers and inventoried resources; had the Battalion members who came from California after their release from duty build a large bowery where he gave much instruction, a good mixture of the practical, moral, and spiritual; built his own adobe house as part of the fort; and started back east on August 26, leaving an organized ecclesiastical-civil government with John Smith to be in charge until the apostles Parley Pratt and John Taylor arrived later in the fall.

On the way back, Brother Brigham soon began meeting the larger wagon trains coming from Winter Quarters (he had left messages and directions all along the route and had sent back guides toward the end of the trail-blazing trek). He usually stopped to rejoice with them, sometimes for a feast and dancing. On September 4 he met the second company, led by Elder Parley P. Pratt, who, arriving from England without being in on the planning at Winter Quarters, had apparently organized differently and brought too large a group. As Bullock reports:

> Prest. Young reproved P. P. P. very strongly for disorganizing all the Winter's work of the Quorum of Twelve. He at first manifested a contra Spirit, but afterwards repented—the Spirit and power of God was poured out—much instruction was given—and it proved a most glorious meeting to all.[31]

On the face of it this seems somewhat harsh, but President Young knew his man. In his autobiography Pratt says, as he had about the earlier chastisement in Iowa, that he deserved it and that he asked forgiveness and was frankly forgiven: "This school of experience made me humble and careful in future, and I think it was the means of making me a wiser and better man ever after."[32]

President Young knew well enough what his own chief fault was; in a speech in 1853 he told the Saints: "Never, in the days of my life, have I hurt a man with the palm of my hand. I never have hurt a person any other way except with this unruly member, my tongue."[33] But though Brigham didn't have complete success in taming his tongue, and though the journals of Clayton, Bullock, Stout, Lee and others reveal that occasionally he could be damaging with that "unruly member," together they bear eloquent testimony, in the devotion of such a diversity of men, to President Young's greatness as a prophet, and reveal the writers' growing sense of the paradox that a man could be both human and a unique spokesman for God.

Brother Brigham, after a journey back that became harrowing, and even mortally dangerous when Indians stole a good portion of the company's horses, moved rapidly to intensify and consolidate the Saints' sense of his calling. The special camaraderie that had been established—of men who have suffered much together, survived against great odds, and in doing so shown much courage and skill—is revealed in the emotion with which Stout and others (who traveled out over two weeks' journey from Winter Quarters) met the returning President on October 18 ("The whole of us was in a perfect extacy of joy and gladness"[34]), and also in Brigham Young's own final speech of gratitude and dismissal to those who had made the difficult journey out to help ("The President said it was more joy, more satisfaction to meet us than a company of angels").

But Brother Brigham knew that they needed and wanted more than respect for himself as a tough, able frontiersman and practical leader; they needed a *prophet*. Bullock tells of sometimes walking ahead of the wagons with President Young and other leaders, and on September 15 reports that they conversed "on Plurality, the rationality of man, and the resurrection; it was a delightful walk to me." On that return journey Brigham had discussed with the Church leaders the need to organize the First Presidency again. There was some opposition to this, but Brother Brigham led the apostles to a complete unity, because Stout reports that, at a conference in the large new "log tabernacle" in Kanesville on Christmas Eve, Elder Orson Pratt discussed this matter affirmatively with the Saints: "His discourse was very interresting and was received with breathless silence. The Spirit rested down upon the whole congregation."[35] And on December 28, Elders Young, Kimball, and Richards were unanimously sustained as the First Presidency, and Joseph's uncle, Father John Smith, as the presiding Patriarch. Stout writes that following President Young's discourse "the Best of feeling prevailed and the Spirit rested down on the Congregation to an uncommon degree."[36]

Again, as in the transfiguration when Brigham had been given Joseph's mantle in Nauvoo, the reality of leadership was more important than the sign. At the beginning of the December conference, the Twelve published a "General Epistle" that in its comprehensiveness of vision and practical wisdom could not help but remind the people of how far they had come with their President, and how exciting and right it would be to go on. The epistle announces the intention to organize a First Presidency, reviews the condition of the Church in all the world, and gives instructions to the Saints from Britain to India, even calling on kings and governors to assist in the latter-day work. It reminds the Saints of their covenant of consecration of all they have to the Lord and of mutual assistance to each other; it advises parents on rearing children; it outlines plans for educational institutions, museums, etc., in the new Zion in the valley; and it affirms loyalty to the U.S. Constitution and institutions and the intention to apply for territorial government. It ends with this expression of what the Mormons conceived themselves to be:

> Come, then, ye saints of Latter-day, and all ye great and small, wise and foolish, rich and poor, noble and ignoble, exalted and persecuted, rulers and ruled of the earth, who love virtue and hate vice, and help us to do this work, which the Lord hath required at our hands; and inasmuch as the glory of the latter house shall excel that of the former, your reward shall be an hundred fold, and your rest shall be glorious.[37]

After he was sustained as President of the Church, Brigham Young spoke, rather less formal when addressing his own people than in a letter to the world — but as expansive in vision:

> I feel glory, Hallelujah! Nothing more has been done today than what I knew would be done when Joseph died. We have been driven from Nauvoo here, but the hand of the Lord is in it, visible as the sun shining this morning; it is visible to my natural eyes; it's all right: and I expect when we see the result of all we pass through in this probationary state, we will discover the hand of the Lord in it all, and shout Amen — it's all right! We shall make the upper courts ring.[38]

Following the speech, the band played and George A. Smith led the Saints in the marvelous Hosanna Shout: "Hosanna, Hosanna, Hosanna, to God and the Lamb. Amen! Amen! and Amen!" The wounds of the Church in the martyrdom of Joseph and Hyrum had begun to heal at last.

But the realities of governing at Winter Quarters continued with Brother Brigham. Only two days after being sustained at the conference he had to deal with a man whose daughter had eloped with a non-Mormon and who wanted the police to go after her. Stout writes, "[The father] went to see the President on the subject, who, on learning that she was anxious to go, said let her go, which ended the matter."[39] He had to cope continually with petty vice.

He even asked to be invited to a hearing with John D. Lee (who had been sealed to him in the formal ceremony of "adoption" then practiced), where Lee was suing for the cost of articles he had dispensed to a Battalion wife, but which she denied getting. Brigham defended Lee's meticulous record-keeping but said he did not want to hear a sister lying, so "was he in Bro. Lee's place he would forgive . . . the debt rather than have feelings, which Lee did." But then President Young, in what seems a characteristic mode of leadership, strongly denounced the husband for letting his wife "trammel him" and her for having a "nasty whining peevish devilish spirit," and then, his point unforgettably made, apologized: "Excuse me for my vulgarity. It is not common for me to use such Language, but I know of no Language too mean to suit the case before us."[40]

For Brigham Young, excessiveness of feeling and even of expression was not inconsistent with being a religious man—even a prophet. On Sunday, July 16, 1848, as the President's company, in his final journey west, was camped at the great landmark of Chimney Rock, he preached:

> [It] is not the good, rel[i]gious, Sa[n]ctified feelings that I have that will present me or any other man blameless and acceptable before the Lord, but it is the good that we do to one another. . . . Esteem it a prevelege to help one another that you may have your reward. . . . I confess my own faults. I am subject to temptation and as liable to do wrong as any other man. . . . I know what is right all the time. I am never at a loss to know what is right, but sometimes I do not think or I am not guarded against the Tempter.[41]

But however unsanctified his feelings at times, Brigham had learned to do good with the same natural spontaneity that he had loved in Joseph. When John D. Lee had reported to Brother Brigham back on May 4 that he was doubtful he could go west with him because of his lack of means, the President said, "You have helped me and I hope that I may have means to help you and you shall prosper." Then he embraced Lee and continued, "Go and prosper and be ye blest"; and Lee reports that a few days later President Young was able to get what was specifically needed and provided it for Lee—as a loan. At the ford over the Loup Fork of the North Platte on June 15, Lee reports that "President B.Y. in person crossed and recrossed back and fourth, untill he saw all over safe."[42] Then on Sunday, June 18, the President praised the company for the peace, love and union in the camps, greater, he said, than since Enoch. But he added:

If [they were going] for the riches, honors, glory, comfort, and enjoyment that they expect to receive in this world. They had better [have] staid in the states or in their own country for they could get the apples and peaches and other luxuries as easy about Pittsburgh as they can in the valley.

Elder Kimball followed with encouragement that they "favor each other as much as their circumstances will allow and not to wait when they saw a team failing until it is entirely done, before assistance is offered." Lee records how effective this preaching and example were, and he mentions his own efforts to help others along, helping a man find his sick son who had wandered off and then taking both in his own wagon, dissuading an impatient "captain of ten" from taking his wagons on by pointing out that because they had stronger teams they should help the others and not rush ahead.

On July 20 they met an express from the valley with "firstrate news from the land that the crops were promising," despite severe losses from crickets and frost, and that "a large majority was well satisfied and had been all the time, though they desired to have Pres. B. Y. in their midst once more to council them under their new and untried climate and circumstances."[43] President Young must have been anxious to get there too, on the evidence of a later description he made of this trek in which the new First Presidency led twenty-four hundred Saints west:

> Instead of 365 pounds of breadstuff when they started from the Missouri river, there was not half of them had half of it. We had to bring our seed grain, our farming utensils, bureaus, secretaries, sideboards, sofas, pianos, large looking glasses, fine chairs, carpets, nice shovels and tongs, and other fine furniture, with all the parlor, cook stoves, etc.; and we had to bring these things piled together with the women and children, helter skelter, topsy turvy, with broken down horses, ring-boned, spavined, pole evil, fistula and hipped; oxen with three legs, . . . This was our only means of transportation, and if we had not brought our goods in this manner we should not have had them.[44]

Brother Brigham also had some *good* times along the route. Lee reports that one night he "rode to Pres. B. Y.'s Camp, found them enjoying themselves firstrate upon the melodious charm of the drum and violin," and that on July 23, "about 2 P.M. Louisa B. Young was delivered of 2 fine boys which verry much del[i]ghted Pres. B. Y. the Father of the children."[45] But the trial of the people of Israel and of their Moses continued. Lee reports that on August 5:

Pres. B. Y. . . . stopped a company that [was] in possession [of] several yoke of cattle, converted to their own use, that had been sent from the valley for the benefit of [all] the companies at the discretion of Pres. B. Y. Said to the man that the catle were the Lord's and that he was Boss of these Prairies and would dictate the teams and see that the poor were not left behind. . . . This is not equality, neither is it bearing each other['s] burden. I am as willing to pull you out of the mud and pick you up on the plains and help as any other man, but I am not willing to have you go ahead with more team than what is necessary, like Daniel Miller and James Bean, who though they got help from the valley, rushed on and left the weak for me to drag along and they shall be cursed and you will see it.[46]

Such evenhanded moral toughness was important to survival and crucial to the perfecting of the Saints. The first winter in the valley had been extremely difficult for the nearly eighteen hundred Saints who remained there. Parley P. Pratt describes how the Saints suffered from want of food in the spring and summer of 1848.[47] His own family had lost their cows and had no milk; they all had to toil incessantly with him in the fields, were compelled to go barefoot several months, and lived on greens and roots. He reports a great feast of thanksgiving on August 10 when some of their harvest was in and tells of the great joy in September at the reinforcement provided by the arrival of the Church leaders and thousands of new immigrants; but still the hardships continued. Of a meeting of the governing Council of Fifty the next February (1849), John D. Lee reports:

The cries and sufferings of the poor were called up in question. The council wer of the opinion that a sufficien[c]y of Bread Stuf was in the valley to sustain all the inhabitants, till more could be raised, could it be equally distributed. P. P. Pratt said that about this time last winter was the most alarming among the People; they suffered more from actual fear than they did from Hunger; the valley was new; ne[i]ther was it proven that grain could be raised here, but when winter broke, grass soon came, milk and butter increased, Thistle Tops and roots togeather with the segos roots were used, which lengthened out the Bread and many that [had] nothing to sell spared a little to those that had none and none starved.[48]

Brigham Young directed that an inventory of supplies be taken by the bishops, and when the report came in he found there was more grain in the valley than had been thought:

Pres. B. Young said that we are safe; still he said . . . he believed all the while that corn was not so scarce as many expected, . . . and if those that have do not sell to those that have not, we will just take it and distribute amoung the poor, and those that have and will not divide willingly may be thankful that their heads are not found wallowing in the snow. There is some of the meanest spirits here amoung the saints that ever graced this footstool. They are too mean to live amoung the gentiles. . . . Still . . . I will talk to the people in public. I know the strongest side are willing to do right.[49]

Characteristically, President Young had vented his feelings in extreme terms in the council meeting but then spoke and acted moderately—and very effectively—with the body of Saints. Back on January 6, after a report that "those that have fat cattle were grinding the faces of the poor" by charging extortionate prices, the council had wanted to control the prices, but Brother Brigham objected and suggested that "every man of the Council use his influence to put down extortion by reasoning with the people and getting up prayer meetings." On the Sunday after his inventory and picturesque threats about heads wallowing in the snow, Lee reported:

Pres. B.Y. addressed the Saints in Public. Spoke of their conditions and of the opression of the poor; said to those that [have] corn to spare, to let it go on reasonable terms; said to those that had to bye, not to be particuelar about what they had to pay, for it would be salvation to them but death to the seller that extortioned.

The speech was effective and "greatly ameliorated the condition of the Poor." Lee reports that "every man that could be touched was stirred by way of remembrance and began to let corn go," and he gives a convincing example: That Sunday morning a William Matthews had charged him forty dollars for an ox, but then:

The same day said Matthews went to meeting, heard what Pres. B. Young had to say about extortioners, came home the same evening and said to [me], kill the ox that I let you have and weigh it and pay me what he weighs. I likely asked you more than what he was worth, etc. Thus [Lee editorializes] the reader may see the effect of the preaching of the man of God.[50]

Brigham Young was intent on building a Zion people who could care for themselves by caring for each other, and he was not about to depend on miracles until they were needed. Occasionally things got to that point of dependence on divine aid, especially with the crickets. Brigham had not witnessed the first of such miracles, which had occurred in the spring of 1848 while he was still at Winter Quarters preparing for his second trek west. The ugly black crawling insects, which Clayton had noticed in vast numbers when they first entered the mountains of Wyoming back in 1847 and which one Mormon described as a cross between a buffalo and a spider, swarmed in from the foothills in May 1848 to devour the young crops, even small trees. Smashing the crickets, burying them, drowning them in ditches—even fire did not stop them. Only the intervention of flocks of seagulls from the Great Salt Lake, which according to the pioneers gorged themselves on the crickets, regurgitated them, and then attacked again, continuing day after day, finally stemmed the plague.[51]

Enough of the crops were saved for survival, but this was certainly not the last of the battles with crickets. The next year, John D. Lee reports, on June 2, "Crickets by millions marched into [my] farm, but luckily the gulls in numbers sufficient visited the fields and repulsed the Destroyers."[52] In the mid-1850s the ravages of crickets, and especially of grasshoppers, which were more fearsome in some ways because they could fly, were devastating. The Mormon struggles to control these plagues eventually became so well known that people in the Midwest wrote Brigham Young for advice based on Mormon experience, eliciting a prime example, in one of his letters of reply, of the rather mordant humor the President was capable of:

> When we had a heavy visitation of [grasshoppers] in the Territory, and the prospects were that we would be troubled with them again, I put in considerable of a crop on purpose for them to eat, hoping that my regular crops might be spared. The crop I put in for them suffered but slightly.[53]

He went on to suggest to his gentile supplicants that, like the Mormons, they do their best and then pray. President Young's advice to his own people was serious and blunt. According to Samuel W. Richards he told the Saints, threatened in 1855 by the real possibility that grasshoppers would totally destroy their bare margin of subsistence, "not to fret their gizzards about the failure of the crops or anything else. The Lord would take care of his people . . . *if they did their duty.*"[54] In 1853 he had already reminded them of the proper relationship between faith and works in any situation of crisis:

> When I cannot feed myself through the means God has placed in my power, it is then time enough for Him to exercise His providence in an unusual manner to administer to my wants. But while we can help ourselves, it is our duty to do so. . . .

While we have a rich soil in this valley, and seed to put in the ground, we need not ask God to feed us, nor follow us round with a loaf of bread begging of us to eat it. He will not do it, neither would I, were I the Lord.[55]

It is easy to imagine Brother Brigham, after hearing of the miracle of the gulls (and especially after learning that some of the Saints had thought they need not irrigate the land because the Lord would miraculously provide rain), telling them, in effect, "That's fine, be grateful, make a joyful noise to the Lord, but then let's dig in and find out what went wrong, and what we can do about it, because we're not going to depend on miracles."

These "children of Israel," who saw in the cricket miracles a sign of God's presence with them as potent as the dividing of the Red Sea, were soon to need—and get—even greater assistance. The second winter was very severe, and with the bad harvest, heavy influx of settlers, and many cattle lost to Indians and wolves, the rations were low by spring—when crickets again did their damage. During the early spring Heber C. Kimball surprised a public gathering by declaring, at the end of a speech of encouragement, that "states goods" would be sold in the streets of Salt Lake City cheaper than in New York "and that the people should be abundantly supplied with food and clothing." When Elder Kimball sat down, the apostle Charles C. Rich leaned over and said, "I don't believe a word of it." Even Heber admitted he was afraid he "had missed it this time."[56] But the prophecy was literally fulfilled by the "gold rush" that spring, in a manner touched with veritable tragic irony.

After Samuel Brannan brought his shipload of Saints in 1846 to what became San Francisco, he traveled overland to meet Brigham Young and passed by John Sutter's mill in the Sacramento Valley, where he learned of Sutter's desire to have the Mormons settle there. When Brannan met Brigham near Fort Bridger, he strongly urged Brigham to take the Saints to California. Brother Brigham not only refused and, to Brannan's great disappointment, settled in the barren Salt Lake Valley, but after Mormon Battalion veterans were among those who discovered gold in Sutter's mill race in January 1848, Brigham still refused to be tempted, though Mormons could easily have taken up many of the gold claims months ahead of the forty-niners, who had to travel overland from the East. Lee reports that when one of the Utah brethren in February 1849 petitioned President Young for leave to go out to the California gold mines with his family to get a better living and pay more tithing to aid the Church, the President chastised him, pointing out that gold was the root of evil and prophesying that "9 tenths of those that went of[f] for gold would go down to hell, and by and by those verry characters would lead mobs in [word illegible] as some did in Missouri." The man "wept like a child and said he would obey counsel."[57]

Not long after this, Elder Kimball's prophecy literally came true. The gold seekers from the eastern states, many of whom passed through Salt Lake, had underestimated the difficulty of the journey and overloaded themselves with merchandise to sell in the gold fields. They began to abandon goods when they reached the more difficult trails in the mountains east of Salt Lake, and when they saw samples of dust and nuggets in the city (brought in by Battalion members), they were so anxious to get fresh teams and move on so they could get rich quickly that the local economy was completely reversed:

> Pack mules and horses that were worth twenty-five or thirty dollars in ordinary times, would readily bring two hundred dollars in the most valuable property at the lowest prices. Goods and other property were daily offered at auction in all parts of the city. For a light, Yankee wagon, sometimes three or four great heavy ones would be offered in exchange, and a yoke of oxen thrown in at that. Common domestic sheeting sold from five to ten cents per yard by the bolt. The best of spades and shovels for fifty cents each. . . . Full chests of joiners' tools that would cost $150 in the east, were sold in that place for $25. Indeed, almost every article, except sugar and coffee, is selling on an average, fifty per cent below wholesale prices in the eastern cities.[58]

John D. Lee reveals the melancholy, even tragic, undertones of the story of the forty-niners in his account of a "picking up expedition" that he and his wife took back along the Mormon trail in July and August. The stragglers they passed said that most of the abandoned goods had been destroyed, but they went on and at the crossing of the Sweetwater met some men whose pack animals were entirely used up and who paid them well to haul their goods to Salt Lake:

> The Road was lined with waggons from the Vally to this point that one would be scarcely out of sight of some train. Dust verry disagreeable but not to compare with the Stench from Dead ca[r]cases which lye along the Road, having died from Fat[i]ge and Hunger. Distruction of Property along the Road was beyond discription, consisting of waggons, Harnesses, Tools of Every discription, Provisions,

clothings, stoves, cooking vessels, Pouder, Lead and allmost everything. . . . Out of necessity, every creek, River or Vally for (10
miles) at le[a]st from the Road was penetrated in search of feed,
which would make the distance from the Missouri river to the great
Basin about 2000 miles. . . . Verry frequent some 20 or 30 person
would suround the waggon and plead for a moment's instructions,
some of them with consternation depicted on their countenances,
their teams worn out, wumen and children on foot and some packing their provision[s], trying to reach some point of Refuge. The
general cry was, are you from the Mormon city or vally? . . . could
we winter in the vally? Do pray tell us all you can that will benefit
us, for we are in great distress. . . . We will pay you all you ask.
. . . The writer here observed truly one of the ancient said that the
love of money was the Root of all Evil. It was the love of it that has
caused thousands to leave their pleasant homes and comfortable
Firesides and thus plunge themselves into unnecessary suffering and
distress.[59]

Lee sensed fully the paradox that these people he now tried to help
were suffering as he had once, they because their love of gold had
moved them to a quest that was now turning to tragedy, he and his
fellow Saints because their love of God had moved them to a way
of life that brought persecution and hardship but had become a
triumph; and he could help because the Saints were beginning to
prosper.

But President Young and the other leaders knew well from the
Book of Mormon the ambiguity of the word *prosper*. They knew
that the Lord promised that those who obeyed him would prosper
— both spiritually and materially — as they lived in harmony with
his created world. But they also knew that such material prosperity
always brought great temptations to pride and the neglect of God
— and thus loss of the truth that had brought prosperity in the first
place. They continued to warn the Saints against gold seeking, even
in Utah, except for special Church-sponsored purposes and with
Church supervision. In their General Epistle of April 12, 1850, they
wrote, "Gold is a good servant, but a miserable, blind and helpless
god, and at last will have to be purified by fire, with all its followers." And Brigham Young in September 1849 said that instead
of gold, the people should have "iron and coal, good hard work,
plenty to eat, good schools and good doctrine."[60]

Brother Brigham once said that he wasn't sure how much of a
prophet he had been to the Saints, but he had certainly been very
profitable to them. And again they understood not only the pun but
the other double meaning of *profit*, for they knew that this modern

Moses had taught them not to live by bread alone, but for a greater profit: They had heard his speech on July 24, 1852 — Pioneer Day — after a parade showing the progress that had been made in five years. President Young reviewed the peace they had found, after being persecuted and driven, reminding them that now they need fear only one thing — that a *cessation* of persecution would mean they had strayed from their religion and God:

> I say to this community, be humble, be faithful to your God, true to His Church, benevolent to the strangers that may pass through our territory, and kind to all people; . . . but never fear the frowns of an enemy, nor be moved by the flatteries of friends or of enemies from the path of right. Serve your God; believe in Him and never be ashamed of Him, and sustain your character before Him, for very soon we will meet in a larger congregation than this, and have a celebration far superior; . . . we only celebrate now our deliverance from the good brick houses we have left, from our farms and lands, and from the graves of our fathers; we celebrate our perfect deliverance from these.
>
> Our lives have been spared, and we are yet upon this planet; and by and by we will celebrate a perfect deliverance from all the powers of earth; and we will keep our eyes set upon the mark, and go forward to victory.[61]

Brigham's
Gospel Kingdom 6

My aunt told me a story as she lay in a hospital bed. She had pioneered in Idaho, as one of the last generation who moved out to the frontier to build the "Great Basin Kingdom" in a process begun by Brigham Young, and she was telling me why she loved Brother Brigham. "You know why it took many years to build that stone wall, the one you can still see a part of east of the Beehive House? When the immigrants would come in the wagon trains, many of them didn't have a thing. They had used up all they had just to get here from England or the East. Sometimes there were a few who didn't even have a place to go for a home or work. So Brigham would hire them to work for him. It was usually some worthwhile, needed job on his farms and orchards, but if those were all taken he would say, 'See the pile of rocks in that corner; I need it over in this corner.' Whatever the job he gave them, he would pay them enough to live on but not as much as the work was paying elsewhere. So they were anxious to leave and start their own farm or shop or hire out to others in the colonies. The next year others would come in and he would say, if there was nothing else, 'See the pile of rocks in this corner; I need it over in that corner.' And that is why it took so long to build that little wall. They thought they were smart to earn what they could and get out of the employ of such a hard man, but he was the smart one. He never gave charity, but he helped many make their new lives." Then, with her face livened by her special form of calm assurance and her thin, strong fingers gesturing, she added, "He didn't tell them what he was doing but he just did it; he made them feel worth something down in here."

Brother Brigham knew what he was doing, and he was sometimes explicit:

My soul feels hallelujah, it exults in God, that He has planted this people in a place that is not desired by the wicked; . . . I want hard times, so that every person that does not wish to stay, for the sake of his religion, will leave. This is a good place to make Saints, and it is a good place for Saints to live; it is the place the Lord has appointed, and we shall stay here until He tells us to go somewhere else.[1]

Of course, it was not mere persecution, or work as an end, that he was after, or even the building of a mighty empire, but that sense of self-worth that my aunt treasured from her own pioneering, that realization of joy-bringing satisfaction that comes only from doing something worthwhile—something honest and developing—with our own divine potential. Brigham Young was intent on fulfilling his growing vision of the promise he had made the Nauvoo Saints in the dark hour of their bewilderment at Joseph's death: "There is an Almighty foundation laid, and we can build a kingdom such as there never was in this world."[2]

And that is what they did—after the trial of people and leaders in the Nauvoo expulsion and the Iowa crossing and the Winter Quarters deaths and the early starvation in the valley. They built, under President Young, a kingdom such as the world had not seen, an unearthly kingdom—though a kingdom partly made of rock walls and nail factories and "rag missions" and sorghum molasses—that molded people into Saints. It was a kingdom that, though it had no dangerous political ambitions, appalled the politicians and economists and the moralists of the Western world and finally had to endure the crushing intervention of the United States government. Meanwhile it attracted tens of thousands of dedicated converts from all over the world and secured the material and spiritual foundations of The Church of Jesus Christ of Latter-day Saints. And it set the vision for all future generations of Mormons, even in the areas where it was defeated, of an ideal someday to be reachieved or completed.

Most Mormons, including those who know little else about him, and many non-Mormon writers, including those who admire nothing else in Mormonism, have been impressed by the kingdom Brigham built. They have called Brigham Young the greatest western colonizer and praised the disciplined dedication and courageous resourcefulness with which he and Church members created a thriving and harmonious commonwealth in a desert wilderness. For instance, Christopher Lasch, a fine non-Mormon historian, while reviewing some books on the Mormon experience, expressed his admiration that "in Utah, under Young's leadership the Mormons created a self-sufficient, cooperative, egalitarian, and authoritarian economy devoted not to individual enrichment but to the collective well-being of the flock."[3] Lasch cited Leonard Arrington who, in his landmark study of the Mormon economy, *Great Basin Kingdom*, "shows how the Mormons accomplished, through a system of cooperative and compulsory labor, impressive feats of planning and development—irrigation, roads, canals, sugar beet factories, iron works—without generating the institutions or the inequalities elsewhere associated with industrial progress." Lasch concludes: "Cooperation and planning caused the desert to bloom, in marked contrast to the exploitive patterns of agriculture which on other frontiers exhausted natural resources and left the land a smoking waste." But even in this high praise, Lasch, like most other commentators, seems to miss the point of Brigham Young's kingdom—and therefore misses its highest achievement. He fails to see the relationship of successful kingdom building to basic Mormon religious principles; he therefore cannot see the continuance in the twentieth-century Church of those remarkable but for him inexplicable pioneer virtues. He cannot see that the principles continue with Mormons as a foundation for other, just as dedicated, forms of kingdom building and remain the basis for a continuing idealism that envisions a kingdom—as literal as Brother Brigham's—to be built in preparation for the coming of Christ.

It is impossible to understand adequately Brigham Young's character and actions, or to appreciate properly his achievement in building "the kingdom of God," without seeing that its greatness did not derive merely from a fortunate combination of people and circumstances that produced a colony successful materially—or even admirable morally—but from a religious vision shared by President Young and his people that produced a school for educating men and women he thought of literally as potential gods: "Intelligent beings are organized to become Gods, even the sons of God, to dwell in the presence of Gods, and become associated with the highest intelligences that dwell in eternity. We are now in the school, and must practice upon what we receive."[4] And Ernst Benz, a non-Mormon theologian who has been uniquely perceptive about the Mormon vision of building a literal kingdom of God on earth, is right in concluding that central to that process were Brother Brigham's commitments in the three areas that have uniquely kept Mormon secularism truly religious: his undeviating loyalty, in all his kingdom building, to establishing and disseminating worldwide an ancient order of truth, the everlasting gospel; his personal reception and wide cultivation of the gifts of the Spirit, including prophecy, both in working out his own and his family's salvation and in blessing the Saints throughout his kingdom; and his constant

talking about, occasional ecstatic exultation in, and consistent planning in terms of the divine potential of every human being in this
earthly school.[5] As my aunt would say it: "He knew what he was
doing; he made them feel worth something down in here."

These resources are the key not only to understanding the
miraculous success of the tangible kingdom in the desert but to
answering certain historical and biographical puzzles. For instance,
a constant mystery to non-Mormons who overlook the background
of Mormon persecution has been the source of Brigham Young's
apparently absolute power over a people raised in democratic traditions—his ability to direct them to make incredible sacrifices, even
to the death, when they could have pulled up and left at any time.
And a puzzle even to some Mormons has been the source of
Brigham's apparently enormous personal wealth—what seems to
critics an inconsistent involvement of a prophet in profits and
politics and a greedy accumulation of a lion's share of scarce resources among a destitute people. But there *are* answers now, which
both Mormons and non-Mormons need to look at.

It is important to see that it was Brigham Young's success in
winning the Mormons' loyalty to him as the true successor to
Joseph Smith—by sharing with them and consistently developing
in them Joseph's vision of their earthly purpose and possibilities
and by truly functioning as a prophet to them—that gave Mormons an other-worldly perspective, but one that paradoxically
freed them for energetic, courageous building in this world. Their
fundamental loyalty, reinforced by bitter persecution and despite
deep-seated, scripturally validated loyalty to the Constitution of the
United States and its principles, was not to Europe or the United
States, or even Nauvoo or Salt Lake City, but to an eternal city of
God, an ideal to be realized in their hearts and minds as well as in
buildings and to be fully realized only in the future; thus they
could endure setbacks and losses, move and rebuild, or move out
to colonize again and again at the call of the prophet. Confident
that President Young was receiving divine direction concerning this
whole unified spiritual and physical kingdom and receiving it according to changing circumstances as they developed, they could
accept, with clear-eyed but persistent obedience, the directions
from their prophet on all aspects of their lives, from health reme-
dies to architecture to marriage choices, and then adjust with
equanimity when the directions changed, even reversed, as conditions changed. These people were not dupes or fools; they were
willing to give such power over their lives only to one whom, on

continuing evidence both of his enjoyment of the gifts of the Spirit and of his practical success, they trusted was indeed God's spokesman.

This turning back to a pre-Enlightenment desire to unite power and goodness in one person, in a prophet-king, appalled most non-Mormons. The federal officials appointed to Utah, who tried magnanimously to interject the individualism and divisions of eastern-style democracy and laissez-faire capitalism into the Mormon theocracy, were amazed at the rejection of their attempts by the people themselves. They failed to understand that Brigham Young's power was freely given him. And those who were (and are) offended at Brigham's imperious, one-man leadership, his involvement in business development, and his seeming carelessness in mixing his own and Church resources simply fail to understand both the times and his fidelity to the basic Mormon concept of stewardship in building the kingdom of God. All—labor and capital, windfalls and profits, talents and time—all was to be used according to his God-given responsibility to direct, and was to be used for one purpose—the good of the kingdom.

Such a perspective also helps us understand Brigham Young's amazing confidence in the kingdom, even from the frightening days of early 1849, when for many of the Saints the issue of survival was still very much in doubt and some were thinking very seriously of moving on to California. At the lowest point of morale, in February of that year, he said to the Saints:

> We have been kicked out of the frying-pan into the fire, out of the fire into the middle of the floor, and here we are and here we will stay. God . . . will temper the elements for the good of His Saints; he will rebuke the frost, and the sterility of the soil, and the land shall become fruitful. Brethren, go to, now, and plant out your fruit seeds. . . . As for gold and silver, and the rich minerals of the earth, there is no country that equals this; let them alone; let others seek them, and we will cultivate the soil. . . . Brethren, plow your land and sow wheat, plant your potatoes.[6]

Indeed, it seems that over the next few years irrigation leached the sterile alkali from the soil, and the combination of plentiful water through irrigation and hot, continuous sunshine, unimpaired by rainclouds, began to produce exceptionally fine crops; it even seems, according to modern climatologists, that a general world-wide warming trend brought sufficiently long growing seasons. But the most important thing is that the Saints, with very few exceptions, did resist the lure of California as well as the temptation to exploit Utah's own mining potential (and thus avoided the mining camp evils of greed, boom and bust economy, and degeneration of morals). They plowed their lands and planted potatoes. And along with the windfall of needed goods, and a market for their surplus teams, wagons, and food, that came with the influx of forty-niners that summer, they began to harvest enough to sustain the fifty-six hundred residents in the valley during the winter of 1849-50 (plus a number of stranded gold seekers) and still leave a large surplus in storage. The next summer continued emigration from the Winter Quarters area raised the population to eleven thousand. The "starving period" was over, and Brigham Young began to act on his already formed plans to colonize the whole area and build the political and economic, the industrial as well as agricultural, base for the literal kingdom.

As he began to build, Brigham, as their Moses, did not forget, in all his apparent self-confidence, the true source of the protection and success the Mormons had enjoyed in their role as modern Israel. On July 28, 1850, he wrote Orson Hyde, in charge back at the Winter Quarters area way-station, by then centered at Kanes-ville, Iowa, where seven thousand still waited their turn and others were coming in from Europe:

> We feel no fear. We are in the hands of our heavenly Father, the God of Abraham and Joseph Who guided us to this Land, who fed the poor Saints on the Plains with Quails, Who gave his people strength to labour without Bread, who sent the Gulls of the Deep as Saviours to preserve (by Devouring the crickets) the Golden Wheat for Bread for his People and who.preserved his Saints from the wrath of their enemies, Delivering them from a bondage more cruel than that inflicted upon Israel in Egypt. He is our Father and our Protector. We live in his Light, are Guided by his Wisdom, Protected by his Shadow, Upheld by his Strength. . . .
>
> Dear Brother . . . we will do the Best we can to Get along with our Domestick affairs with the Blessing of the almighty. We shall none of us have to Die but once.[7]

But as we have seen, Brigham thought a man a fool — worse than a fool, a neglectful steward of God's gifts — if he relied only on such miracles. He was certain God was in charge and thus he was able to work without fear or even undue haste or anxiety, especially after the chastening of the Iowa experience. He was confident that he must only do his best and God's will for the kingdom would be realized, even if God occasionally had to take up the slack of human failure or inability with his miracles. This confidence helped greatly in freeing Brigham to act decisively and to move others to do their best — both through his actions and through his exhortations such as that letter to Orson Hyde.

So President Young sat down in the spring of 1849 with the Council of Fifty (by this time a kind of town meeting of the chief leaders of the Church and community) and began to plan the kingdom. It did not surprise him later when the enterprise was saved from failure by the exceptionally good harvests of 1849 and 1850 and the windfall profits of various kinds from the gold rush. He was willing to take the Lord's blessing, without blinking at the irony (any more than he did again in 1858-60 when the economy was bolstered by the U.S. Army trade and surplus), that the kingdom was profiting from something that was in some ways a serious threat to it — and without compunction at charging what the market would bear: "What! sell bread to the man who is going to earn his one hundred and fifty dollars a day, at the same price as you do to the poor laborer, who works hard here for one dollar a day? I say, you men who are going to get gold to make golden images . . . pay for your flour!"[8] Those two profitable years gave President Young the confidence to move rapidly ahead with bringing west the thousands of Saints still remaining in Iowa and to plan for emigrating the thirty thousand converts from England; to send out missionaries, especially beginning in 1852, to many parts of the world; and to spread out colonies up and down the central corridor and even into distant parts of the huge provisional State of Deseret confidently envisioned in those meetings in 1849.

That "state" functioned quite fully, with the Church President also as its "governor," for two years while the Mormons unsuccessfully sought federal approval, and again it functioned as a kind of "ghost government" from about 1860 to the 1870s, during a time when the executive and judicial branches of the central territorial government were regarded as an alien collection of carpetbaggers. Late in 1849, Brigham's astute friend, Thomas Kane, who knew the ways of Washington, had warned the Mormons against settling for less than statehood. Wilford Woodruff reports an interview with him in Philadelphia, in which Kane described President Polk's continuing animosity (spurred in part by Missouri Senator Benton) and Polk's clear intention, despite Kane's efforts with him, to appoint territorial officials from the East who would not be friendly. Woodruff quotes Kane as saying:

> You are better off without any government from the hands of Congress than with a Territorial government. The political intrigues of

government officers will be against you. You can govern yourselves
better. . . . You do not want corrupt political men from Washington
strutting around you. . . . You have a government now, which is
firm and powerful, and you are under no obligations to the United
States. . . .

Brigham Young should be your governor. His head is not filled
with law books and lawyers' tactics, but he has power to see through
men and things.[9]

Unconcerned with Mormon preferences, Congress created the
Utah Territory under the Compromise of 1850, which settled the
controversy over slavery in the new territories acquired from
Mexico (California was given statehood with slavery forbidden,
and Utah and New Mexico were made territories and left to decide
about slavery, which they both rejected). This decision also reduced
the ambitious size of the original "state," which had included all of
present-day Utah and Nevada, large parts of Arizona, New
Mexico, Colorado, Wyoming and Oregon, and, to make possible
what Brigham envisioned as a corridor to the sea, most of southern
California. And though Brigham Young was appointed governor
(in what was, given the national opposition to Mormons, a rather
courageous choice by President Millard Fillmore), being made a
territory brought the first of many presidentially appointed, non-
Mormon officials to Utah.

There was difficulty almost immediately, of the kind Kane had
foreseen. Shortly after his arrival, Associate Justice Perry Brocchus,
one of the non-Mormon officials, asked to speak to the Saints in a
special conference in September 1851. There he made some
remarks about polygamy that were insulting, especially to the
Mormon women present. President Young, responding in obvious
anger, in turn publicly criticized Brocchus and the other officials.
After other disagreements developed in the next few weeks, especially over control of a twenty-four-thousand-dollar federal
appropriation to the territory and determining the prerogatives of
the elected (and therefore essentially Mormon) territorial legislature, most of the non-Mormon presidential appointees left, taking
with them the money and also the first of a series of vindictive
reports about Brother Brigham and the Mormons that led eventually to much trouble, including a threatened occupation by federal
troops, and to a set of circumstances which contributed to a
massacre.

The departure of these officials created a central judicial
vacuum, which Brigham Young filled ingeniously and to the

general benefit of the Saints but, as with many other such actions, to the consternation and eventual opposition of outsiders. Governor Young had the territorial legislature extend criminal jurisdiction to the county probate judges. As a result, even when federal courts were again able to be in session, accused persons, as well as applicants for citizenship, etc., could choose the probate judge, often the natural leader of the town, the Mormon bishop, rather than an anti-Mormon federal appointee who was dead set, for instance, against polygamy. This combining of local Church authority with government authority (usually including both judicial and executive power) was attacked by outsiders as subversive of American principles. But to Brigham and the Mormons (and ironically to some Utah non-Mormons, who preferred the spirit of amicable arbitration in Mormon courts) it seemed by far the best way to reach substantive, as opposed to merely procedural, justice.

President Young's attitudes and actions concerning the non-Mormons structured much of the Mormon history of the 1850s. Soon after he first arrived, on July 28, 1847, he had lectured the then-isolated Saints:

> We do not intend to have any trade or commerce with the gentile world, for so long as we buy of them we are in a degree dependent upon them. The Kingdom of God cannot rise independent of the gentile nations until we produce, manufacture, and make every article of use, convenience, or necessity among our people. . . . I am determined to cut every thread of this kind and live free and independent, untrammeled by any of their detestable customs and practices.[10]

He then proceeded to spend two thousand precious dollars of Battalion pay to buy out the only non-Mormon landholder in the area, Miles Goodyear, who had a homestead at what became Ogden. Despite the economic costs in transportation and the lack of capital goods and know-how, he continually rejoiced in the isolation that resulted from moving a thousand miles beyond the frontier into a land that had as its chief virtue the fact that "nobody else wanted it." He planned and developed the kingdom using the beehive (*Deseret* means honeybee) as a symbol and model — of unified (even to the edge of uniform), orderly, cooperative work for the public well-being rather than individualistic struggle for private profit. These values, expressed both in the colonization and irrigation process and in industrial development, though antagonizing to proponents of the new rugged individualism and laissez-faire capitalism that gained sway in the rest of the United States after 1850, were quite similar to the economic policies of the earlier Puritan Northeast. In fact, in a final irony that Leonard Arrington has noted, the very policies of central direction, cooperation, and long-run planning that Mormons had developed earlier in the face of government opposition—these policies, "as a result of the failure of individuals, the success of large corporations, and the impositions of government, came to characterize national policy with respect to the West in the twentieth century" and have become the policies the United States government has advocated in its efforts to help many developing countries.[11]

In forming the root values of the kingdom and persisting in action that conformed to those values, Brigham Young was able to be patient, even optimistic, in what many felt to be a hopeless task (and which in fact brought many failures) because of absolute faith in his calling and in the divine guarantee of ultimate success in what mattered. Thus, though some colonies had to be abandoned (a few at great economic loss when they were called back during the 1857 Utah War) and many developed in ways quite different from the original intent, and though the ambitious attempts at developing a wholly self-sufficient industrial base seemed more often than not to end in drastic cut-back or abandonment, without Brother Brigham's prophetic vision and drive much less—perhaps nothing—would have been achieved.

Of course, great success did come in the more important matters. The towns were built and the schooling in faith and endurance, in ingenuity and unselfishness, went on. The first expansion from the Salt Lake Valley formed an "inner cordon" of settlements in the irrigable valleys along what is now known as the Wasatch Front, a 250-mile, north-south barrier of mountains that produces rain and snowfall sufficient to bring yearlong streams into the nearby valleys. Sending out colonies north and then south and then north again, by 1856 Brigham Young had fully established settlements along the two- to twenty-mile-wide arable strip from Cache Valley south to Parowan, and these towns were constantly growing from an influx of immigrants. In the meantime he had ringed the kingdom with colonies at strategic points of entry: Carson Valley where the California Trail crossed the Sierra, Fort Bridger and Fort Supply on the Oregon Trail in Wyoming, and Lemhi in northern Idaho. Also, following a systematic exploration under Parley P. Pratt between Salt Lake City and San Diego, Brigham had formed the skeleton for a great "Mormon Corridor," a proposed trade and immigration route to the sea, with twenty-seven settlements, including present-day Las Vegas, Nevada, and San Bernardino, California.[12]

The Mormon colonization process was developed in part under Joseph Smith: preliminary exploration, followed by a "call," much like a mission assignment, issued to a carefully chosen company, who were fully equipped and extensively exhorted to properly build the kingdom and who then moved out in the fall or winter to build a fort and homes before beginning spring planting. This was turned into a smooth routine by President Young, as we can see in the Iron County Mission sent out in December 1850 under the apostle George A. Smith: The 167 persons reached their site, an untouched sagebrush valley 250 miles south of Salt Lake City, on January 10, immediately nominated county officials, and on January 15 conducted elections. By January 28 a meetinghouse was being built, and letters were now sent to Washington, D.C., for a post office charter and meteorological instruments. Houses were up by the end of February, and work was progressing on a school, canals, roads, a gristmill and on development of the iron works that were, along with establishing a link in the Mormon Corridor, one of the colony's major responsibilities. On July 4, Smith reported in his journal, "All was silent, not a gun fired, nor a drunken man seen in the streets," feeling no need to note that what six months before had been an empty wilderness now had peaceful lanes and ripening crops and a full civil and religious society — a school for making Saints. But he and the other leaders, under Brigham's tutelage, were well aware that that is what they were doing, as we see from a comment made the next year on this same group of people by the apostle Erastus Snow. He had gone to Parowan with the apostle Franklin D. Richards to spur development of the iron industry that had been successfully begun by these pioneers but was having some cooperation problems:

> We found a Scotch party, a Wel[s]h party, an English party, and an American party, and we turned Iron Masters and undertook to put all these parties through the furnace, and run out a party of Saints for building up the Kingdom of God.[13]

Despite the achievement of the colonists in turning out quality iron in just one year and the boost given the work by the reorganization and capitalization under Elders Snow and Richards, the effort to establish an iron industry (which Brother Brigham favored because iron, unlike gold, was a "civilizing" metal) suffered a series of setbacks and finally failed. This was true in varying degrees of other major industries attempted by President Young in his efforts to provide a self-sufficient commonwealth.

Development of a paper mill was the most successful enterprise and gives us insight into Brigham's methods: After one abortive effort in 1851 under a skilled paper-maker converted in England, better machinery was obtained and the first successful mill west of the Mississippi established — mainly to provide for the Church's newspaper, the *Deseret News*. A more superior set of engines was purchased in 1860, and, to meet the continuous and growing need for rags to make a good quality paper, George Goddard was called by the Prophet to serve a "rag mission":

> When President Young first made the proposition, the humiliating prospect almost stunned me [Goddard had been a merchant, had gone to Brigham Young for business advice, and now found himself called to "go from door to door with a basket on one arm and an empty sack on the other, enquiring for rags"], but a few moments' reflection reminded me that I came to these valleys of the mountains from my native country . . . for the purpose of doing the will of my Heavenly Father. . . . I therefore answered President Young in the affirmative, and for over three years . . . my labors extended, not only visiting many hundreds of houses during the week days, but preaching rag sermons on Sunday. The first time I ever spoke in the Tabernacle, Salt Lake City, . . . was a rag discourse, and Presidents Brigham Young and Heber C. Kimball backed it up with their testimony and enlarged upon it.[14]

A pottery plant, "Deseret Pottery," also established in 1851 by skilled converts from England, was much less successful and was abandoned at a substantial loss in 1853, though a profitable pottery business was established privately by 1856. Attempts to establish wool manufacturing with imported sheep, machinery, and convert experts from Europe met a similar fate, the effort dragging out over ten years and finally failing due to insufficient sheep, many having been killed by coyotes and wolves; it was revived years later with several mills.

What are we to make of such "failures"? For one thing, daring major Church enterprises like the sugar factory (in "Sugarhouse" near Salt Lake City) and the iron mill came close enough to success that they encouraged sporadic continuing efforts that eventually led to some of Utah's major private industries. For another, such bold efforts to establish economic foundations for a totally new and independent religious commonwealth had special goals — to utilize the skills of European immigrants in building a literal kingdom of God to function as a divine school—that paradoxically made the usual forms of "success" more difficult but also assured that even in "failure" the enterprises would achieve the most important goals and the kingdom would press on. As Leonard Arrington has suggested, the Mormons were crippled by a fundamental problem of lack of sufficient capital to see the projects through to final success, and their efforts would have achieved a more traditional *financial* success if knowledgeable private interests had been allowed a freer hand in the day-to-day direction and a stronger voice in the making of basic decisions.[15] But mere financial success was not the main goal; the Mormon businessman "was not a capitalistic profit-calculator, but an appointed overseer of a part of the Kingdom," and besides serving the more basic religious goals, "this concept of collective entrepreneurship and administration . . . saved the Great Basin Kingdom from the oblivion which seemed inevitable when so many of its major projects fell through."[16]

So, despite the harsh environment, formidable setbacks from poor harvests in 1847-48 and 1855-56, and the failure or near failure of many major experimental efforts, Brigham Young continued to build his kingdom. He succeeded because of major windfalls, yes, but also by achieving superior organization of what scarce capital was available, including willing and skilled human labor as well as machinery, livestock and money; by motivating in the original pioneers an almost unbelievable individual sacrifice and cooperative, obedient effort in a great cause; and by maintaining that vision in the new generation that grew up and the thousands of new immigrants that came in a constant stream—nearly seventy thousand by the time of his death.

It was, of course, Brother Brigham who, in Liverpool in 1840, had organized the real beginning of LDS immigration to the United States from Europe as well as leading in the establishment of a missionary effort so fruitful that it continued to bring in converts by the thousands each year, all anxious to "gather to Zion." Although a significant purpose in the immigration was to fulfill the Mormon religious principle of gathering a modern Israel out of the world to build a separate, exemplary kingdom, the special economic and organizational needs of that kingdom were also important. Even in 1840 Joseph Smith had instructed Brigham Young to first emigrate those with the skills and capital to build an economic base for those who would follow. In 1850, when a "Perpetual

Emigrating Fund" was organized under the laws of the provisional State of Deseret, President Young's instructions to Church agents in Europe were to first find iron and textile manufacturers, metal workers, and potters, "artisans and mechanics of all kinds," to have them emigrate immediately in preference to anyone else, and to bring machinery, tools, and blueprints with them.[17]

The emigration system was developed on the foundation laid by Brigham in 1840: It began with a member's application to a local Church agent in Europe; the gathering and organization of companies for each ship at Liverpool followed; then came the long voyage to New Orleans and up the Mississippi to St. Louis and the Missouri to Kanesville (after 1854 to New York and by train as far west as possible); and the trek along the pioneer trail to Utah and assignment to an established community completed the journey. It became the most successful privately financed immigration system in United States history, praised not only by Charles Dickens, who saw it operating in Liverpool, but by modern scholars who have studied its overall achievements.[18]

Most interesting in understanding Brother Brigham is the spirit of consecration which, under his direction, informed and motivated the system of emigration. If emigrants had been required to pay their own way many would have been left behind or doomed to a long wait in saving the hundred dollars needed. Companies were therefore formed according to ability to pay: self-supporting "cash" emigrant companies (about 40 percent); "Ten Pound" companies frugally designed to cost about that much — about fifty dollars per adult and twenty-five dollars per child (another 40 percent of the total companies); and "P.E." companies, consisting of those who could pay nothing. Systematic saving in established funds was encouraged in the European Mission of the Church, and added to this were nearly all European tithing receipts and contributions of more well-to-do converts (beginning with Jane Benbow's gift to Brigham back in 1840). But by far the main contributions to the Perpetual Emigrating Fund — labor, produce, and cattle, as well as cash — were those of the Saints already in Zion, estimated in 1900 to have totalled eight million dollars. Of course, those aided were then expected to make the Fund "Perpetual" by repaying the loan as fast as they could (they pledged by signed contract to "hold ourselves, our time and our labor, subject to the appropriation of the Perpetual Emigration Fund Company, until the full cost of our emigration is paid"), and many did work for the Church through Brigham's public works, which in turn gave tithing resources to the Perpetual Emigrating Fund.

Brigham Young's ingenuity in marshaling these diverse resources—including such things as stray cattle and other unclaimed
property which was turned over by the territory—into a working
process is impressive. Especially important, and possible only
because of the trust and spirit of consecration President Young
shared with the Saints, was the use of what Arrington calls "sight
drafts," by which resources physically present in one place could be
used in another form elsewhere. For instance, the Saints left any
cash they had in Europe or at outfitting stations like St. Louis to be
used by the Church to pay ship and wagon costs, etc. These members were in turn given drafts for food, implements, and other
supplies in Utah that had been donated there to the fund. Or a
Utah Saint could contribute labor or food to his local tithing office
and receive a draft on the Church's tithing resources in Europe to
emigrate his family. Brother Brigham was much involved in this
process, not only as planner and motivator but as personal guar-
antor in his complex role as spiritual and temporal leader. And
when he was not able to meet all the drafts coming in he spoke his
mind with characteristic verve:

> When Br. Erastus Snow arrived on the first of this month, he came
> in the morning and informed me that he had run me in debt nearly
> fifty thousand dollars to strangers, merchants, cattle dealers, and our
> brethren who are coming here; he said, "Prest. Young's name is as
> good as the bank."
>
> . . . I will pay you when I can, and not before. . . . It is the poor
> who have got your money, and if you have any complaints to make,
> make them against the Almighty for having so many poor. . . . I
> cannot chew paper and spit out bank bills that will pass in payment
> of those debts.[19]

Sometimes he came down hard on the immigrants who were
still in debt: "I want to have you understand fully that I intend to
put the screws upon you, and you who have owed for years, if
you do not pay up now and help us, we will levy on your property
and take every farthing you have on earth."[20] But, as in other cases,
Brigham was merely barking to make a point and motivate the
genuine backsliders rather than making a threat with much bite in
it. Most immigrants could not really generate a surplus, and the
chief form of "repayment" was contributions of labor and tithing,
as is revealed by the growing total of accrued debt (counted up
each year by the "block teachers" who visited each home monthly),
which reached over a million dollars by the time of Brigham's
death.

Rather than "put the screws" on those unable to repay, President Young put his energy into cutting down expenses and finding better ways to use the variety of resources he had in the kingdom. For instance, when immigration was resumed in 1860, after the "Utah War" hiatus, Brother Brigham took advantage of a surplus of teams and wagons obtained from the abandonment of his Express Company and the army surplus sales, both brought on by that war, and after careful experimentation in 1859 began to send ox trains out from Utah to bring the immigrants from the Missouri Valley. Brigham's nephew Joseph W. Young found that properly-cared-for oxen could make the twenty-two-hundred-mile round trip in six months, and he delivered a sermon in October conference on "the science of Ox-teamology." By order of the First Presidency, needed men, teams, and equipment were apportioned to various communities and gathered in Salt Lake City in April, where they were inspected and organized. Surplus cattle and other expendable goods were taken east to be sold, thus reversing the cash flow that had been draining resources at the outfitting stations. And the President didn't miss a chance for other, more spiritual benefits. Those who went were called as "missionaries" and carefully shepherded by good leaders; they were often unmarried men who looked for and found prospective brides among the immigrants they brought back. On the economic side, during the 1860s the equivalent of about $2,400,000 was utilized for immigration, but very little actual money changed hands. As the transcontinental railroad moved west the trips to the railhead became shorter and shorter until, with the meeting of the Union Pacific and Central Pacific railroads at Promontory Summit on May 10, 1869, "ox-teamology" ended.

A more dramatic example of Brigham Young's ingenuity in bringing over the immigrants to his kingdom was the handcart companies, his response to economic depression. Despite the hostile environment and failure of some early enterprises, the kingdom survived the crucial building period of the early fifties, largely on the strength of a series of increasingly good harvests; but beginning in 1855, crop failures (harvests reduced one-half to two-thirds by grasshoppers and drought) and the loss of nearly half the cattle in the disastrous winter of 1856 completely depleted surpluses and quickly reduced the thirty-five thousand settlers to a condition of semistarvation similar to early 1849. President Young used every resource of wit and power at his command — emphasizing more thorough gleaning, more efficient seeding, better land use — but his ultimate resource was the faith of the Saints, and in the extremity of the 1855-56 winter he asked them to adapt to the crisis the long-standing but sporadic custom of fasting, by going without food on the first Thursday of each month and donating for the poor the food thus saved, a practice that was so effective it has been continued in the Church as the monthly first Sunday "fast day." Ultimately Brigham had to ask each head of family to place his household on close rations (a half pound of breadstuff per day) and use all surplus in feeding those in need:

> Set the poor to building your houses, to making fences . . . or doing something, and hand out your grain to them. . . . If you do not pursue a righteous course, we will separate you from the Church. Is that all? No, if necessary we will take your grain from your bin and distribute it among the poor and needy, and they shall be fed and supplied with work, and you shall receive what your grain is worth.[21]

This is hyperbolic rhetoric again, Brother Brigham's half-humorous but effective way of making sharp enough a serious point (there is no evidence that a forced levy was ever used, any more than in getting immigrants to pay debts to the Perpetual Emigrating Fund). What he actually *did* was feed nearly three hundred persons throughout the famine with the resources directly available to him, employing many of them in building an extra house and barn and in work on that wall my aunt told me about:

> I build walls, dig ditches, make bridges, and do a great amount and variety of labor that is of but little consequence only to provide ways and means for sustaining and preserving the destitute. . . . Why? I have articles of food, which I wish my brethren to have; and it is better for them to labor, . . . so far as they are able to have opportunity than to have them given to them.[22]

President Young called an additional three hundred unemployed men in Salt Lake City on missions — both colonizing (to Las Vegas, Carson Valley, etc.) and proselyting (the East Indies, Australia, etc.). Though most of the missionaries had to be supported from Church resources, they were nonetheless productively building the kingdom.[23]

With such efforts the kingdom survived; but, though none died, the community came close to starvation, and, with tithing and Perpetual Emigrating Fund donations next to nothing, it seemed the expensive "gathering of the poor" from Europe would have to stop. But President Young, unwilling to curtail such an essential part of the purpose and success of the kingdom, instead revived an idea first suggested in a General Epistle in 1851, when he had ventured that immigrants could come on foot, like the forty-niners with their wheelbarrows, in seventy days.

> I am . . . thrown back upon my old plan—to make handcarts, and let the emigration foot it, and draw upon [the carts] the necessary supplies. . . . They can come just as quick, if not quicker, and much cheaper—can start earlier and escape the prevailing sickness which annually lays so many of our brethren in the dust.[24]

That letter was to Franklin D. Richards, who was in charge of the European Mission. On the same day Brigham Young wrote his son-in-law Edmund Ellsworth, who was serving on a mission under Elder Richards:

> I do believe that I could bring a company across without a team and beat any ox train if I could be there myself. Would you like to try it? It will by much relieve our Brethren from sickness and death, which I am very anxious to do. There is a railway from New York to Iowa City and will cost only about 8 dollars for the passage, then take handcarts, their little luggage with a few good milk cows, and come on till they are met with teams from this place, with provisions.[25]

It was a good plan on paper and there is great optimism in the General Epistle which Brigham sent to Europe on October 29, 1855, to be published in the *Millennial Star* ("let them gird up their loins and walk through, and nothing shall hinder or stay them"). Such promises infected Elder Richards, who wrote a series of enthusiastic editorials for the *Star*. This brought an excited response, and nearly two thousand signed up for the much cheaper (under fifty dollars) though untried method. Perhaps too many signed up, or there was some other misunderstanding between Church agents in Liverpool and those at the outfitting stations in Iowa, because the last two of five companies had to wait for their handcarts to be built—many from green lumber that later broke up—and were disastrously late on the trail.

The first three companies seemed to justify President Young's confidence, arriving in remarkable time (about sixty-five days) by the end of September without suffering more than the usual number of wagon-train deaths and still proudly carrying letters they had meant to send on ahead but couldn't because no one passed them. Church leaders were extremely pleased. Elder Woodruff wrote: "As I gazed upon the scene, meditating upon the future result, it looked to me like the first hoisting of the floodgates of deliverance to the oppressed millions. We can now say to the poor and honest in heart, come home to Zion, for the way is prepared."[26]

As if on cue from a Greek tragedy, this expression of pride was followed immediately by the arrival of Franklin D. Richards and other missionaries returning from England (including Brigham's son, Joseph A.) with the sobering news that two more companies were still behind them. Elder Richards was still optimistic and could speak in the general conference the next day about the handcart pioneers' faith that God would turn away the storms so that they would not suffer more than they could bear. But President Young was as usual not about to *wait* for a miracle. As soon as he understood that there were still a thousand walking immigrants over five hundred miles out on the trail, where winter storms could come at any time, he announced a new theme for the conference:

> The text will be—to get them here! I want the brethren who may speak to understand that their text is the people on the Plains, and the subject matter for this community is to send for them and bring them in before the winter sets in.
>
> That is my religion; that is the dictation of the Holy Ghost that I possess, it is to save the people. . . .
>
> . . . This is dividing my text into heads; first, forty good young men who know how to drive teams . . . second, sixty or sixty-five good spans of mules, or horses, with harness . . . thirdly, twenty-four thousand pounds of flour, which we have on hand. . . .
>
> I will tell you all that your faith, religion, and profession of religion, will never save one soul of you in the celestial kingdom of our God, unless you carry out just such principles as I am now teaching you.[27]

Wallace Stegner, who has written a most perceptive and moving account of this episode, describes what followed:

> "You may rise up now," he told them, "and give your names."
>
> They rose up and gave their names, and more than their names. Though they had no information on exactly how bad the condition of the companies might be, they had enough experience to guess. With the unanimity of effort which had always been their greatest strength, they oversubscribed Brigham's first request, and when new requests were made, they met those too. By October 7, three days after Richards' arrival, the first contingent of the rescue party was heading eastward into the mountains. . . . The presence of . . . Brigham's son Joseph A. Young, Cyrus Wheelock, and others, was significant. They were the missionaries who had converted a good

many of the handcart emigrants in the first place. . . . They may have felt partially responsible, or have felt the Church to be responsible, for the delays at Iowa City. Whatever may be said of their excessive zeal in the first place, they were neither indifferent nor cowardly once they knew the handcart companies might be in distress. Separated from their families for two years or more, restored to the valley no more than forty-eight hours, they turned unhesitatingly around and drove out again with the rescue wagons.[28]

President Young sent 250 wagons out to keep the trail open and to provide a relay of supplies and fresh teams down to the valley. He goaded the vanguard rescuers (who at one point turned back because of the blizzards) until they pushed themselves at a desperate pace up through the already snow-blocked passes and reached the two companies camped in snowdrifts, out of food, and waiting for the end. They were literally angels of mercy for people among whom death was a constant presence after the delays from collapsing carts and loss of their supply wagons in a buffalo stampede had put them into the increasing mountain cold, nearly exhausted and without sufficient food. Stegner writes:

> It is hard to imagine the emotions of rescue, the dazed joy of being snatched from the very toppling brink. . . . It is quite as hard to visualize the hardship that even rescue entailed — that jolting, racking, freezing, grief-numbed, drained and exhausted 300 miles on through the winter mountains to sanctuary. In Echo Canyon, between the battlements of red sandrock [where a year later, some of these rescuers would face an advancing U.S. Army], a child was born in one of the wagons. . . . He was wrapped in the "garments," the holy underwear, of one of the young rescuers, and they named him, with a haunting appropriateness, Echo. Against all probability, both he and his mother lived.[29]

But the deaths continued along that three hundred miles until the number reached over two hundred, compared to eleven and forty in the more famous Fremont and Donner disasters:

> Perhaps their suffering seems less dramatic because the handcart pioneers bore it meekly, praising God, instead of fighting for life with the ferocity of animals and eating their dead to keep their own life beating, as both the Fremont and Donner parties did. And assuredly the handcart pilgrims were less hardy, less skilled, less well equipped to be pioneers. But if courage and endurance made a story, if human kindness and helpfulness and brotherly love in the midst of raw horror are worth recording, this half-forgotten episode of the Mormon migration is one of the great tales of the West and of America.[30]

It is clear who the victims of this classic tragedy of overreaching were: not only those who died of cold and hunger and exhaustion, but the many more who wore lasting scars of body (almost all had frozen hands and feet) and spirit (some later apostatized). Even the rescuers suffered lasting damage. William Kimball, for instance, spent a whole day carrying women and children through floating ice on a crossing of the Sweetwater, and according to the journal of one of them, "staid so long in the water that he had to be taken out and packed to camp and he was a long time before he recoverd as he was chil[le]d through and in after life he was allways afflicted with rhumetism."[31]

The heroes are fairly obvious too: the rescuers like Kimball and Joseph A. Young, who bucked his way back and forth along the trail many times; perhaps especially Levi Savage, the lone voice raised in opposition when the decision to go on despite being over a month behind was made at a mass meeting of the two companies back on the Missouri in mid-August. After arguing forcefully against risking their lives in blind trust that snowfall would be late, and seeing everyone else vote to go on, he is reported to have announced, "Brethren and sisters, what I have said I know to be true; but, seeing you are to go forward, I will go with you, will help you all I can, will work with you, will rest with you, will suffer with you, and if necessary I will die with you."[32] Savage did not die, and he saved the lives of less hardy and experienced companions in the final agony; but he endured Elder Richards's allegation (when the missionaries from England passed the companies) that his opposition had been simply lack of faith in God.

To those trying to identify a scapegoat for the tragedy, blame might seem to have been fixed publicly by the Church President on Elder Richards:

> Are those people in the frost and snow by my doings? No, my skirts are clear of their blood, God knows. If a bird had chirped in brother Franklin's ears in Florence [Nebraska], and the brethren there had held a council, he would have stopped the rear companies there, and we would have been putting in our wheat, etc., instead of going on to the Plains and spending weeks and months to succor our brethren.[33]

But to anyone who has read many of Brigham Young's speeches — or examined his actions carefully enough — that speech of rebuke is fairly standard in tone and color, actually quite mild compared to some. It might even be read as providing, in the face of growing anxiety on the part of relatives and friends of the pioneers still struggling toward them, authoritative explanation of what had happened and a *defense* of Elder Richards: "Here is brother Franklin D. Richards who has but little knowledge of business . . . and here is brother Daniel Spencer . . . and I do not know that I will attach blame to either of them." At any rate, the speech is largely a very frank discussion of what had caused the disaster (the late start, not prevented as it should have been by the Church agents) and how the problem would be prevented in the future: "I am going to lay an injunction and place a penalty, to be suffered by any Elder or Elders who will start the immigration across the Plains after a given time; and the penalty shall be that they shall be severed from the Church, for I will not have such late starts." Elder Richards and the other missionaries had encouraged the emigrants to rely on miraculous intervention to protect them from the consequences of needless folly in a practical decision — something Brother Brigham would never do; he understood and forgave such a mistake but wanted no misunderstanding about what the mistake was.

At the same time there is a certain defensiveness in Brigham Young's speech. The President was clearly wounded by this disaster in a way that the failures of dozens of industries could not threaten him. Here was where his stewardship touched human lives and where his old abhorrence of violence and unneeded, unredemptive suffering came to the fore — and he wanted very much not to feel responsible. He was right most of the time and wanted to be right all the time. When he made some of the usual miscalculations that plague us all, considering the stakes with which he played, the costs were proportionately much greater. Even in these, such as the economic failures of various enterprises, he maintained a singular equanimity, essentially because of his unbounded faith that he was God's steward and God would overrule all according to His will, salvaging good out of his unwitting errors and weaknesses, or providing strength, as God had given him in the Iowa crossing, to regroup and try again. But when it came to violence, there is a new dimension: avoidance if possible at whatever cost; deep pity and haunting heartbreak on the positive side; but a certain resentment of those responsible, including himself, and a desire for vindication. In this case, determined that the handcart scheme should prove itself despite the tragedy, President Young sent a company of seventy missionaries back along the trail by handcart (and without commissary wagons) to Florence in forty-eight days as soon as possible in the spring. He then made other ambitious efforts to facilitate continuing the scheme, but bad publicity and the interference of the Utah War kept the numbers very small; and in 1860 the round-trip ox-team caravan from Utah was established.

Deeper than any need for vindication, however, was Brother Brigham's heroic acceptance at a personal level of the pain of responsibility. Those two months of rescue operations must have been the longest two months of his life. Speaking to the Saints in the Old Tabernacle on Sunday, November 2, he reminded them how comfortable they were despite the recent famine:

> We can return home and sit down and warm our feet before the fire, and can eat our bread and butter, etc., but my mind is yonder in the snow, where those immigrating Saints are, and my mind has been with them ever since I had the report of their [late] start. . . . I cannot talk about any thing, I cannot go out or come in, but what in every minute or two minutes my mind reverts to them; and the questions — whereabouts are my brethren and sisters who are on the Plains, and what is their condition — force themselves upon me.[34]

A classic and much quoted statement of the LDS doctrine of faith and works is the sermon President Young gave on hearing that some survivors of the Martin Company were entering the valley on Sunday morning, November 30, 1856. He instructed the bishops and other brethren on placing the refugees in good homes, and then he announced:

> The afternoon meeting will be omitted, for I wish the sisters to go home and prepare to give those who have just arrived a mouthful of something to eat, and to wash them and nurse them up. . . . Were I in the situation of those persons who have just come in, . . . I would give more for a dish of pudding or a baked potato and salt, . . . than I would for all your prayers, though you were to stay here all afternoon and pray. Prayer is good, but when baked potatoes and milk are needed, prayer will not supply their place.[35]

But some of Brother Brigham's deepest anguish is seen in the luminous autobiography of Mary Goble Pay, who as a child of thirteen in the Martin Company froze her feet at the last crossing of the Platte, and who saw her two little sisters die on the trail and her mother finally expire on the day they arrived, December 10:

> Three out of four that were living were frozen. My mother was dead in the wagon.
>
> Bishop Hardy had us taken to a home in his ward and the brethren and the sisters brought us plenty of food. We had to be careful and not eat too much as it might kill us we were so hungry.

Early next morning Bro. Brigham Young and a doctor came. . . .
When Bro. Young came in he shook hands with us all. When he
saw our condition—our feet frozen and our mother dead—tears
rolled down his cheeks.

The doctor amputated my toes using a saw and a butcher knife.
Brigham Young promised me I would not have to have any more of
my feet cut off. The sisters were dressing mother for the last time.
. . . That afternoon she was buried.[36]

The girl refused to have her feet cut off, despite the pressing advice
of another doctor when they didn't heal:

One day I sat there crying. My feet were hurting me so—when a
little old woman knocked at the door. She said she had felt some
one needed her there for a number of days. . . . I showed her my
feet and told her the promise Bro. Young had given me. She said,
"Yes, and with the help of the Lord we will save them yet." She
made a poultice and put on my feet and every day after the doctor
had gone she would come and change the poultice. At the end of
three months my feet were well.

Brother Brigham was not one to linger long in self-doubt or
despair. He not only sent out the missionary company that spring
to revive faith in his handcart scheme, but he immediately set to
work planning the extremely ambitious Brigham Young Express
and Carrying Company (known as the Y.X. Company), with a
series of way stations along the trail to carry freight, mail and
immigrants:

As the largest single venture yet tackled by the Mormons in the
Great Basin, the Y.X. Company was a bold and well-conceived enterprise, which, if "war" had not been its outcome, would undoubtedly have changed the whole structure of Mormon, and perhaps
Western, economic development. . . . [It] anticipated the Pony
Express, the Ben Holladay Stagecoach line, and the Russell, Majors,
and Waddell freight trains of the late '50's and '60's.[37]

After it was learned, in February 1857, that the U.S. mail contract
had been awarded to Hiram Kimball, an agent for the Church,
President Young spent much time that spring choosing the spots
for the way stations, which were to be actual settlements with
farms; solicited and organized the contributions of men, wagons,
cattle, material, provisions (over a hundred-thousand-dollars' worth
in the first half of 1857); and counseled and set apart the "express
missionaries," who were to see their work as religious duty and live
accordingly—including treating their teams with kindness. The

effort proceeded rapidly; mail was being carried by the middle of February, and by July many of the way stations were nearly completed and stocked. But as the chorus in a Greek tragedy would have pointed out, even while Brigham Young was proudly reporting the progress of this enterprise to the Saints in the April conference, bragging that "the company is the Latter day Saints . . . this is the only people that can do it,"[38] President James Buchanan was considering actions that would not only destroy the Y.X. Company at a great loss but bring the Church to the very brink of battle with federal forces and put Brigham and the succeeding leaders in a defensive position against the government and outsiders for the next forty years.

Events had come together as if ordained by a perverse fate. In 1856 the new Republican Party formed itself around opposition to slavery and to popular sovereignty, which would allow territories to decide about slavery. It used the practice of polygamy in Utah as a sensationalistic example of what could happen under such popular sovereignty. The Republicans resolved that "it is both the right and the imperative duty of Congress to prohibit in the Territories those twin relics of barbarism—Polygamy and Slavery." They lost the election, but many antipolygamy resolutions subsequently appeared in Congress, and Democratic President Buchanan, unwilling to move against slavery in the South where his major support was, chose to oppose polygamy so he would not be vulnerable to Republican attack on both issues. In this mood he reacted precipitately to a vitriolic letter of resignation in March 1857 by W. W. Drummond. Drummond was a non-Mormon who had been appointed associate justice in Utah in 1854 and had soon come into wide-open conflict with President Young and the Mormons when he attacked the probate court jurisdiction and especially when it was discovered he had deserted his family and brought with him a mistress, who actually sat beside him in court. Without investigating Drummond's character or the substance of his false charges that Governor Young had destroyed court records and was heading what amounted to a rebellious dictatorship, and without even notifying the Mormons, Buchanan cancelled the mail contract and dispatched an expeditionary force of twenty-five hundred troops to install a newly appointed Utah governor, Alfred Cumming.

There was fine dramatic irony in the patriotic displays in which Brigham Young led the unknowing Saints on July 4 and July 24, even while troops were marching against them under the flag the Mormons were saluting. In fact it was on July 24 that definite word arrived of the army's approach, though there had been rumors before. President Young and the Church leaders were gathered at the top of Big Cottonwood Canyon with twenty-five hundred Saints for a jubilant celebration of their entrance into the valley a decade before, when Abraham Smoot, who had heard in Missouri of the government actions and rushed back the thousand miles to Utah in twenty days, rode up to Brigham's tent with the news. Brother Brigham calmly let the Saints continue their celebration in peace that night, but to his close colleagues he began a characteristically hyperbolic call to arms that clearly grows out of the bitter experiences of the preceding twenty years:

> I said if [Expedition Commander] General Harney came here, I should then know the intention of the government; And it was carried unanimously that if Harney crossed the *South Pass* the *buzards* should *pick his bones.* The feeling of mobocracy is rife in the "States." The constant cry is Kill the Mormons. *Let them try it.*[39]

Even when faint rumors of possible trouble had begun to come in earlier in July, Brigham had taken a hard line: "I wish to avoid hostilities with the United States, but before I'll see this people suffer as they have done heretofore I will draw my sword, in the name of Great God, and say to my Brethren let our Swords fall upon our enemies."[40] On August 20 he reflected: "The Day I entered Salt Lake Valley 24 July 1847 I remarked—if the devil will let us alone for 10 years—we will bid them defiance. July 24 1857 —10 years to a day—I first heard of the intended expedition to Utah under Genl. Harney. I feel the same now. I defy all the powers of darkness."[41]

In the absence of contrary evidence, Governor Young chose to regard the expedition as an enemy mob and girded Zion for battle. He called back missionaries from the East and Canada and eventually from foreign lands; he called in the outpost settlements at San Bernardino and Carson Valley; he mobilized the Nauvoo Legion and sent out guerrilla forces to spy on and then harass the troops and destroy supply trains and Mormon forts that might be used by the enemy; his sermons and letters escalated the rhetoric of total war (for example, the Secretary's Journal for August 16: "Warning the brethren to prepare for the worst. And bring their minds to making every town a 'Moscow' and every mountains pass a 'Potters field,' ere they would permit a mob to desecrate the Land which God has given us"); finally on September 15, he, as governor, declared the territory under martial law.[42]

On the other hand there was a clear strain of calm, assured pacifism. President Young forcefully instructed the guerrillas under his counselor, General Daniel H. Wells, commander of the Nauvoo Legion, to burn forage, drive off cattle, even burn supplies — all as delaying tactics — but absolutely to shed no blood. On August 30, he said to the Saints:

> Cannot this Kingdom be overthrown? No. They might as well try to obliterate the sun. God is at the helm. . . .
>
> Sow your grain early this fall. Many wish to know whether I think we shall reap. I do not care whether we do or not, but I intend to sow early this fall so that it will ripen next season. . . .
>
> The Lord has suffered the wicked to drive us about, that we might accomplish his designs the sooner. . . .
>
> . . . do not be angry with [the army], for they are in the hands of God. Instead of feeling a spirit to punish them, or anything like wrath, you live your religion; and you will see the day when you will pray God to turn away from your eyes the sight of their afflictions.[43]

And indeed forces were already at work to defuse what by the end of the year became known in the East as "Buchanan's Blunder." Commanding General Winfield Scott had early seen the military folly of the expedition, but his letter of opposition was kept secret from Buchanan by Secretary of War John B. Floyd. General Harney saw the same problems and found an excuse to resign his command in Kansas, which resulted in its being given to Colonel Albert S. Johnston, whose name thus became notorious in Mormon legend. A Captain Stewart Van Vliet was sent ahead, arriving on September 8, to convey the troops' "peaceful intent" and secure cooperation by the displaced governor (who was addressed in the letter from Harney as "President Young of the Society of the Mormons" in what Brigham saw as calculated insult) and to buy provisions for the troops. Van Vliet was treated courteously but firmly by President Young, who considered him a "gentleman" who "understood our position," and the officer returned sobered by the Saints' unanimous determination (he had been present at a large meeting where they all shouted "Amen" to the proposition, "All of you that are willing to set fire to your property and lay it in ashes, rather than submit to their military rule and oppression"[44]). Despite the reluctance of his superiors to believe him, Van Vliet then began to work toward securing the peace commission from Washington that successfully negotiated a truce nine months later.

The Lord did seem to be at the helm, because the harvest that fall, in sharp distinction to the previous two, was huge (according to Wilford Woodruff "the largest ever known in these valleys"[45]), big enough to support the settlers and missionaries who had been called in and the militia, as well as compensating for the disruptive evacuation of northern Utah the next spring. The guerrillas succeeded in slowing down the army until snow had so blocked the passes that they had to winter in misery near the burned-out Fort Bridger. Though they finally marched through Salt Lake the next June, it was a somber triumph. They set up Camp Floyd in the desert about forty miles south of Salt Lake and finally left in 1860, after providing the Mormons another great windfall through trade supplies and through the eventual disposal, for next to nothing, of the army's surplus property.

But Brother Brigham's rhetoric, effective in meeting his goal of rousing the Saints to faith and energetic action, may this time have helped tip the balance toward a tragedy that caused great suffering and hurt the kingdom badly in terms both of national sympathy and internal confidence. During the tinderbox conditions of August 1857, a company of emigrants was making its way south from Salt Lake City toward southern California. There were constant irritations caused by the unwillingness of the Saints — mobilized for defense and suspicious of any strangers — to carry on normal sales of food. More seriously, there was also a firing of the smoldering hatred for Missourians, caused by a band of them attached to the company who boasted of their part in the murder and rape of Mormons in 1838 and now threatened more of the same. The company had a series of run-ins with Indians, and it was rumored that some Indians — and one Mormon — had died after eating an ox the emigrants poisoned. The impending war between their friends the "Mormonees" and the gentile "Mericats" had made the Indians even more hostile than usual toward the emigrants. The Indians finally attacked on September 7 and then besieged and sporadically fired upon the company at Mountain Meadows in southern Utah. A few days previous in Cedar City the emigrants, furious at the citizens' continued refusal to sell food, had destroyed some property and threatened that they would return with troops from California to drive the Mormons out. After the emigrants left Cedar City, angry and frightened civil and Church authorities had sent a rider the 260 miles north to get President Young's advice. But when three emigrants broke out of the Indians' siege and had an encounter with some Mormons in which one emigrant was killed and the other two fled, it seems that some of the local Mormons feared certain retaliation from California if the main body escaped, and they decided to take action on September 11. A group of them, led on the field by John D. Lee, who had been called in as a local Church agent among the Indians and who later claimed the Indians had threatened to kill him and his family if he did not help them, somehow got the emigrants to disarm and leave their barricades for safe passage to Cedar City. Apparently Lee's command, "Do your duty," started the massacre—which called for the 50 Iron County militiamen to slaughter the men and the 200 Indians to kill the women and older children. About 120 were killed. Only seventeen small children survived to be eventually returned to the East.[46]

The messenger rode in to Salt Lake City while Brigham Young was entertaining the U.S. Army emissary Van Vliet and remained only four hours before turning back for another hard three-day ride under Brigham's command, "Go with all speed, spare no horse flesh," and with a letter to Isaac Haight, presiding Church authority at Cedar City:

> You must not meddle with them. The Indians we expect will do as they please, but you should try to preserve good feeling with them. There are no other trains going south that I know of. If those who are there will leave, let them go in peace.[47]

But the messenger was two days late. An official report to Governor Young on September 30 by the local Indian agent described the massacre as wholly the work of Indians, and Brigham, preoccupied with an impending war, seems to have had no contrary suspicions until some time later, when non-Mormon investigations and the pall of guilt that gathered over Cedar City must have slowly made the truth apparent to him. The process of determining guilt and responding to it was complicated by distance and the delay caused by the war; by the fact that, as the historian Nels Anderson has written, "most investigators were not so much interested in the facts as in using the incident to indict Brigham Young";[48] by the oath of secrecy the participants made with each other; and by the incalculable tragic emotion and traumatic defensiveness felt not only by them and their friends and families but by many other Mormons, who had come to think of themselves as God's chosen people, veritable Saints—the victims, not the perpetrators, of massacres.

It would seem impossible to understand Mormon history without understanding *both* the Haun's Mill Massacre, where Mormon men and children were murdered and mutilated and Mormon women tortured and raped, *and* the Mountain Meadows Massacre, where Mormons murdered many men and consented to the murder of women and children. Levi Peterson has written an intelligent and compassionate essay on how Juanita Brooks, in her studies of the massacre and of John D. Lee, has brought to Mormon historical consciousness much of the truth of the tragic massacre and the tragic cover-up and scapegoating that followed. He claims that in doing so she has functioned both as a truth-revealing historian and as a classic tragedian in that her work not only arouses the tragic emotions of loss of innocence, of pain and anguish and sympathy at intolerable loss, but does it in a way, because of her own empathetic commitment to the Mormon people and the kingdom, and because of her courage and skill, that is healing and redemptive.[49]

Brigham Young must have felt those tragic emotions, and probably more acutely than most because of his more acute aversion to bloodshed than many of his frontier-conditioned associates. On January 27, 1857, with the handcart tragedy still weighing on him, the President had talked to his office staff, meditatively, almost obsessively, about the terrible crime of shedding innocent blood: "If I should hereafter, say 50,000 years, in the spirit world meet a man in my journeys . . . [who] asked me 'did you not . . . spill my blood 50,000 years ago.' . . . I never wish to have this feeling in the eternal world."[50]

In 1866, while challenging non-members in the audience at the Old Tabernacle to prove in court the private insinuations some were making that he had been involved in a recent murder in Salt Lake, he said:

> I will tell the Latter-day Saints that there are some things which transpire that I cannot think about. There are transactions that are too horrible for me to contemplate.
>
> The massacre at Haun's mill, and that of Joseph and Hyrum Smith, and the Mountain Meadow's massacre and the murder of Dr. Robinson are of this character. I cannot think that there are beings upon the earth who have any claim to the sentiments and feelings which dwell in the breasts of civilized men who could be guilty of such atrocities; and it is hard to suppose that even savages would be capable of performing such inhuman acts.[51]

We know that Brigham Young's enemies were wrong in accusing him of perpetrating or condoning the massacre, but his role in the cover-up and in the fate of John D. Lee is still unclear. Blame was increasingly focussed on Lee by those who broke silence, and he was summarily excommunicated by the Church in 1870 and was executed by civil authorities on the massacre site nearly twenty years after the event, March 23, 1877, just five months before Brigham's own death.

There are a few hints of Brother Brigham's complex feelings. John D. Lee was part of Brigham's own family, a son through the sacred early Mormon ceremony of "adoption," a loyal and tried Saint and an intrepid builder of the kingdom. But it apparently became clear to the President that Lee had participated in a kind of thing Brigham most intensely abhorred and that he had lied to Brigham about it. In addition, the cancer of that action threatened the kingdom from within and without. The complexity of response is indicated in John D. Lee's continuance for a while in positions of trust in southern Utah that could not have been possible without President Young's approval, and then, after a certain point, the sudden withdrawal of Brigham's support and association. In this tragic dilemma, Brother Brigham may have experienced a loss of innocence, in choosing the kingdom over full candor and then over loyalty, even greater and more painful than the one in Iowa. It is difficult to speculate how he might have done better, given the narrow alternatives. If he could have, but did not, it is difficult to feel other than empathy for a prophet of God who so deeply and personally suffered the tragedy. And it is possible to gain insights into what it may cost an imperfect mortal to be called to the role of prophet.

Brigham Young was always perfectly candid about being imperfect. In the year following the Mountain Meadows Massacre he had ample opportunity to show as well that he was a prophet. Perhaps most impressive is his firm and well-vindicated reliance on God's protection of the kingdom: "It is a solemn time. The armies of the Gentiles are making war upon us because of our religion. . . . We have to trust in God for the result. We shall do what we can, and leave the work in his hands."[52] And yet he was constant in his recognition—and in reminding the Saints—that whatever the outcome of this attack on the kingdom they had built with their hands, the adversity they were passing through could serve, de-

pending on their righteous response, to further the basic goals of
the kingdom: "Should we live in peace, year after year, how long
would it be before we were glued to the world? . . . it would be
contrary to our feelings to attend to anything but our own individual concerns to make ourselves rich. . . . This shows to us that
all things pertaining to this world are subject to change, and such
changes as we cannot control."[53]

It is true that President Young continued to make dramatic
and invigorating speeches to the Saints as God seemed to them to
fight their battle—to close up the passes with snow and bring
Buchanan under congressional attack:

> If [the soldiers] come here, I will tell you what will be done. . . .
> Men shall be secreted here and there and shall waste away our
> enemies. . . .
>
> . . . I want you to prepare to cache our grain and lay waste to this
> Territory; for I am determined, if driven to that extremity, that our
> enemies shall find nothing but heaps of ashes and ruins. . . .
>
> . . . with us it is the Kingdom of God, or nothing; and we shall
> maintain it, or die in trying—though we shall not die in trying.[54]

Throughout the "war," however, Brigham constantly affirmed
his readiness to negotiate with anyone who would deal with him
fairly and not under threat of force. According to one non-
Mormon's report, Brigham's constant emphasis was to avoid bloodshed "so that if another course should be adopted . . . the feeling of
revenge should not hinder the . . . peace."[55] Thus when his old
friend Thomas Kane suddenly appeared as a mediator from President Buchanan in February 1858, after a heroic journey through
Panama and up from southern California that injured his health,
Brigham welcomed him as an answer to his prayer for a bloodless
solution: "Friend Thomas, the Lord sent you here, and he will not
let you die . . . till your work is done. You have done a great work,
and you will do a greater work still."[56] President Young later reflected on this crucial time:

> When Colonel Kane came to visit us, he tried to point out a policy
> for me to pursue. But I told him I should not turn to the right nor
> the left, *only as god dictated*. I should do nothing but what was right.
> When he found that I would not be informed, only as the Spirit of
> the Lord led me, he felt discouraged, and said he would not go to
> the army. But finally he said, if I would dictate he would execute. I
> told him that as he had been inspired to come here, he would go to
> the army and do as the Spirit of the Lord led him, and all would be
> right. He did so—and all was right.[57]

This was, of course, a memory recorded after successful resolution of the conflict, but in fact Kane did make another dangerous trip, out through the snow to the army camped at Fort Bridger. There, after some difficulties with the belligerent General Johnston, he convinced Cumming, the appointed governor, to travel unescorted to Utah to investigate the situation. When he arrived in April, Governor Cumming was treated with good-humored respect by the Mormons. Brigham Young convinced him of the falsity of Drummond's charges and that he would be accepted fully as governor if the army kept out.

In March the Church leaders had agreed with President Young's feeling that, if Kane were unsuccessful and Johnston marched on them when the passes opened up, resistance would lead to much futile bloodshed and that evacuation and the "scorched-earth" policy considered earlier was the best course. Some have pointed out that this tactic served to turn world opinion in favor of the Mormons and thus was designed to allow Brigham Young to save face after his more violent public threats of the previous fall. There is no doubt that Brigham played a cagey and effective game with the federal powers. But the "Big Move," as it came to be called, was no game, and the thirty thousand people leaving their homes and trekking south in wagons was an awesome sight that greeted Cumming as he traveled down Weber Canyon and then south from Ogden to Salt Lake City. President Young was dead serious, bringing to fulfillment a plan that had been in his mind since the first news of invasion. He had written on January 6, 1858, to W. I. Appleby, president of the Eastern Mission:

> Rather than see my wives and daughters ravished and polluted, and the seeds of corruption sown in the hearts of my sons by a brutal soldiery, I would leave my home in ashes, my gardens and orchards a waste, and subsist upon roots and herbs, a wanderer through these mountains for the remainder of my natural life.[58]

Whatever the outcome, Brother Brigham knew this was a way of testing, and therefore developing through its exercise, the faith of the builders and beneficiaries of the kingdom. Their feelings, as they responded immediately to President Young's call to leave all behind again, are captured by a teenage participant:

> We packed all we had into father's one wagon and waited for the command to leave. . . .
>
> . . . One morning father told us that we should leave with a large company in the evening. . . .

Along in the middle of the day father scattered leaves and straw in all the rooms and I heard him say: "Never mind, little daughter, this house has sheltered us, it shall never shelter them." . . .

That night we camped on Willow Creek in the south end of the valley, and at ten o'clock every soul with bowed head knelt in prayer to God. As I dropped to sleep I heard my mother whispering that the Lord had heard our prayers and that our homes should not be burned.[59]

But the Saints were *ready* to burn those homes, and Brigham Young stood firm in the face of Cumming's pleas, even commands, to have the people return. They remained, Brother Brigham with them, in Provo and further south until late in June, by which time Buchanan's peace commission had arrived and had successfully negotiated a settlement. In it the Mormons received a full "pardon." (President Young commented, "I thank President Buchanan for forgiving me, but I really cannot tell what I have done.") Johnston led his army in an eerie "triumphal march" through the city, which was completely deserted except for the men who stood ready to set it to the torch if one soldier stepped out of line.

The ten years that followed the peace were full of irony for the Saints. The occupation by a huge non-Mormon army (Camp Floyd became the largest military post in the United States) and its vice-filled satellite community of camp followers would seem to have ended Brigham Young's drive for an isolated and self-sufficient kingdom. But the Church leaders held firm to their policy, even financing their efforts at home industry with profits from such windfalls as the occupation and trade with gentile-developed mines—thus turning to their own purposes the very forces that threatened self-sufficiency.[60] The soldiers, who jeered the impoverished and somewhat humiliated Saints when the latter returned from the "Big Move" to their hard-won homesteads, were pulled out of Utah to fight in the bloody Civil War, leaving to the Mormons the camp and surpluses; and Johnston, an effective commander who reduced potential antagonisms with his fairness but remained implacably disdainful of the Mormons as rebels, ironically joined the Southern rebellion, as did those other rather self-righteous instigators or participants in the crusade to put down the Mormon "secession," Governor Cumming and Secretary of War Floyd.

Meanwhile the Mormons, expected by many (including some who thought them justified) to join the Confederacy—and, in fact, despite many who felt that the Civil War would perhaps destroy

the country and usher in the Millennium—remained firmly loyal
to the Constitution and the Union. But they did not send soldiers
and only participated in the war by responding to Abraham Lincoln's request to Brigham for a company of cavalry to protect the
mail route through Wyoming. Even this ended when Colonel
Patrick Connor arrived from California in October 1862 at the
head of the Third California Volunteers, took over the postal guard
duty from the Mormons, and built Camp Douglas on Salt Lake
City's east bench expressly to intimidate Brigham and the Saints.
Connor joined with other non-Mormons in the city who were
determined to destroy Mormon hegemony, especially involving
himself in prospecting activities in Utah mountains with the explicit
purpose of attracting so many non-Mormons to these riches that
the Mormon culture would be overwhelmed.

Brigham Young remained quite aloof from all this, actually
going into a year of near isolation in his home and office after
Cumming took over; this was a precaution against the threats of
Gentiles encouraged by the presence of Johnston's soldiers and it
also helped show that, whatever the title bestowed on Cumming,
the Utah government could not operate except with Brother Brigham's consent. Though Utah's applications for statehood continued
to be denied in the growing crusade against polygamy in the
1860s, President Young operated the "ghost" government of the
State of Deseret and that political reality was recognized by Lincoln
in his direct approach to the Mormon leader for guards for the mail
route. Lincoln told a visitor from Utah that the Mormons were like
the logs he learned to plow around as a youth clearing timber, "too
hard to split, too wet to burn, and too heavy to move," and added,
"You go back and tell Brigham Young that if he will let me alone I
will let him alone."[61] And generally that is what Lincoln did,
attempting to be fair with Utah appointees and refusing to push
prosecution of the Morrill Anti-Bigamy Act of 1862, which dis-
incorporated the Church and limited its real estate holdings to fifty
thousand dollars.

It was partly in response to the Morrill Act, and subsequent
acts aimed at destroying the Church's power through direct economic attack, that President Young made what were to him very
sensible transfers of Church property into his own name. But these
actions have resulted in misunderstanding and suspicion about him.
Jack Adamson, in his perceptive and moving introduction to Dean
Jessee's edition of *Letters of Brigham Young to His Sons*, quotes from a
hasty note written in 1856 to Joseph A. in England: "I want you to

be faithful that you may [be] worthe of your stashon in my Kingdom." And then Adamson comments: "My Kingdom? Did he mean
in my Father's kingdom where there are many mansions. . . ? It was
late and Brigham was wearier than he realized. Who can know
what he meant?"[62] But there is no mistake, and no mystery. Brigham meant "my" kingdom — and in a way that ought to be clearer
than it is, even to Mormons themselves, inheritors of the tradition
of consecration and stewardship President Young so firmly established. He meant it in precisely the way he said "my family" —
meaning the nearly one thousand people at any one time included
in the total of his wives and children, those sealed to him by
"adoption," and the families of men hired by him to work on "his"
various and expanding projects — all those to whom he felt responsible as a patriarch. And that use of "my" ought to be understandable, since it is close to the same sense in which the head (or
any member) of a closely knit modern family might refer to that
unit, where he feels responsible to all and all of whose resources he
shares and helps direct for the common good.

President Young's position as prophet and his special skills
combined to make it natural for him to be the center of the process
of developing the new economy in Utah — especially given the
integrated vision of temporal and spiritual effort and success that
he shared with his followers. As an outsider saw it:

> Brigham Young is at the head of everything; . . . he receives the
> revenue, and he spends them — both without any apparent account-
> ability; the best farms are his, the largest saw-mills, the most pros-
> pering manufactories; . . . There is immense wealth in his possession;
> but what proportion of it he calls his own, and what the church's, no
> one knows — he apparently recognizes no distinction.[63]

Actually President Young did recognize a distinction, especially in
his clerk's carefully kept books; but the distinction was not absolute
because it was not very important to the central purposes of the
kingdom. Brother Brigham used the available resources in whatever way his judgment and inspiration told him was for the good
of the kingdom — whether in using the Church's tithing resources
to feed unemployed people to whom he had given work on "his"
farm or in making drafts on his personal accounts to pay for emigrating people to Utah when "the Church's" Perpetual Emigrating
Fund resources were insufficient.

Brigham Young did develop great "personal" wealth and holdings. Originally this happened through his own basic abilities, as

craftsman, farmer, and entrepreneur, and then it continued and increased through his use of the resources and trust accorded his position to get the pioneer economy going—especially through personally directing a book credit system by which labor and material resources could be put to use in the time before a money and an industrial economy had been created. His wealth seemed greater than it actually was because he at the same time managed the similar—and interchangeable—Church system as "Trustee-in-Trust." The confusion became even greater—and has unfortunately persisted—because, beginning in 1862, much Church property was consciously put in private hands (other trusted leaders' as well as President Young's) to avoid escheatment by the federal government in its "legal" attack against Mormonism.

Non-Mormons were mystified, eventually infuriated, by this casual mixing of religious and economic power, by what seemed to them a primitivistic affront to the new American ways that the Enlightenment and the Revolution had made possible. But it is non-Mormons who provide us with some of the best evidence concerning Brother Brigham's honesty and ability. Fitz Hugh Ludlow, who visited in 1868, concluded that if Brigham Young had to support himself by farming, "he understands soils, stock, tools, rotation, irrigation, manures, and all the agricultural economies so well that he would speedily have the best crops within a hundred miles' radius. With his own hands he would put the best house in the settlement over the heads of himself and his family."[64]

Ludlow described President Young as sitting in the Church office "managing a whole nation's temporalities with such secular astuteness that Talleyrand or Richelieu would find him a match . . . and the Rothschild family could not get ahead of him if the stakes were a financial advantage." These qualities, and Brigham's style of operating as if all were included in his kingdom, continued to be perplexing, even offensive, to some, but it is easy to see that the advantages to the Church and the community—the gospel kingdom—were at least as great as to himself.

For himself, Brother Brigham actually claimed nothing, except that God had appointed him steward over the kingdom—which of course meant everything. It is true that one notes in his life a developing love of quality that led him, not to personal luxury in lifestyle (though he appreciated well-made watches, carriages, etc.), but to build and furnish with fine things homes in Salt Lake City and St. George and perhaps occasionally indulge some of his wives' and daughters' special tastes. Even these indulgences are revealed mainly by his strong, even public, efforts to *curb* luxurious tastes in his family and others (for instance, his formation of the Retrenchment societies), and his efforts to achieve quality in his homes and decorations were mainly a part of his felt responsibility to set standards for the pioneer community struggling to build a civilization in the wilderness. Certainly he cannot be seriously faulted (although he might well have prepared better) for the difficulties that attended settlement of his estate after his death, when some members of his family did not understand fully his tacit assumptions about the holdings all belonging to the kingdom.[65] Just as Joseph did not succeed in making clear to everyone the proper mode of succession of authority that should follow his death, Brigham did not succeed in making clear to everyone before he died his vision of consecration to the kingdom.

Brother Brigham understood that all the world is God's, to be used for God's purposes in providing eternal joy and progress for all his children, and that he uses human beings to safeguard and develop those resources. President Young believed he happened to be placed at the head of God's earthly kingdom and to be given commensurate gifts, and that it was his job to make the most of them:

> Man is destined to be a God—and has to act as an independent being—and is left without aid to see what he will do, whether he will for God, and to practise him to depend on his own resources, and try his independency—to be righteous in the dark—to be the friend of God and do the best I can when left to myself, act on my Agency as the independent Gods, and show our capacity.[66]

And of course, by acting responsibly with his capacities as God's steward, and by consecrating everything to the building of the kingdom, he felt he was able to receive God's aid, not only in making up for his inadequacies and the losses incurred at the hands of nature and the kingdom's enemies, but in making the kingdom into a blessing for all.

Brigham Young's efforts to build "his" kingdom did not come to success in all the details he intended, or even in its apparently central religious goal, that of self-sufficient unity and order, but it did succeed in building the Utah commonwealth in ways that have been a blessing to Mormons and non-Mormons alike. Leonard Arrington has pointed out that the remarkable thing about Brother Brigham's building of his kingdom was not his pragmatic flexibility, great as that was. It was rather his stubborn adherence to policy he believed was revealed from God, in the face of those who saw Mormonism as a barrier to the spread of individualistic and competitive economic and political principles and who therefore produced the "stream of laws, administrative directives, judicial decisions, and occupation armies which progressively reduced the scope of church and group economic activity."[67] And Arrington has also pointed out the irony that despite its natural and human obstacles the kingdom "by the end of the century . . . had provided the basis of support for half a million people in an area long and widely regarded as uninhabitable," and thus "demonstrated the effectiveness of central planning and voluntary cooperation in developing a large semi-arid region."

Though Mormons gradually during Brigham Young's lifetime and then altogether in the 1890s gave up what seem his central goals of self-sufficiency and isolation from the gentile "Babylon," when to persist would have done even greater harm, they have continued to hold fast to Brother Brigham's ideals of community and order. In fact, in Arrington's words, Mormons, "having no doubt of its attainability and inevitability, . . . still discuss the type of society that will exist when the Kingdom is finally realized."[68] They continue to prepare themselves — in committing to the gospel kingdom whatever that kingdom requires of their means, their abilities, and their time; in storing a year's supply of food and clothing; in practicing gardening, canning, sewing, and many other skills of self-sufficiency; and in continual sharing with the needy through fast offerings and the welfare plan — for a time when they firmly believe God will call them by his prophets to step forward and complete the building of the kingdom.

President Young continued to build throughout his life, adding over 150 new communities in the 1860s, with the impetus for self-sufficiency brought by the Utah War and by the peace ironically given Utah by the Civil War. For example, the prototypical and heroic "Dixie Mission" was sent to southern Utah in 1862 to grow cotton for the kingdom. As late as 1872, Brigham was discussing with Thomas Kane, who came to Utah and visited the southern settlements with him, the prospects for expanding the colonization into Mexico. Even at the end of his life, Brigham was planning and beginning to develop additional colonies in Arizona, since irrigable land in Utah was becoming fully used. Always his vision remained constant, as a letter to the editor of the *New York Herald* in 1873 indicates. He explains with terse wit his resignation from various business responsibilities in favor of others "competent to succeed me," and then gives us, in his unique personal voice, the essence of his life and its continuing challenge:

> For over forty years I have served my people, laboring incessantly, and I am now nearly seventy-two years of age and I need relaxation. . . .
>
> We intend establishing settlements in Arizona, in the country of the Apaches, persuaded that if we become acquainted with them, we can influence them to peace. . . .
>
> In Utah we have a fine country for stock raising and agriculture and abundance of minerals awaiting development, and we welcome all good citizens who love peace and good order to come and settle with us. . . .
>
> It has been frequently published that I have a deposit of several millions of pounds sterling in the Bank of England. Were such the case I would most assuredly use the means to gather our poor Church members. . . . All my means are invested here improving this Territory. . . .
>
> All my transactions and labors have been carried on in accordance with my calling as a servant of God. I know no difference between spiritual and temporal labors. God has seen fit to bless me with means, and as a faithful steward I use them to benefit my fellow men — to promote their happiness in this world in preparing them for the great hereafter.
>
> My whole life is devoted to the Almighty's service, and while I regret that my mission is not better understood by the world, the time will come when I will be understood, and I leave to futurity the judgment of my labors and their result as they shall become manifest.[69]

President
Brigham Young   7

We remember Brigham Young most vividly—and perhaps always will—as the builder of his kingdom in the Great Basin. But he would probably much prefer to be remembered as Prophet and President of the Lord's Church and to be honored not for the many thriving settlements he founded but for the religious structure and spirit that informed them; not for the economic strength that his genius produced in a nineteenth-century desert commonwealth, but for the legacy of spiritual strength and idealism for which The Church of Jesus Christ of Latter-day Saints is indebted to him. Of course, the point of the previous chapter is that for Brother Brigham such matters could not be separated. But it cannot be emphasized enough that he thought of the kingdom essentially as "a good place to make Saints" and that that was truly the heart of his vocation—to make literal Saints, genuine followers of Christ.

President Young's goal, after the double trauma of Joseph Smith's death and the exodus, was not only to shepherd a bewildered people to some kind of safety and recovery but to renew the fires of their faith as builders of a kingdom such as the world had never seen. He did that as a prophet as well as a colonizer, and he succeeded in isolating his people long enough in a self-sufficient set of unified, cooperative towns that they were able to build up certain institutions and attitudes, legends and symbols, resources and commitments that are the continuing foundation and vitality of the Church. Brigham built in the mountains a kingdom that continues to serve as a model, etched in the habits and imaginations of the Saints, and a perpetual reservoir of economic, organizational, and motivational strength for the building of the Church and kingdom throughout all the world. He did this through emphasizing, even during the desperate times of flight and near starvation and even in the face of all-out conflict with federal armies and judges, the basically spiritual dimensions of his leadership—through the many prayer circles with other leaders, the steady voice of sensible inspiration in sermons week after week, the reaching back to Joseph's teachings and the "ancient order of things" for the religious foundation of his central economic efforts such as the cooperative movement and the United Order of Enoch. His regular visits to the outlying settlements, necessary for efficient planning, evaluation, and communication, were even more important as a means for him literally to bless and counsel the Saints and to increase and celebrate the extraordinary spiritual unity of the kingdom. His attention to the building of temples and to highly sacred ordinances of the endowment and the sealing of families for which the temples were intended began within days after his arrival in the Salt Lake Valley, when he saw in vision the great six-spired temple and marked with his cane its building spot;[1] and it continued unabated to the last year of his life, when he saw the St. George Temple dedicated and two others (Logan and Manti) begun. The central work of that last year, climaxing a gradual relinquishing of his more obviously temporal responsibilities in government and business, was a vigorous reorganization of the Church at the local level and a redefinition of the duties of the apostles that set the Church's course for many years.

President Young's last official act, on August 19, 1877, just four days before he was struck with his final illness, was to reorganize the Box Elder Stake in Brigham City, replacing the president, Lorenzo Snow, so that that gentle, inspiring apostle could join in the newly redefined Churchwide spiritual duties of the Quorum; and there Brigham held up to the people his continuing prophetic vision:

> We have a multitude of traditions to overcome, and when this people called Latter-day Saints will be free from these traditions, so that they can take hold of the Gospel and build up the kingdom according to the pattern, I am not able to say; . . . but still on the whole there is an increase of faith, of knowledge, of wisdom, of understanding. When we get to understand all knowledge, all wisdom, that it is necessary for us to understand in the flesh, we will be like clay in the hands of the potter, willing to be moulded and fashioned according to the will of him who has called us to this great and glorious work, of purifying ourselves and our fellow-beings, and of preparing the nations of the earth for the glory that awaits them through obedience.[2]

For thirty years Brigham had graphically imprinted that vision in the hearts of the pioneers, in good part through the power of his oratory, speaking to them regularly, first from the top of a wagon on the first Sunday, the day after their arrival in the valley: "He told the brethren that they must not work on Sunday; that they would lose five times as much as they would gain by it. None were to hunt on that day; and there should not any man dwell among us who would not observe these rules."³ A bowery of posts to support leafed branches for shade was next built and served both summer and winter; it is there that Brigham rallied the starving and desperate Saints, shivering as they stood before him in the snow on February 4, 1849:

> As the Saints gather here and get strong enough to possess the land, God will temper the climate, and we shall build a city and a temple to the Most High God in this place. We will extend our settlements to the east and west, to the north and to the south, and we will build towns and cities by the hundreds, and thousands of the Saints will gather in from the nations of the earth. . . . Take courage brethren. . . . It is our duty to preach the gospel, gather Israel, pay our tithing, and build temples. The worst fear that I have about this people is that they will get rich in this country, wax fat, and kick themselves out of the Church and go to hell.⁴

Absurd as it may have seemed to Brigham's listeners in 1849 to worry about getting rich and going to hell, the profits from trading with gold rush emigrants and then the successive good harvests in the early fifties made the danger real by 1855. Then a disastrously poor crop and destructive winter chastened the Saints, and the Church leaders, especially Jedediah M. Grant, who had replaced Willard Richards as the President's second counselor, used the disasters as an object lesson to bring repentance and rededication. In August, President Young rose before the Saints in the Bowery at the rear of the Old Tabernacle (an adobe structure built in 1851) and sounded the theme of what became known as the "Reformation":

> How slow many of us are to believe the things of God, O how slow. . . .
>   . . . I have no confidence in faith without works. . . .
>   . . . The past year was a hard one for us with regard to provisions, but I never had one faltering feeling in reference to this community's suffering, provided all had understood their religion and lived it. . . .
>   . . . If all our cattle had died through the severity of the past winter, if the insects had cut off all our crops, if we still proved faithful to our God and to our religion, I have confidence that the Lord would send manna and flocks of quails to us. But He will not do this, if we murmur and are neglectful and disunited.⁵

Brigham Young and the other leaders, who had been pre-occupied with fulfilling his prophecy about "extending the settlements" and with one of the rare periods of difficulty with Indians, now traveled throughout the territory, "bearing down in pure testimony" as the Book of Mormon prophet Alma had done in similar circumstances. In the fall of 1856 President Young forbade dancing and public theatre — and even discontinued the sacrament of the Lord's supper (until April 1857). The leaders were able to spark a zeal for reform that manifested itself in public confessions, in private interviews by Church representatives to encourage soul-searching, even in the rebaptism of thousands (including the entire all-Mormon legislature on December 30, 1856). All of this disciplinary activity, though there is evidence that some Saints got carried away to extremes, produced a spiritual reunification and toning-up that may well have made possible their remarkable response to the invading federal forces the next year.

Ten years later, in October of 1867, the Saints faced a different kind of invading force that threatened even greater disruption to the kingdom — all the intrusions of Babylon to be brought by an intercontinental railroad bearing down on Zion from east and west. President Young again rallied his people, this time by calling them together in the first conference in their new tabernacle, even though the great organ was only about one-third completed.

This was the world-famous building that still stands on Temple Square, with its striking, almost modernistic dome and its extraordinary acoustics — incredible achievements of that subsistence culture of the 1860s. It was also a fascinating example of President Young's leadership style and power: He apparently had the original idea for the size and shape. (Various legends say the shape was suggested to him by his umbrella, a turtle, the roof of his mouth, or the elongated half of an egg; but whatever the source, the huge open space is a remarkably pure formal expression of the central Mormon desire to meet together in large groups for instruction and inspiration from their leaders and for communion with each other.) Then Brother Brigham asked others to find a way to give the idea practical form — which the architect Truman Angell and Henry Grow, the engineer, proceeded to do, using an unprecedented application of truss-bridge-span construction by arching it and thus, without the usual massive iron bracings, making essentially a curved, rigid beam. President Young oversaw the work daily and ultimately brought it to conclusion by asking for all plasterers in the Salt Lake area: 250 responded and completed the full interior in sixteen days in the summer of 1867.[6]

The people felt great pride and completely overflowed the nearly six-thousand-seat building through four days of October conference, in which their President often repeated his encouragement not to fear the railroad but to prepare to meet its new challenges:

> On their former history [the Saints] had been tossed from pillar to post and driven from place to place; but here the people will stay, if they keep the commandments of the Lord, till they receive the word to gather up, go back and build up the Center of Zion.
>
> Some entertained the idea that we came here to hide ourselves up from the world; but we very soon learned that our light had been placed where the inhabitants of the earth could see that we had the Gospel of Jesus Christ, the Light of the world. . . .
>
> . . . The Lord wishes us to show to our neighbors, friends and foes, how to live, how to be great, how to live a hundred years in the beauty of life.[7]

Eight years later, while continuing to pursue economic policies that successfully met the challenge of the railroads, and only two years before his death, President Young dedicated the finished tabernacle, with its completed organ and the free-standing balcony, that both increased the seating room (to about eight thousand) and perfected the acoustics. He left a special glimpse of the spiritual concerns undergirding his economic and organizational efforts:

> We do pray to the Latter-day Saints to yield themselves obedient to the Spirit of God. When we do this we shall be one . . . but as long as we permit selfishness in our hearts we shall be divided, we shall have individual and self interest. But when we are actuated by the Spirit of the Lord, our interest is general, it is for the whole people, it is for the Kingdom of God upon the earth, it is to sanctify the people, to prepare for redeeming the nations of the earth, to assist all that is in our power, our Savior, our Elder Brother, who calls upon us to do our part; He has fulfilled his part, so far as the sacrifice is concerned, and He is still laboring, still toiling, still directing, to prepare the inhabitants of the earth that He may come and receive them, that He may come and reign in their midst. . . . Now we pray you, be reconciled to God; and the word of the Lord is, directly, to those who call themselves Latter-day Saints; Son or daughter, give me thy heart. Let us give our hearts and our affections to God our father.[8]

It seems that even Mormons have tended to downplay Brigham Young's role as a directly spiritual (as opposed to political and economic) leader. And a stereotype has emerged, formed partly by his genuine deference to the memory of Joseph, the great Prophet of the Restoration, partly by his forceful and visible effectiveness in other areas, and perhaps partly by the otherwise excellent film made by Darryl Zanuck in 1940 that portrayed Brigham as a competent and charismatic leader but uncertain of his divine calling, more surprised than anyone else at God's occasional help. That image is not true. Heber C. Kimball, who knew him longer and better than any man, testified to the Saints during the height of the Reformation, on October 12, 1856, that President Young had received ministrations of Jesus Christ, Michael, Elijah, Moses, and the ancient apostles.[9] And late in his life the President himself departed from his usual reticence about his prophetic gifts to tell the Saints in Ogden:

> I know that Joseph Smith was a Prophet of God, and that he had many revelations. . . . I have had many revelations; I have seen and heard for myself, and know these things are true, and nobody on earth can disprove them. . . . What I know concerning God, concerning the earth, concerning government, I have received from the heavens, not alone through my natural ability, and I give God the glory and the praise. Men talk about what has been accomplished under my direction, and attribute it to my wisdom and ability; but it is all by the power of God, and by intelligence received from him. I say to the whole world, receive the truth, no matter who presents it to you.[10]

As telling as direct claims for his spiritual power and effectiveness are, the best indication is the quality of President Young's daily conversations, feelings, and ministrations as revealed in his various journals, correspondence, and of course his sermons. Speaking with Bishop Edwin Woolley in January of 1857, while still physically ill and just beginning to recover from the chastening of the handcart disaster, Brigham revealed his understanding of the patient spiritual basis for his governing:

> [People] cannot all be governed together, unless with the even steady hand of mercy and justice. Men don't understand those things, or they would not commingle such spirits as they do, and try to measure all in one half bushel.
>
> Let this people become pliant in my hands, that I can lead them into celestial glory, then I am prepared to set them in order to beget Tabernacles for celestial Spirits, but now as they are, and their minds

set on this one thing forgetful of the weightier matters, I do not wish to hurry this matter.[11]

And, despite the lingering excitement of the 1856 Reformation, President Young did *not* hurry matters; he worked slowly but consistently with the means at hand, his developing kingdom, to purify the Saints and himself. We see him giving permissions for plural marriages—and for divorces. He counseled one couple against separation: "Go and live peaceably and try and live in peace . . . do not be arbitrary—Let the woman have her own way in cooking and don't be peevish." To a woman uncertain whether to be sealed in eternal marriage to her dead husband, who had been a good man but very cross to her, he counseled, "The grave is a purifying place to mortals—you will be proud of the connection."[12] He spent much time in carefully checking through his sermons (recorded in shorthand by George D. Watt, Thomas Bullock, and others) for correctness before having them published in the *Deseret News*, because he then expected, as he made clear, that they were to be taken as scripture. Despite the incredible press of business matters, especially in the early fifties when he was serving as governor, Indian agent for the territory, and both administrator and entrepreneur for the developing kingdom, he took time to review tracts and sermons by various apostles. And he was often involved, with other members of the Presidency, in officiating in the Endowment House (used for the sacred temple ordinances), even to the point of exhaustion ("sealed some 35 persons yesterday and must have spoke 20,000 words"[13]). One day the clerk records that in the midst of the usual press of business, "Sister Naomi Young [Brigham's fifteenth plural wife] being sick, was administered to by Prest. Y[oung], Wells, and TDB [Thomas D. Bullock, the clerk himself] . . . high fever soon abated. After the administration Prest. Y[oung] kept his hands on her head for some Minutes. She became calm, composed and seemed as if she would sleep."[14]

The President's extended journeys through the settlements were a major interruption in the office routine. At first they were mere jaunts out to nearby settlements, by horseback or carriage, to check on the development of the physical kingdom. But before long they took on something of the aspect of a royal "progress," with a full caravan of leaders, clerks, and guests making a month-long swing through the northern or southern communities, greeted in each town by banners and parades—school was let out and the prophet was honored by flower girls in white, and great feasts. This is Brigham Young's own description of an early trip:

From the 22nd of April to the 21st of May we spent our time accompanied by several engineers, and near fifty of the brethren, in visiting all the settlements south of this, in the Territory, and many places which had not before been visited; instructing, comforting, and blessing the Saints, selecting new locations, forming acquaintances with and striving to promote peace among the different bands of Indians; and, by the blessings of heaven, accomplished all we could reasonably anticipate.[15]

By the late sixties, a reporter for the *Deseret News*, traveling with one such caravan, mentioned that, whereas in the early days the President had camped out along the way, the settlements were now so near each other he could always stay with the Saints. But despite this growth and the emergence of good local leaders, "a visit from the Presidency and Twelve is refreshing to the officers and people. They partake of the spirit which prevails at head-quarters and can better keep pace with their brethren who reside there. Without these visits the people might become harrowed up in their feelings and sectional."[16] In 1871 President Young reported on one such journey without taking himself quite that seriously: "Our visit and travels have proved of great mutual advantage. . . . We started on this trip on the 24th of November, and returned on the 10th of February . . . teaching, counseling and exhorting the Saints in the various settlements, doing all the good, and the very least portion of harm we possibly could."[17] But the President, besides genuinely enjoying such grass-roots contact with the people he constantly called on for extreme sacrifice, clearly *cared* about these Saints who not only were what the kingdom was *for*, but *were* the kingdom, and he would not let distance or changing circumstance separate him from them. He had been through Iowa and Winter Quarters and the famine of 1848-49 with them and remembered what they had suffered and achieved, and they knew again with each visit that he did.

By the sixties, the trips increasingly involved preaching to the Saints, effecting ecclesiastical organizations, and making checkups. A friend of mine in Kaysville, Utah, whose grandfather often hosted the President during that period, remembers being told how President Young always sternly reviewed all assignments and unsolved problems discussed on the previous visit. Brigham Young was slowly becoming more of a public man, a symbolic motivator as well as doer. During the year of withdrawal following the Utah War, Wilford Woodruff had become concerned that the absence of this warning voice, in preaching regularly to the people, would allow them to fall away, but Brigham expressed only confidence in the Saints' continuing spirit as he began public appearances again in 1859:

> In our testimony meeting yesterday, I could not refrain from weeping for joy. What a peaceful, joyous, happy, heavenly spirit rested upon the congregation. . . .
>
> Brethren and sisters, I feel as calm and serene as the autumn sun of our mountain home. All is right. . . . God is at the helm. He guides the ship, and will bring it safely to port. All we have to care about is to take care of ourselves and see that we do right.[18]

In the relative peace of the 1860s it is interesting to see this mellowing continue and Brother Brigham gradually be given — and accept — the dimensions of a legendary figure, receiving with perfect aplomb such notables as Emerson, Richard Burton, Mark Twain, and Horace Greeley, and impressing them with his sturdy honesty and simple attractiveness of mind and manner as well as his obvious practical and administrative skills. His own people increasingly honored him with a striking combination of familiarity and obedience: one dropped into his office with an apple; he answered a knock at the office door one day to find a woman there whom he embraced and called by name and then, according to the clerk, found she had walked in from Draper (fifteen miles) to bring him a pair of socks she had knitted;[19] and the Saints universally called him "Brother Brigham." They sought his counsel in every conceivable matter and usually followed it (even though, as he complained, they sometimes went ahead to do what they wanted to, convincing themselves and others that he had approved); they responded to his sudden "calls" on them for everything from money to proselyting in India; and they gathered by the hundreds on Salt Lake streets to welcome him back from his trips.

By 1869 President Young, approaching seventy and bothered with rheumatism in the cold Salt Lake winters, began to turn his long trip to the southern settlements into a three- or four-month stay in St. George; there, though busy running the Church by telegraph, he got an important period of peace. Brigham's friend Thomas L. Kane came west again and with his family took part in the journey south in December 1872. We are fortunate to have Elizabeth Kane's witty, sharply perceptive, but (given her forthright antagonism to polygamy) amazingly sympathetic account of his journey; it provides us much insight into Mormon society — and into Brother Brigham. Among other things, Mrs. Kane tells us of his regular custom, on the evening of their arrival in each settlement, of having a kind of "open house" for all who wished to see him:

> At these informal audiences, reports, complaints, and petitions were made; and I think I gathered more of the actual working of Mormonism by listening to them than from any other source. They talked away to Brigham Young about every conceivable matter, from the fluxing of an ore to the advantages of a Navajo bit, and expected him to remember every child in every cotter's family. And he really seemed to do so, and to be at home, and be rightfully deemed infallible on every subject. I think he must make fewer mistakes than most popes, from his being in such constant intercourse with his people. I noticed that he never seemed uninterested, but gave an unforced attention to the person addressing him, which suggested a mind free from care. I used to fancy that he wasted a great deal of power in this way; but I soon saw that he was accumulating it. Power, I mean, at least as the driving wheel of his people's industry.[20]

This sense of growing power in his calling, derived from the combination of his steady and intimate service to his people and their sustaining acceptance and response, was recognized in a sermon ten years before by Brigham Young himself:

> I am better now than I was 20 years ago, . . . my spirit is more vigorous and more powerful. . . . more quick to comprehend, more ready to discern, the understanding is more matured, more correct in judgment, the memory more vivid and enduring, and discretion more circumspect.[21]

He is not bragging, but rather illustrating a principle of religious living. In an intriguing reversal of Wordsworth's notion that the child is "father of the man" because it comes "trailing clouds of glory," innocence, and natural wisdom from the premortal existence, President Young teaches in this sermon that the righteous aging man takes on spiritual intelligence from the postmortal paradise he is approaching:

> If we live in our holy religion and let the spirit reign, it will not become dull and stupid, but as the body approaches dissolution the spirit takes a firmer hold on that enduring substance behind the veil, drawing from the depths of that eternal fountain of light, sparkling gems of intelligence, which surround the frail and sinking tabernacle with the halo of immortal wisdom.

At about the same time we have independent justification for Brigham's self-confidence (in a private letter by George A. Smith to a fellow apostle in England):

> President Young enjoys excellent health; cares multiply around him. He personally superintends everything of a public nature as far as possible. To conduct his private affairs would seem work enough for any man. He attends the bishops' meetings, visits the Endowment House, on almost every occasion, being as near as a man can be "everywhere present"; preserving in his communications with the brethren the same simplicity of intercourse and implicit dependence upon the providence of God, as when he used to travel and preach without purse or scrip.[22]

Or, if a critical outsider might be believed more than a close colleague, this is how the noted explorer Richard Burton viewed him at about the same time (1860):

> . . . fifty-nine years of age: he looks about forty-five. . . . Scarcely a grey thread appears in his hair, which is parted on the side, light coloured, rather thick, and reaches below the ears with a half curl. . . . The forehead is somewhat narrow, the eyebrows are thin, the eyes between grey and blue, with a calm, composed and somewhat reserved expression. . . .
>
> The Prophet's dress was neat and plain as a Quaker's, all gray home spun, except the cravat and waistcoat. . . .
>
> . . . His manner is at once affable and impressive, simple and courteous. . . . He shows no signs of dogmatism, bigotry, or fanaticism, and never once entered—with me at least—upon the subject of religion. He impresses a stranger with a certain sense of power. . . . He is neither morose nor methodistic, and where occasion requires he can use all the weapons of ridicule to direful effect, and "speak a bit of his mind" in a style which no one forgets. . . . His powers of observation are intuitively strong, and his friends declare him to be gifted with an excellent memory and a perfect judgment of character. If he dislikes a stranger at the first interview, he never sees him again. . . . His life is ascetic: his favourite food is baked potatoes and a little buttermilk, and his drink water.[23]

President Young may have refrained from buttonholing Burton in person on the subject of religion, but he did not hold back in the sermons he preached in the Bowery with Burton present:

> Let everyone get a knowledge for himself that this work is true. We do not want you to say that it is true, until you know it is; and if you know it, that knowledge is as good to you as though the Lord

came down and told you. Then let every person say: "I will live my religion, though every other person goes to hell! I will walk humbly before my God and deal honestly with my fellow beings." . . .

Out of this Church will grow the kingdom which Daniel saw. This is the very people that Daniel saw would continue to grow and spread and prosper; and if we are not faithful, others will take our places, for this is the Church and people that will possess the kingdom forever and forever.[24]

This leaves us however with perhaps too somber and narrow a view of Brother Brigham near the height of his power physically and when he was increasing in wisdom and effectiveness spiritually. On September 1, 1860, the night before the sermons Burton heard, the clerk keeping the Secretary's Journal records: "In the evening the President's children had a dance at the 'Social Hall school room.' The President was with them a short time and seemed to enjoy himself very much participating in one or two cotillions." The night after the sermon he "had some General conversation . . . subject, the gathering of the Jews to Jerusalem" and later "alluded to a joke between him and Dr. Willard Richards. The Pres. once said . . . 'If you will make a gentleman of me I will make a rich man of you.'" And a few days later, "In the evening several of the brethren met in the office and sung songs and Hyms to the President. . . . Some of the clerks of the office also played on instruments of music."[25]

It was not, of course, in the systematic development of doctrine — or the announcement of revelations of seminal ideas or of whole new bodies of concepts, in the manner of Joseph — that Brigham exercised his stewardship as President. It was rather in the steady application of gospel fundamentals concerning the nature and destiny of men and women as the children of a personal God, called to act for God in building an earthly kingdom as a preparatory school for heavenly kingdoms. It was in his unique combination of sturdy but witty good sense with exalted and exalting visions of the possibilities of common people in their common life. In June 1860, for instance, President Young took one of his extended journeys through the settlements of northern Utah, with a caravan of thirty carriages. He told the Saints in Brigham City:

The people here are rich. . . . The Lord had increased our flocks and herds until some are sorry that they have so many for the Indians and thieves to drive away. . . . Throughout the Territory you see a people more industrious than any other people in the world. . . .

Those who live their religion will enjoy the Spirit, and that enjoyment will increase; and if we will be faithful, the Lord will make our feet as firm in these valleys as are the everlasting riches in these mountains, and no power can remove us. He will give us a sure place in these mountains until we go forth to redeem Zion.[26]

Moving up over the mountain to Wellsville in Cache Valley, where he was welcomed with a great feast, he reminded the new settlers that though they came poor that spring they were already better off than they ever were in Europe:

This is a splendid valley, and is better adapted to raising Saints than any other article that can be raised here. . . . It is the best country in the world for raising Saints. . . .

. . . pray and exercise faith that the Lord will make our feet fast here — that they shall never be removed until we have the privilege of going to build up the center stake of Zion.[27]

Across the valley in Logan the next day he advised the brethren to build sawmills and make lumber so they would not use up the scarce timber so fast with log houses:

Keep the valley pure; keep your towns as pure as you possibly can; keep your hearts pure; and labor what you can consistently, but not so as to injure yourselves. Be faithful in your religion. Be full of love and kindness towards each other.[28]

Back in Ogden, on the way home, he spoke in the handsome tabernacle built where a swamp had been just a few years before:

Cultivate the earth and cultivate your minds. Build cities, adorn your habitations, make gardens, orchards and vineyards, and render the earth so pleasant that when you look upon your labors you may do so with pleasure, and that angels may delight to come and visit your beautiful locations. In the meantime seek to adorn your minds with all the graces of the Spirit of Christ.[29]

That his people would adorn their minds and spirits while they were adorning their valleys was a central preoccupation of President Young:

Not only does the religion of Jesus Christ make the people acquainted with the things of God, and develop within them moral excellence and purity, but it holds out every encouragement and inducement possible, for them to increase in knowledge and intelligence, in every branch of mechanism, or in the arts and sciences, for all wisdom, and all the arts and sciences in the world are from God, and are designated for the good of His people.[30]

As the Lutheran scholar Ernst Benz has pointed out, Brigham Young was freed by that assurance to escape the fear of many Christian pietists that "the warning of Christ [Matthew 12:31] against the blasphemy of the Holy Ghost was a warning against modern science."[31] President Young actually had the expansive vision and courage to reverse that traditional interpretation; he saw such blasphemy as a stop to learning rather than learning as the cause of blasphemy:

> If we continue to learn all that we can, pertaining to the salvation which is purchased and presented to us through the Son of God, is there a time when a person will cease to learn? Yes, when he has sinned against God the Father, Jesus Christ the Son, and the Holy Ghost — God's minister; when he has denied the Lord, defied Him and committed the sin against the Holy Ghost. That is the time when a person will cease to learn, and from that time forth, will descend in ignorance, forgetting that which they formerly knew. . . . They will cease to increase, but must decrease. . . . These are the only characters who will ever cease to learn, both in time and eternity.[32]

Despite his rather more pragmatic turn of mind, President Young, like Joseph Smith, had the courage even to improve on an earlier prophet, especially in order to reinforce his basic message of encouragement:

> Paul says, in his Epistle to the Corinthians, "But the natural man receiveth not the things of God," but I say it is the unnatural "man that receiveth not the things of God." . . . That which was, is, and will continue to endure is more natural than that which will pass away and be no more. The natural man is of God. We are the natural sons and daughters of our natural parents, and spiritually we are the natural children of the Father of light and natural heirs to his kingdom; and when we do an evil, we do it in opposition to the promptings of the Spirit of Truth that is within us. Man, the noblest work of God, was in his creation designed for an endless duration, for which the love of all good was incorporated in his nature. It was never designed that he should naturally do and love evil.[33]

Such optimistic expansiveness extended in all directions. Brigham, again taking his cue from Joseph, constantly encouraged the Saints to seek and accept genuine truth from whatever source — other churches, the sciences and arts, anywhere — because they were all embraced under God's plan of redemption for all:

> How gladly would we understand every principle pertaining to science and art, and become thoroughly acquainted with every intri-

cate operation of nature, and with all the chemical changes that are constantly going on around us! How delightful this would be, and what a boundless field of truth and power is open for us to explore! We are only just approaching the shores of the vast ocean of information that pertains to this physical world, to say nothing of that which pertains to the heavens, to angels and celestial beings, to the place of their habitation, to the manner of their life, and their progress to still higher degrees of perfection.[34]

And that easy blend of desire for worldly knowledge with yearning for spiritual insight leavened all of President Young's perceptions and activities, even something as seemingly temporal as building a telegraph line.

After the completion, with Mormon help, of the transcontinental telegraph in 1861 (the final connection in Salt Lake with President Young sending the first message—one of loyalty to the Union), Brigham planned the development of a north-south line connecting the settlements. Equipment could not be purchased until after the Civil War, but by February 1867 the entire five-hundred-mile line from Logan to St. George was in operation and President Young dedicated it with a telegraphed message:

> Greeting. In my heart I dedicate the line which is now completed . . . to the Lord God of Israel, whom we serve, and for the building up of His Kingdom; praying that this and all other improvements may contribute to our benefit, and the glory of our God; until we can waft ourselves by the power of the Almighty from world to world, to our fullest satisfaction.[35]

Here we see another side of the paradox mentioned earlier. Mormonism was a religion founded in the nineteenth century that affronted contemporary politics and economics, as well as other religions, by looking back to an "ancient order of things" which included visits of angels, God speaking from the heavens, the acceptance of ancient rituals, and a literal prophet who, as the mouthpiece of God, could direct people in temporal as well as spiritual matters. But despite this apparent primitivism in their fundamental principles and rituals, Mormons have not (like the Shakers, for instance) retained a nineteenth century rural life-style but have consistently adopted the latest knowledge and technology, down to the present day when they use the contemporary media for their missionary work and the most advanced computer systems to process genealogical data—which then is used in rituals whose roots go back beyond Solomon's Temple.

Under the enthusiastic direction of Brigham Young, who like Joseph was always an adventuresome innovator almost playfully alive to new knowledge and possibilities but who was also an experienced craftsman, the Utah Mormons were able to use technology, despite gentile hopes and expectations of the opposite, to *slow down* rather than increase secularization and dissolution of the kingdom. This was true not only of the telegraph but even of the potentially overpowering transcontinental railroad, which outsiders hoped—and many observers have since assumed—marked a sudden and drastic change in the uniqueness and cohesiveness of Mormon institutions. President Young perhaps showed his greatest application of his combined temporal and spiritual powers in his response to this threat, which for him was merely another opportunity. Even while he was leading the first group of pioneers west in 1847, he later recalled:

> I remember that, when riding in advance of that company, with my first Counselor, Heber C. Kimball, and others, to search out the route for the wagons to follow we were carefully watching for and frequently conversing about a route for a railroad across the continent.[36]

He had made continual efforts to secure such a railroad, including petitions to Congress in 1849 and 1853. So when the widespread view that the railroad would destroy Mormonism was taken up by the Eastern press ("When the United States goes to Utah, Mormonism will disappear like a puddle with Niagara Falls turned into it"[37]), Brigham paid them no mind: "We want to hear the iron horse puffing through this valley. What for? To bring our brethren and sisters here."[38] To his son in England he wrote:

> Traveling to the states is not what it was before the Rail Road had been pushed so far this way. . . . It will be sure to help us, and be advantageous to the Zion of our God, though the wicked are contemplating terrible things respecting us as soon as they can and finish the Rail Road. . . .
>
> . . . Improvements will progress; Rail Roads and Telegraph Lines and Cables will be built and stretched; but instead of these things acting as a check to the growth of the Kingdom of God, and as an aid to our enemies, they will increase our facilities and accelerate the progress of the work of the Lord.[39]

Brother Brigham knew the dangers of this potentially massive intrusion of Babylon into Zion, but he also knew the advantages, from the easier gathering of Israel and sending out of missionaries to improved travel and communication within the kingdom; and besides, as he expressed it, Mormonism "must, indeed be a poor religion if it cannot stand one railroad."[40]

The most important tools Brigham used in turning the challenge of the railroad into a great opportunity were the reorganization of the Relief Society in 1867, with its indomitable "Presidentess" Eliza R. Snow, and the School of the Prophets (also organized by Brigham in that same year). Sister Snow was a prolific and popular poet among the Saints, and a persuasive champion of women's rights and responsibilities, including suffrage and support of the kingdom. She enjoyed a powerful reputation as the wife of two prophets, Joseph Smith and then Brigham Young, and with Brigham's strong backing and her own formidable talents and energy she developed the basic mission of the Relief Society (to provide help for the poor) into a comprehensive program of improving the lives of women and their families: teaching home industries and congruent tastes in clothing, etc., that would save their husbands' money for building the kingdom; committing women to obey the Word of Wisdom, for both economic and religious reasons; encouraging the storing of wheat and the operation of cooperative general stores, both as outlets for their own craft work and as part of the development of a more cooperative and independent, priesthood-directed economy. The women also participated in a revealing example of President Young's audacious pragmatism in seeking self-sufficiency. Having asked the women to "adorn themselves with the workmanship of their own hands," Brigham responded to their continuing taste for finer things by assigning them to develop a silk industry; in the 1870s nearly all of the 150 local Relief Societies had their own mulberry tree plots and raised the worms, treated the cocoons, and spun and wove the thread.

Most of the direct guidance of the effort to maintain a theocratic commonwealth was centered in the School of the Prophets. Named after Joseph Smith's educational organization for Church leaders in the early 1830s, the new group was really an extension of the Council of Fifty, or General Council, the town-meeting-like association of Church and community leaders who had done the central planning for the kingdom both in Nauvoo and in the first ten years in Utah. Directed by the Church's General Authorities, with a central "school" in Salt Lake City and branches in all the main settlements, this new organization of over five thousand Mormon priesthood leaders involved them in high-level Church instruction and in confidential civil government and economic planning conferences directly responsive to the concerns raised by the approaching railroad. The School of the Prophets reinforced, with sermons of exhortation and actual signed pledges, commitment to such principles as the Word of Wisdom; it planned and carried out specific policies; and it even was the forum for Church response to what became known as the "Godbeite heresy," the effort of some prominent Mormon merchants and intellectuals, led by William Godbe, to accommodate Utah to the national economy (by developing mining and cooperating with Gentiles) and to subvert Mormonism in the direction of Protestantism and spiritualism.

It was the School of the Prophets that actually voted to disfellowship Godbe's group after they had openly challenged President Young's authority, as well as his policies, in their *Utah Magazine* (Brigham himself was remarkably patient and lenient, considering the provocation).[41] The school also took a series of positive actions under Brigham's leadership. To prevent an influx of rowdy railroad workers and camp followers who would in turn invite non-Mormon merchants in to trade with them, they sponsored a contract in the name of Brigham Young to build the Union Pacific line for a distance of nearly a hundred miles, from Echo Canyon to Ogden. They also acted to discourage a rush of undesirable mine workers, by first attempting to deflate reports on mining potential and then by encouraging Mormons to work for the eastern concerns which finally moved in. In order to prevent large intrusions of cheaper gentile goods and consequent unemployment, they acted under close direction of the First Presidency to encourage development of cooperative enterprises and brought strong—and only partially successful—pressure to bear on Mormons to patronize these Mormon cooperatives. Laborers and craftsmen made a significant sacrifice for the kingdom by accepting substantial reductions in wages in order to be competitive (which was the first policy of President Young's that the Godbeites publicly criticized).

Perhaps most significant, in terms of furthering President Young's long-term goal of unity and cooperation, was his use of the School of the Prophets to establish, in order to control imported goods, a wholesale trading establishment—Zion's Cooperative Mercantile Institution—with a main store in Salt Lake City and over a hundred local community branches. A boycott of unfriendly non-Mormon merchants had been started in 1865 by Brigham, who bore a continuing grudge against those who had profited from the Saints but refused to defend them against false reports in the East. In the October 1868 conference, for essentially economic reasons, this boycott was extended to all "outsiders." Within a few weeks ZCMI was formed as an alternative, and great verbal pressure was exerted on Mormons through the School of the Prophets and the Relief Society to buy only through its stores.

With all of these carefully coordinated means President Young and his associates managed, in the words of Leonard Arrington, to introduce "a deliberate program whereby the machinery of civilization, usually designed for breaking up isolation, would make isolation more complete and better organized—or, at the least, make isolation sufficiently complete and well-organized to preserve the integrity of Mormon institutions.[42] Though he knew he was fighting a losing battle, President Young used the Church organization to establish protective economic institutions and policies and to mobilize the faith and sacrificial energy of Mormons in support. By this means, though not achieving all his goals, he prevented or delayed what seemed to many, including Mormons, would be the inevitable results of the railroad's coming: a shift to a mining economy and an influx of mining camp morality; an increase in gentile imports and therefore degenerate fashions and luxurious tastes; an increase in unemployment and decrease in money for immigration because of economic intrusion; and a loss of control over the kingdom's temporal institutions to eastern capitalists.

President Young's efforts avoided, at least for a time, the fate that overtook surrounding states, similar in geography and resources, which became chiefly colonies providing raw materials to the industries of the eastern United States. These efforts, carried on by his successor, John Taylor, "left the Mormons in 1884 nearer the realization of their ancient goals than when the ox-cart was outmoded in 1869."[43] And though substantial accommodation was eventually forced on the Mormons by the full power of federal agencies at the turn of the century, this two-decade delay preserved the Mormons as a "peculiar people" and allowed them to continue their colonizing process into isolated rural communities. This in turn preserved their uniqueness and influences on the formation of Mormon faith and character well into the twentieth century—long enough to provide an enduring structure of ideals and models that continues to energize and direct the Church.

The historian Charles Peterson seems right in his argument that Mormon peculiarity peaked in the Mormon village, which served as a place "where the withdrawal from the world was re-enacted and protected for many decades"—most of the towns being preserved in their essential nature until about 1940. As Peterson points out, President Young, in the last years of his life, fought the rearguard action that made that preservation possible and left a priceless legacy:

> Thus while Salt Lake City met the world and yielded under its impact, the point of creative withdrawal was perpetuated by southern Utah towns in preparation for the momentarily expected time when Christ's second advent would overturn all worldly systems and build on the beachhead so carefully developed and sustained.[44]

The Mormon towns, which Brigham Young and other leaders established and then protected, thus preserved and continued the conscious rejection of mainstream American institutions and values that had been given maximum practical expression in the flight to the desert in 1847. The confrontation with the Great Basin environment encouraged, and the continual expansion outward into towns allowed, perpetuation of the essential program for making Saints—a self-governing community, cooperative irrigated farming, practices of resource utilization based upon stewardship and the public good rather than speculation and competition, and an economy of unified self-sufficiency.

But Peterson, because of the necessary limits of his study of the Mormon village, describes only part of the picture. Those fundamental values, developed in a cooperative, self-sufficient society that was indeed preserved far past its expected time, in the Mormon village, depend mainly on the basic doctrine of "Consecration and Stewardship," which was the key both to Brother Brigham's own life and his sometimes misunderstood economic actions and also to the isolationist policies that he consistently advocated. It is the legacy of that vision that enables the "unprecedented" creative withdrawal from American society, which Peterson rightly recognizes as characteristic of the exodus and the Mormon village, *to continue even today*—when, as he also recognizes, the Mormon village has finally surrendered to "defense industry, federal spending, reclamation projects, expanding tourism, uranium booms and oil strikes."[45] President Young's ideal (still fostered by the Mormon village experience of many of the Church's present ecclesiastical and intellectual and artistic leaders and perhaps even more by the enduring memory of the President's tangible efforts to develop a truly consecrated society) lives on in the hearts and expectations of faithful Mormons, fostered by a number of concrete religious experiences in their congregations, even while they engage quite fully in the American economic institutions that were once seen as a threat. A powerful test of the faith continues to be the serious question the Saints sometimes ask each other, or in their own hearts: "Could you live the United Order?"

This means that just as the purpose and success of Brigham Young's efforts as *colonizer, governor*, and *entrepreneur* can only be understood in terms of his religious goals—for building a place for making Saints, a veritable school for potential gods—so his purposes and success as *President of the Church* can best be seen in efforts to establish a temporal and political order that would provide the proper base in cooperative, unselfish living for such a school. In this he was not original but only being a faithful disciple of Joseph Smith, who had originally received the Law of Consecration and Stewardship by revelation in 1831, less than a year after the Church was organized.

In an excellent study of this subject, *Building the City of God*, the authors state that a deeply felt aspect of Joseph Smith's sense of his commission from Christ as the prophet of the Restoration was to provide, by means of this "Order of Enoch" (as it was called after its ancient pattern), "a structured haven in a society that seemed about to disintegrate from the excesses of individualism and pluralism" and also to form "the model upon which all human society would be organized when the Savior returned to the latter-day Zion in Missouri."[46] The central values of this ideal—order, unity, and community—were at odds with those forces of antebellum America that were already threatening small town and rural life. Thus the very success of initial efforts to practice the "Law" provoked persecution that drove the Mormons out of Missouri and Illinois. But the Mormons tended to put the blame for such failures on themselves—as not having reached the degree of moral development necessary; in this reform movement, in sharp distinction from most other communitarian movements then and since, the Mormons tended to be very pragmatic and experimental, to see a reformed society as the *expression* not the *cause* of reform in character, to see their faith, not the institutions imposed upon them, as the most powerful instrument of change.

Thus, the covenant of consecration that the Saints entered into to help each other escape Nauvoo led naturally to the Perpetual Emigrating Fund—which failed as a business but succeeded in its basic purpose of redeeming the poor of Nauvoo and immigrating thousands who otherwise would have been unable to come from Europe. Cooperation became a habit essential to survival in the desert crossing and the early desperate years. But in 1855 and 1856, partly in connection with the new zeal sparked by the "Reformation" and partly through failure of needed Church resources for immigration, etc., because of dwindling tithing payments, especially when crops began to fail, President Young called for a literal "consecration" to the Church of all property of the members; the local bishop would in turn give back to them, as stewards, an "inheritance" of farms, tools, shops, etc., according to their needs and abilities, and they would manage these and periodically give to the bishop any surplus — to be used for the common good.

To the accompaniment of much religious enthusiasm, which merged into the Reformation, about 40 percent of the seven thousand families, of much and little means, signed over all they had to the Church on standard printed forms — including President Young's own property valued at $199,625. But the process never culminated in Church control and assigned inheritances: non-Mormons and apostates saw this as one more evidence of Brigham's theocratic despotism; Congress further delayed passing laws to give legal land ownership in Utah; the press took up the attack; and a visiting U.S. Land Office commissioner called the consecration movement "incompatible with our system" and asked Congress to investigate. These developments, and most directly the advance of Johnston's federal troops in 1857, caused President Young to drop the plan and resort again to the "lower" law of tithing.[47]

In a speech to the Saints at Parowan in 1855, Brigham gives us insight into his basic motivations in attempting to revive literal consecration in order to be true to God's plan for the economic order as revealed to Joseph:

> If the people had done their duty and consecrated all their property to the Church of Jesus Christ of Latter-day Saints, they could not have gone away and lost their souls. . . . I want to have you consecrate your property if you wish it, if not, do as you please with it. If any man will say, "I am going to apostatize," I will advise him to consecrate all he has that he might be kept with the Saints and saved, so that if you are tempted to go away, you may feel it best to stay where your treasure is.[48]

It is interesting that Elder Orson Pratt, who certainly did not always see eye to eye with Brother Brigham, was the most articulate and energetic advocate of President Young's effort to fully re-establish the Law of Consecration and Stewardship. In a sermon printed in July 1854, Elder Pratt quoted from Christ's words to Joseph Smith: "Be one; and if ye are not one, ye are not mine." He then showed from that original context that temporal equality and unity as well as spiritual unity were enjoined upon true Saints, just as they had been the distinguishing quality of early Christians both in Jerusalem and in ancient America.[49] Later that year, even before the standard consecration form was ready, Elder Pratt made his commitment specific: "I long for the time to come when I can consecrate everything I have got; all the cattle I have; . . . also my books, and the right and title I have to publish my works, also my wearing apparel, and my houses."

Somewhat less than half of the Saints made the consecration, thus perhaps vindicating Elder Pratt's judgment that the Saints were still devoted to "the Gentile god of property" and were still in a position of having to live up to "preparatory laws" such as tithing "because of the hardness of our hearts, and the blindness of our minds, and our covetousness."[50] But another way to see the results of President Young's efforts in the mid-1850s is as a remarkable evidence that nearly half the Saints were willing, in the New Testament pattern, literally to come forward and lay all they possessed at the apostles' feet.

The years from 1857 to 1865 were a time of constant threat and trial, mainly from misunderstandings with Washington that twice resulted in federal troops "occupying" the territory. As the Utah Expedition approached in 1857, President Young asked, "Do you not see that we are coming to where the Lord will *make* us consecrate?"[51] Indeed, during the time of stress, including the temporary mass abandonment of their homes in the "Big Move," the Saints practiced of necessity a number of forms of cooperative consecration to meet each other's needs and those of the kingdom (for instance, there was emergency aid to the handcart companies and dedication of time and means for the ox-team missions to bring immigrants in the 1860s). But by the late 1860s Brigham found himself pressed by a number of circumstances to try to protect the kingdom and its goals by invoking explicit forms of sacrificial cooperation — even, despite his basic dislike of merchandising, creating the huge mercantile trading system, ZCMI.

The Church-directed ZCMI did not achieve as wide a distribution of shares as the leaders desired — or as would be necessary for a truly "cooperative" institution (four people held 1,772 of 1,990 original shares). But the organizers, men of the priesthood in the School of the Prophets who worked hard to broaden the owner- ship, refused to take advantage either of scarcity demands or wind- fall profits and thus retained the aims and effect, if not the strict form, of a cooperative. For the private Mormon merchants, who had for a time benefited from a boycott against non-Mormons to make huge profits but were now being themselves squeezed out by the Mormon cooperative, Brother Brigham had no sympathy. In the first place he thought it suspicious for a man to be engaged in such "non-productive" occupations, and he resented the profits merchants had already taken "from an innocent, confiding, poor, industrious people. . . . If they do not repent, they will go to hell." He had been well taught by Joseph to oppose gradations of wealth and status, especially the formation of a wealthy privileged class, as inimical to everything the gospel and the kingdom stood for:

> Take any community, three-eighths of whom are living on the labor of the remaining five-eighths and you will find the few are living on the many. . . . If the members of this community wish to get rich and to enjoy the fruits of the earth they must be producers as well as consumers. . . .
>
> . . . Our Female Relief Societies are doing immense good now, but they can take hold and do all the trading for these wards just as well as to keep a big loafer to do it. It is always disgusting to me to see a big, fat, lubberly fellow handing out calicoes and measuring ribbon. . . .
>
> The capitalists may say "What are we to do with our means?" Go and build factories and have one, two or three thousand spindles going. . . . Some of you go to raising flax and build a factory to manufacture it, and do not take every advantage and pocket every dollar that is to be made. You are rich and I want to turn the stream so as to do good to the whole community.[52]

Using his well-developed ingenuity for combining the personal and Church resources of the kingdom, President Young stepped in with various means, including at one point assuming charge himself, to keep ZCMI solvent during some crises in the early 1870s — such as delays of merchandise by snow and the National Panic of 1873 — and the institution has evolved to become a leading commercial enterprise of Utah in the twentieth century. At the same time many other such cooperative ventures (mills, livestock, etc.) were also developed in Mormon villages under the impetus of President Young's efforts and expressed ideals.

President Young had emphasized that the cooperative movement was a step toward realizing the revealed ideal of Joseph the Prophet that had been thwarted in Missouri. The various successes, especially the development by Elder Lorenzo Snow at Brigham City of a truly self-sufficient set of cooperatives forming a community order, led naturally toward the efforts to establish completely integrated communal systems in 1874. In fact, it may well have been the remarkable success of the Brigham City Mormons (who with their independent cooperative system survived the Panic of 1873 essentially untouched, while Mormon communities tied to the national economy suffered) that moved Brigham to contemplate deploying such a system in various forms throughout the kingdom. President Young had counseled Lorenzo Snow, as the two rode north to visit Brigham City in 1864, that for the "moral, spiritual, and financial interest of the Saints" they follow "all the elements and principles of [what he later called] the United Order." Elder Snow, who was one day himself to become President of the Church in one of its darkest hours and was able to save it financially with an inspired and inspiring call to greater consecration through tithing, recalled that early conversation in a letter to President Young in 1875. He claimed that his success (which had become a matter of international reputation) had come from following the President's program outlined back in 1864:

> I stripped myself and put on the harness for the conflict, so I could say to this people, Come and follow in my footsteps. They have felt the influence of this until prejudice and opposition have been gradually giving way, and moving along, step by step, we have succeeded in arriving at a position of some prominence in spiritual and financial union.
>
> I do not for a moment consider that we are worthy to be called a people of the United Order, but we are slowly progressing toward that position.[53]

The effort, which began with a simple joint-stock enterprise to which Elder Snow and others subscribed, had developed a number of home industry ventures and a cooperative store that were so successful in building the cooperative spirit that Brother Brigham later said, "Brother Snow has led the people along, and got them into the United Order without their knowing it."[54] This success may even have directly encouraged President Young to initiate ZCMI in 1868, in the hope of developing a Great Basin economy based on a number of such nearly self-sufficient cooperative communities. After some laboring on Elder Snow's part to teach them "a knowledge of their duty and obligations as elders of Israel and servants of God," the participants had agreed to take dividends not in cash or imported merchandise but in kind, so that accumulation could be made to establish the home industries. By 1873 the community was approaching genuine self-sufficiency. That winter the President, on his trip south to St. George, began preaching that the Saints should follow the Brigham City example and develop from the retail cooperatives already established toward a more complete obedience to the Law of Consecration. Then in the spring, beginning with St. George, he began to establish "United Orders" in the communities responsive to his message.

The seventy-three-year-old President took upon himself an unprecedented task in attempting at one stroke to bring eighty thousand people into a communal order, but the initial responses in the southern communities were extremely promising. After a series of meetings of explanation and encouragement in February 1874, President Young called for formal organization of the St. George Order: "Now is the accepted time and blessed are the Latter-day Saints, but if we are not disposed to enter into this Order, the curses of God will come upon the people. I cannot help it. I will not curse them, but the time has come for this work to be commenced."[55] Three hundred enthusiastically came forward to sign the United Order roll, thus registering commitment to specific rules of religious living as well as consecration of properties and labor. They then presented themselves for rebaptism in a solemn covenant of renewal and obligation. This procedure was followed in many other communities as Brother Brigham traveled north to Salt Lake, and it was carried out by other apostles in other settlements. President Young postponed April conference a month so he could proceed with these organizations and then promote the new cause to the metropolitan Saints in the conference, and by fall organization throughout most of the Great Basin was completed.

There were four basic types of "Orders," each with different problems and degrees of success: Most followed the St. George model, where members contributed property to the Order and received different wages and dividends depending on their contributions in labor and capital; hostility between those in the community who were in and those who were not, plus indolence that in turn produced jealousy and selfishness concerning fair distribution of benefits, broke most of these down before very long. In the north the Orders were mainly mere variations on cooperatives, which required no deep religious commitment. President Young headed one such order in Salt Lake City that seems to have been designed mainly to provide a large pool of capital for industrial development. Each ward was responsible for an enterprise, much in the manner of modern LDS "welfare projects," which are cooperatively maintained by each stake or ward for assisting the needy. United Orders modeled on the Brigham City Order, which itself made no change, merely increased community ownership of manufacturing and agricultural enterprises while maintaining individual property ownership. These were the most successful economically but they did not challenge the members to reach the complete purposes of consecration, and they were disbanded in the 1880s under the attack of federal officials in the polygamy persecutions (Elder Snow himself was sentenced to the penitentiary) without ever having achieved the power to evoke the lingering sense of loss and hope we feel for a utopia.

One type did evoke such feelings and memories—the kind established in 1875 at Orderville, Utah, by a group of impoverished refugees from a failed colony on the Muddy River in Nevada. The success of this Order, the one that endured longest and has been fastened in Mormon memory as the symbolic representative of all the others, seems to have been at least partly based on the unity fostered by the members' previous deprivation and their desire somehow to succeed this time. The undivided nature of their totally new community and the opportunity to enter the Order without the problems of transition that plagued other established settlements also helped—as did the effort to prove themselves to doubters living just a few miles away. But perhaps most of all they succeeded because they came closest to living the ideal community envisioned in Joseph Smith's original revelations, a success described by the historians James Allen and Glen Leonard:

> By cooperative labor they built all the apartment units, shops, bakeries, barns, and other buildings needed for a well-regulated community. Each family had its own apartment, but at first everyone ate together in a large dining room with the women taking turns at kitchen duty. They operated farms, orchards, dairies, livestock projects, and various manufacturing enterprises. They produced an excess of furniture and sold it to surrounding communities in exchange for funds for expansion. They wore the same kind of clothes, all manufactured at Orderville, and no member of the community could improve his situation unless all were likewise improved.[56]

Despite its advantages, Orderville, like all the others, eventually "failed"—that is, moved to a less cooperative economic order. Its particular problems centered on lack of a needed minimal amount of initial capital. This helped cause a persistent poverty and created consequences such as drab clothing that reduced morale, especially among the young, who compared their situation to the improving conditions for their friends in nearby towns. This was compounded by too much liberality in accepting new members without any capital contribution (against Brother Brigham's advice) and, on the other hand, excessive charity in allowances to those leaving the order.

Other communities that tried to reach for this most perfect form of order also had a variety of related problems. In the established community of Kanab the most dedicated adherents to the original "ideal" covenant were intolerant of others, especially leaders who tried to adapt the plan, as President Young had given them leave to do. That is, paradoxically, some orders broke down when, in an attempt to meet the complaints of those who saw inequities (or thought they saw indolence), they reverted back toward legalistic forms of equal pay for equal work; thus, the essential spirit of unselfish sharing was lost, mercy destroyed by justice. In Richfield, Brigham Young's son Joseph A. was the first to sign over all his property, even though "it was a trial to me"; he advised his cosigners, "The feeling of 'Mine' is the greatest feeling we have to combat." When he died only a year later, the Order was breaking up and his heirs were fighting to get back the property he had given so selflessly in 1874.

Despite these problems, as Arrington has noted, it took the marshaled power of the U.S. government to finally end the Orders: "It is a testimony to the effectiveness of the cooperative and United Order movements that Mormon cooperative ventures and collective institutions had to be destroyed, as most of them were during the [federal] 'Raid' of the 1880s, before the 'peculiar' theocratic economy of Zion could be accommodated and absorbed into the general economy of the nation." Indeed, though it is common to speak of the United Orders as "failures," they succeeded admirably in contributing to President Young's fundamental goal, not of establishing set institutions but of tempering "the growing spirit of acquisitiveness and individualism with a more saintly selflessness and devotion to the building of the Kingdom" and of keeping Utah "economically independent of the East longer and more completely than would otherwise have been the case."[57]

All the Orders bore the stamp of Brigham Young's vision—both in their difficulties and in their successes. At this time the growing inequities and social trauma, created by the very success of capitalistic industrialization in Europe and America, were moving reformers to promote various schemes of state ownership and government-forced cooperation and equality. On the contrary, President Young sought to inspire the Mormons to build *voluntary* cooperative and sharing communities, units—whether towns or wards in a city—that could exist within a larger society yet be self-sufficient and thus be unaffected in times of emergency like the 1873 Panic. Joseph Smith's revelation enjoining such voluntary sharing was the basic guide:

> For it is expedient that I, the Lord, should make every man account-able, as a steward over earthly blessings, which I have made and prepared for my creatures.
>
> And it is my purpose to provide for my saints, for all things are mine.
>
> But it must needs be done in mine own way; and behold this is the way that I, the Lord, have decreed to provide for my saints, that the poor shall be exalted, in that the rich are made low.
>
> For the earth is full, and there is enough and to spare; yea, I pre-pared all things, and have given unto the children of men to be agents unto themselves.
>
> Therefore, if any man shall take of the abundance which I have made, and impart not his portion, according to the law of my gospel, unto the poor and the needy, he shall, with the wicked, lift up his eyes in hell, being in torment.[58]

This fundamental principle of total consecration *freely entered into* motivated President Young's forceful teaching and yet led him to allow a variety and flexibility in the Orders that, as Mormons exercised their freedom unwisely, was the undoing of many. As Arrington has pointed out:

> "It was not a part of this Order," concluded Brigham Young [in 1877], "to take away the property of one man and give it to another, neither to equally divide what we possessed." Its primary purpose, he said, was "to afford to all the opportunity of enriching themselves through their diligence" and to devote the surplus property thus made available to the task of "carrying on the work of God gener-ally."[59]

Brother Brigham recognized that even though the cooperatives were a step toward complete consecration, they were part of an economy still functioning in largely individualistic terms, with measured returns for labor and investment, so he did not require immediately that all possessions be consecrated to the Order. Instead he emphasized during the transition that labor was the main source of wealth (". . . our time and the power to choose in the disposition of the same. This is the real capital that is bequeathed unto us by our Heavenly Father"[60]). If members were fully dedicated, whatever the material resources committed, consecrated labor would bring such benefits to the system that material consecration would follow.

But President Young's hopes in this regard proved overly optimistic. Most United Orders failed before the thorny task of transition was properly completed. Some of the Saints felt, though many Orders held on until bludgeoned with federal intervention, that the Orders lost their motivating spirit with the death of Brother Brigham in 1877. Much later, his son John R. wrote:

> President Young was the pilot, the guiding star. When he died the master mind was gone.
>
> The visible leader, who said, "Unless you are one in temporal things, how can you be one in spiritual things?" and "The way the world does business is a sin, the strong build themselves up by putting the weak ones down." That was the voice of the Good Shepherd to that people, and when that voice was hushed in death, the light was gone — and the community dissolved. It needs the Leadership of the Priesthood to establish the United Order.[61]

But this supreme achievement of President Young's vision lived on, sometimes in memory: "We were happy in the Order. A spirit of true brotherhood prevailed," one said; another, "I never was so much attached to a people, I never experienced greater joy nor had better times. . . . The United Order is a grand institution."[62] And in 1950 two Harvard sociologists interviewed representatives of five very different cultures living close to each other in New Mexico, asking about their ideals for human community. A Mormon farmer responded:

> I've often commented to myself that I'd like a newly man-made community. I think we ought to have a big reservoir the first thing to take care of the water supply. I believe I would put it under the United Order. . . . There would be just one people, all of one belief, where they treat everybody equal, no injustice to any of them, each looking out for the other's welfare. I think that used to be done in years back.[63]

It is not just an ideal that remains. When floods from the collapse of a dam wiped out whole towns in Idaho's Teton Valley in June of 1976, the predominantly Mormon people organized themselves under standing Church procedures and rallied to each other's aid—the Church immediately dispatching truckloads of supplies for the victims, whether Mormon or not, busloads of Latter-day Saints coming from hundreds of miles away to help as well—in a way that amazed federal officials. In the cooperative and efficient process of their recovery these Mormons proved to be among the best practical communitarians that America has produced.

Indeed, there is enduring in every faithful Mormon heart a vision given tangible form by Brother Brigham's "work of a lifetime." Their spirits respond to the ancient story of Enoch, who built a city based on the Law of Consecration and Stewardship that became so perfected in unselfish love that its people were taken bodily into the heavens. Mormons look forward with complete faith in the Lord's promise that when he so directs through a modern prophet they shall return to the ancient site of Eden, in Missouri, and build just such a city as Enoch built, one to which in fact Enoch will return from heaven with his people. And, then, because we too have learned how to achieve the joy of the perfect social order, we will fall on each other's necks with embraces of recognition.[64] The authors of *Building the City of God* trace the continuing shape of that city—especially the enduring image created by President Young—in the Mormon mind. They conclude:

> The ordered hierarchical structure of the Mormon lay priesthood organization could turn itself quickly to the task of building upon the economic superstructure of the Welfare Plan and undertaking direction of economic as well as religious and political affairs among the Saints. The force of such a people, willingly responsive to church authority and fired by the assurance that they were being granted the inestimable privilege of bringing Joseph Smith's plan to fruition in preparation for ultimate cosmic events, could be staggering. It would be a curious twist of history if Mormon communitarianism and cooperation in the past had indeed prepared a people capable of preserving an enclave of order in the face of spreading chaos. Holding union and order "as a precious jewel," the Latter-day Saints, no doubt, would stride boldly forth to put the finishing touches on their city of God.[65]

Despite his son's reflection that the impelling spirit of the United Orders was lost when President Young died, a number of the Orders survived until the antipolygamy raids of the 1880s robbed them of their local leaders. It seems now a special blessing that Brother Brigham did not live to see those cruel days. It almost seems, in retrospect, that—in a way that comes rarely to mortal men, even the best—his final years were providentially structured to allow him to be protected from extremities of disappointment and danger and to enable him to complete essential tasks that form a perfect capstone to his long stewardship. He lived long enough to see beloved colleagues and lifelong friends—even a mature son— die before him, and to express his special appreciation for them and his secure faith in their continued life and future association with him. When his oldest and closest friend, Heber C. Kimball, died after an accident in June of 1868 he told the Saints:

> He was a man of as much integrity I presume as any man who ever lived on the earth. . . . a man of truth, a man of benevolence. . . . I have not felt one particle of death in his house nor about it, and through this scene we are now passing I have not felt one particle of the spirit of death. . . . the same Heber C. Kimball . . . will be resurrected, and he, in the flesh, will see God and converse with Him; and see his brethren and associate with them and they will enjoy a happy eternity together. . . .
>
> . . . What can we say to one another? Live as he lived; . . . If we do so, our end will be peace and joy.[66]

In 1875, Brigham lost his eldest son, Joseph A., who had become ill on his way to take charge of the building of the Manti Temple, and then his first counselor, George A. Smith, the cousin of Joseph Smith who had been Brigham's much younger companion on the way to England. Brigham had come to depend on George A. more than anyone after Heber's death; at the funeral he mourned: "He gave his heart, his mind, his energy, his life, in fact his all, to the furtherance of the great purposes of our God. In youth and in manhood, in sunshine or in storm, in peace or in persecution, he was true to his religion, his brethren and his God."[67]

Late in the sixties, with the aid of George A., President Young had begun to focus on specifics of Church organization that gave the Church much of its essential modern form. Besides the development of various auxiliaries such as the Relief Society and youth organizations already mentioned, he began to restructure the stake and ward organizations and functions in order that they might better serve ecclesiastical and spiritual purposes. Previously, wards had functioned as economic and somewhat political units; religious meetings and activities took place on the community-wide basis, even in large and growing cities like Salt Lake where the central tabernacles were used for preaching meetings on Sunday. In 1868-69 President Young organized five new stakes to make a total of nine; in the 1870s he expanded the number of stakes to thirteen, and in the last year of his life he reorganized many — especially in order to release apostles from local responsibility as stake presidents so that they could be freed for more Churchwide preaching and for centralizing counseling together. In the fall of 1872 President Young reported in a letter to Albert Carrington in England the beginning of the Church's modern sacrament meeting:

> For several weeks past the Tabernacle has been closed on Sundays, and meetings for Sacrament and instruction are held in the various wards. We expect one result of this arrangement will be a better attendance at meetings during the winter, as the ward meeting houses are generally commodious, and within easy distances. At present these meetings are well attended and are becoming very interesting.[68]

In 1873 Brigham resigned his position as trustee-in-trust for the Church to George A. Smith (with twelve men as assistant trustees) and turned his attention even more away from economic to ecclesiastical concerns, adding five counselors to assist him. Planning and directly motivating the formation of the United Orders occupied President Young in 1874 and 1875, but he also during that time worked out a unanimous agreement on seniority in the Twelve Apostles, based on longest *continuous* service, by which John Taylor and Wilford Woodruff (who both thus became future presidents of the Church) were placed ahead of Orson Pratt and Orson Hyde (who had both been excommunicated for a short time at Nauvoo and then reinstated in the Quorum).

The last year of Brother Brigham's life was a veritable crescendo of administrative reform. As he reorganized stakes he set up the practice of quarterly stake conferences and monthly priesthood meetings. Elders quorums were organized with ninety-six members each and directed to participate in forming United Orders and in welfare services. Ward organization was strengthened by the requirement for the first time that all bishops be formally called and ordained high priests — and that they serve with two counselors who were also high priests. The bishop's position as presiding authority in the wards was clarified and his responsibility as head of the priests quorum in the Aaronic Priesthood confirmed. President Young saw the Aaronic Priesthood as a good training ground for young men, and many more were called at an earlier age than previously? Aaronic priesthood quorums were identified clearly as ward rather than stake units, and in general the role of the ward as the primary unit of ecclesiastical organization was for the first time clearly established.

At the October 1877 General Conference, just a month after Brigham Young's death, George Q. Cannon declared:

> I do not believe myself that President Young could have felt as happy, as I know he does feel, had he left the Church in the condition it was in when he commenced his labors last spring. I am convinced that it has added greatly to his satisfaction; it has been a fitting consummation to the labors of his long life that he should be spared to organize the Church throughout these valleys in the manner in which it now is organized.[69]

But perhaps the most fitting consummation (and the most satisfying to Brigham) was his temple building in the last years of his life, climaxed with the dedication of the St. George Temple — the first since Nauvoo was left to his enemies thirty years before — and the beginning of others at Manti and Logan. One of his first acts on entering the valley was to mark the place for the great Salt Lake Temple. Though he pushed construction of that remarkable building constantly throughout his life, the ambitiousness of the project was such that it was not completed until twenty years after his death. The original vision, however, of the six main spires, echoing the granite peaks to the east from where Brigham had first looked down on a promised land, remained constantly before him as the temple was built, just to the west of his home, from huge blocks of that mountain granite. After meditating on the temple's destiny to stand through the Millennium, and having heard complaints of imperfect workmanship, he had the original foundations of sandstone ripped out and replaced with granite. He later had those foundations and the stone for the walls buried under the semblance of a plowed field to avoid possible desecrations at the hands of Johnston's occupying army. And the walls continued upward and reached the beginning of the spires as he died.

Sacred endowments and sealings were performed in the Endowment House, but President Young continued always to be anxious. He said in 1863 to the Saints, "There is not a house on the face of the whole earth that has been reared to God's name and which will in anywise compare with his character, and that he can consistently call his house."[70] But he went on to prophesy what would have seemed utterly absurd to a non-Mormon visitor to that struggling oasis in 1863 — that "there will be hundreds of [temples] built and dedicated to the Lord." In 1871, as part of his program to encourage cooperative labor, especially in the hard-pressed Dixie Mission, he broke ground for the St. George Temple.

Much less ambitious than the Salt Lake Temple, the one in "Dixie" was pushed through to completion in six years and dedicated at President Young's last general conference (April 1877), which was held in St. George for the occasion. This first temple in the West, and the first the Church was not driven away from, came to symbolize two great successes for Brother Brigham: It demonstrated that the kingdom had a safe location, at least for a long time; and it enabled him, by reinstituting for the first time since Nauvoo endowments and marriage in behalf of the dead, to provide tangible completion to Joseph Smith's revealed vision of the unity of mankind, especially of family ties, across the gulf of death. President Young's anxiety to make available these sacred ordinances in order to extend redemptive love to those who had not been privileged to receive the gospel in this life, and to unite them in eternal families, led him to dedicate part of the temple as soon as the roof was on so that this work could proceed.

The temple was a great evidence of self-sufficient home industry, built by local craftsmen and furnished with local materials, including stone quarried nearby and timber hauled sixty-five miles from Mount Trumbull and even the rag and wool carpets and silk decorations, and Brother Brigham loved to personally supervise this work as it progressed through the last years of his life. In the winter of 1874-75, though not in good health, he rode to the temple each day to encourage, instruct, and aid the workers, moving George A. Smith to write in a letter, "President Young is our only architect."[71] The next year, 1876, the President postponed his trip south until after April conference, in which he strongly encouraged faster work on the Salt Lake Temple, calling for more workers from the wards — and also asked for (and got) two hundred volunteers to travel south and push the St. George Temple to completion. When he arrived in St. George he found the temple whitewashed and standing in dramatic contrast to the striking reds and browns and purples of the southern Utah landscape; though approaching his seventy-fifth birthday, he climbed up on the walls and tower to inspect and enjoy the view. He returned again in December, and by January 1, 1877, the lower story was completed, and twelve hundred Saints gathered for dedicatory prayers by

Erastus Snow, Wilford Woodruff, and Brigham Young, Jr. President Young, apparently not feeling strong, spoke "a few encouraging things":

> Now we have a Temple which will be finished in a few days, and of which there is enough completed to commence work therein, which has not been done since the days of Adam, that we have any knowledge of. Now those that can see the Spiritual Atmosphere, can see that many of the Saints are still glued to this earth, and lusting and longing after the things of this world, in which there is no profit. It is true we should look after the things of this world and devote all to the building up of the Kingdom of God . . . [but] suppose we were awake to this thing, namely the salvation of the human family, this house would be crowded . . . from Monday Morning until Saturday Night. This house was built here in this place purposely, where it is warm and pleasant in the winter time, and comfortable to work, and also for the Lamanites [American Indians] and all those coming from the South and other places to receive their Endowments and other blessings . . . All of the angels of heaven are looking at this little handful of people, and stimulating them to the salvation of the human family. . . . When I think upon this subject I want the tongues of Seven Thunders to wake up the people.[72]

Erastus Snow asked in a prayer:

> Bless especially thy servant Brigham Young, whom Thou hast given us for a leader and President over all thy people, by whose hand Thou didst lead them into this land, and plant their feet in the tops of the mountains, inspired him to build this house unto Thee. . . . Comfort him in his old age, heal up his body, relieve him of aches and pains, fill him with the revelation of thy Spirit to speak thy word unto thy people, and that he may be able to order all things in this Thine House, and among thy people as thou wilt.[73]

Elder Snow's prayer was well answered, as President Young *was* strong enough to put in order the Lord's house and to participate in the ordinance work for the dead as it began within a few days. He remained in St. George until after the special April conference, directing the Church from a small office and enjoying continued participation in the temple ordinances. Again he did not give a dedicatory prayer when the temple was finally completed in April, but he spoke briefly in the conference:

> We have no business here other than to build up and establish the Zion of our God. . . .
>
> . . . We will continue to grow, to increase and spread abroad. . . . the Lord Almighty has said [to our enemies], Thus far thou shalt go

and no farther, and hence we are spared to carry on his work. . . . The hearts of all living are in his hands and he turns them as the rivers of water are turned. . . .

As to my health I feel many times that I could not live an hour longer, but I mean to live just as long as I can. I know not how soon the messenger will call for me, but I calculate to die in harness.[74]

As we have seen, he also received another strength Elder Snow prayed for—to "order all things . . . among thy people"—as he participated in a whirlwind of activities that summer, dying "in harness" right after returning from reorganization of the stake in Brigham City.

Brother Brigham had indeed been the St. George Temple's "architect" in terms of immediate supervision of the building process, but he was not its designer; in fact he disliked acutely and vocally the small original tower, which offended his carpenter's eye as badly out of proportion. He did not embarrass the local craftsmen by directly *insisting* on a change, but on August 16, 1878, about one year after Brigham's death, the tower was struck by lightning and, though the temple was miraculously preserved from burning, the tower was badly damaged—and was replaced by a much larger one.

There is another way President Young's voice was still heard after his death. He died on August 29, 1877. Twenty-five thousand of the Saints filed by his bier on Saturday, September 1, and the next day at his funeral George Q. Cannon reflected on the loss:

> From the greatest details connected with the organization of this Church, down to the smallest minutiae connected with the work, he has left upon it the impress of his great mind. From the organization of the Church, and the construction of Temples, the building of Tabernacles; from the creation of a provisional state government and a Territorial government, down to the small matter of directing the shape of these seats upon which we sit this day; upon all these things, as well as upon all the settlements of the Territory, the impress of his genius is apparent. . . .
>
> His value has not been properly estimated by the Latter-day Saints. There are none of us who will not feel this more and more. . . . The time will come when the Latter-day Saints will appreciate him as one of the greatest Prophets that ever lived.[75]

The new prophet and leader of the Church, John Taylor, looked back to the time thirty-three years before when he had seen Joseph

Smith, the Church's first prophet, die "by the hand, and in the midst of vindictive and blood-thirsty foes, who, in the absence of legal offense, surcharged with deadly, venomous hate, clamored for his blood." In contrast, he said:

> President Young, after leading the Church [for those thirty-three years since], and buffeting the trials and persecutions to which the Church has ever been subjected, has, at length, in these valleys of the mountains, after having accomplished the object of his life . . . lain down to sleep in the midst of a loving and affectionate family, and surrounded by faithful and tried friends.[76]

But perhaps most fitting for the occasion was the reading of Brother Brigham's burial instructions, made in his own irrepressible personal voice back in 1873.[77] He had given a carpenter's very explicit and matter-of-fact directions about his coffin ("made of plump 1-1/4 inch [redwood] boards, not scrimped in length . . . my body dressed in my temple clothing, and laid nicely to the coffin, and the coffin to have the appearance that if I wanted to turn a little to the right or the left, I should have plenty of room to do so"); he had urged frugality in mourning ("all of my family present that can be conveniently, and the male members wear no crepe . . . the females to buy no black bonnets, nor black dresses"); and he had named the burial spot ("the little burying ground, which I have reserved on my lot east of the White House on the hill, and in the southeast corner of this lot [presently 140 A Street in Salt Lake City]"). And then he had concluded, with the calm assurance at his heart's core:

> There let my earthly house or tabernacle rest in peace, and have a good sleep, until the morning of the first resurrection; no crying or mourning with anyone as I have done my work faithfully and in good faith.
>
> I wish this to be read at the funeral, providing that if I should die anywhere in the mountains, I desire the above directions respecting my place of burial to be observed; but if I should live to go back with the Church to Jackson County, I wish to be buried there.

Notes

Notes to Chapter 1

1. Norris R. Werner, *Brigham Young* (New York: Harcourt, Brace & Co., 1925), p. 5.

2. Susa Young Gates, in collaboration with Leah D. Widtsoe, *The Life Story of Brigham Young* (New York: Macmillan Company, 1930), pp. 2-3.

3. *Journal of Discourses*, 26 vols. (London: Latter-day Saints' Book Depot, 1854-86), 2:94, 6 February 1853; hereafter cited as *JD*.

4. *JD*, 5:97, 2 August 1857.

5. *Manuscript History of Brigham Young, 1801-1844*, comp. Elden J. Watson (Salt Lake City, 1967), p. 1; hereafter cited as *Ms. History*.

6. *JD*, 12:287, 8 October 1868.

7. James A. Little, "Biography of Lorenzo Dow Young," *Utah Historical Quarterly* 14 (1946): 130.

8. *JD*, 8:37, 6 April 1860.

9. *JD*, 10:360, 6 November 1864.

10. Mary Van Sickle Wait, *Brigham Young in Cayuga County, 1813-1829* (Ithaca, New York, 1964), p. 24.

11. Ibid., p. 41.

12. Ibid., p. 47. In 1977 this desk was given to The Church of Jesus Christ of Latter-day Saints and is now in the care of the Church Curator in Salt Lake City.

13. Ibid., p. 41.

14. Captain George Hickox to Brigham Young, 7 February 1876, Brigham Young Papers, Historical Department, The Church of Jesus Christ of Latter-day Saints, Salt Lake City; hereafter cited as Church Archives.

15. Brigham Young to George Hickox, 19 February 1876, Brigham Young Letterbook No. 16, Church Archives, pp. 206-7.

16. *JD*, 8:37, 6 April 1860.

17. *JD*, 18:247, 23 June 1874.

18. *JD*, 8:38, 6 April 1860.

19. Gates, p. 20.

20. Wait, p. 54; see also S. Dilworth Young, *"Here is Brigham": Brigham Young, the Years to 1844* (Salt Lake City: Bookcraft, 1964), p. 41.

21. Hiram McKee to Brigham Young, 4 April 1860, Brigham Young Papers, Church Archives.

22. Brigham Young to Hiram McKee, 3 May 1860, Brigham Young Papers, Church Archives.

23. Minutes of Young Family Meeting, Nauvoo, Illinois, 18 January 1845, Brigham Young Papers, Church Archives.

24. *JD*, 14:197-98, 3 June 1871.

25. Minutes of Young Family Meeting, 18 January 1845.

26. *Ms. History*, p. xvii.

27. *JD*, 11:254, 17 June 1866.

28. *Ms. History*, p. xix.

29. *JD*, 3:91, 8 August 1852.

30. *JD*, 8:38, 6 April 1860.

31. *JD*, 1:90, 13 June 1852.

32. *Ms. History*, p. 2.

33. *JD*, 8:37, 6 April 1860.

34. *JD*, 13:211, 17 July 1870. The date of Brigham Young's baptism was incorrectly recorded as April 14 (Saturday) in the Manuscript History. He called attention to this error in a sermon on February 16, 1862 (*JD*, 9:219), and further confirmed that the day was a Sunday in the quotation from this sermon.

35. *Ms. History*, p. 3.

36. Ibid., p. 3.

37. See Elinore Hughes Partridge, "Nineteenth-century Spelling: The Rules and the Writers," *Ensign* 5 (August 1975): 74-80. The four holograph diaries are in the Brigham Young Papers, Church Archives. For ease in reading I have modernized and regularized the punctuation of quotations from nineteenth-century sources. Any other changes are indicated with brackets.

38. Werner, see preface.

39. *JD*, 3:320, 20 April 1856.

40. Heber C. Kimball Journal 94b, Church Archives, p. 4.

41. *JD*, 8:173, 16 September 1860.

42. *JD*, 4:21, 17 August 1856.

43. *JD*, 5:96-97, 2 August 1857.

44. *JD*, 10:193, 31 May 1863.

45. Gates, p. 280.

46. *JD*, 1:264, 14 August 1853.

47. *JD*, 9:140-41, 28 July 1861.

48. *JD*, 8:346, 20 January 1861.

49. Stanley B. Kimball, manuscript "Biography of Heber C. Kimball," Church Archives, p. 27.

50. *JD*, 5:97, 2 August 1857.

51. Wait, p. 36.

52. *Ms. History*, p. vi. When Joseph Smith, Sr., was later ordained he was the first *presiding* Patriarch.

53. Ibid., p. 4.

54. *Deseret News*, 31 March 1858.

55. Reported by Daniel G. Millett in *Church News*, 30 August 1975, p. 16. The Artemus Millett journal is in the Church Archives.

56. *Ms. History*, p. 5.

57. Manuscript Diary, 1832-35, Brigham Young Papers, Church Archives.

58. *Ms. History*, p. 7.

59. Ibid.

60. Gates, p. 11.

61. *Ms. History*, p. 8.

62. Kimball, pp. 72-80. The revelation quoted was given to Joseph Smith on June 22, 1834; see D&C 105:19.

63. George A. Smith, "Memoirs of George A. Smith," typescript, George A. Smith Papers, Church Archives.

64. *Ms. History*, p. 9.

65. Ray B. West, Jr., *Kingdom of the Saints: The Story of Brigham Young and the Mormons* (New York: Viking Press, 1957), p. 57.

66. Minutes of Young Family Meeting, 18 January 1845.

67. *Ms. History*, pp. 11-12.

68. Manuscript Diary, 1832-35. (Spelling modernized.)

69. Journal of Joseph Millett, see appendix, Church Archives.

70. Helen Mar Whitney, "Life Incidents," *Woman's Exponent* 9 (1 February 1881): 130.

71. D&C 110:4, 6-7.

72. *Ms. History*, p. 13.

73. This summary of the Kirtland troubles is based on B. H. Roberts, *A Comprehensive History of The Church of Jesus Christ of Latter-day Saints*, 6 vols. (Salt Lake City: The Church of Jesus Christ of Latter-day Saints, 1930), 1:396, 410; hereafter cited as *CHC*. See also James B. Allen and Glen M. Leonard, *The Story of the Latter-day Saints* (Salt Lake City: Deseret Book Co., 1976), pp. 110-15.

74. *Ms. History*, p. 16.

75. *Millennial Star* (10 September 1864): 585.

76. *Ms. History*, p. 21.

77. Ibid., p. 23.

78. Ibid., pp. 29-30.

79. Joseph Smith, Jr., *History of The Church of Jesus Christ of Latter-day Saints*, ed. B. H. Roberts, 7 vols. (Salt Lake City: The Church of Jesus Christ of Latter-day Saints, 1948), 3:250; hereafter cited as *HC*.

80. *Ms. History*, p. 34.

Notes to Chapter 2

1. Journal of Wilford Woodruff, typescript, 4 and 5 April 1841, Wilford Woodruff Papers, Church Archives.

2. Heber C. Kimball to Vilate Kimball, 25 May 1841, Church Archives.

3. Heber C. Kimball to Vilate Kimball, 27 May 1841, Church Archives.

4. Woodruff, 22 March 1841.

5. *Manuscript History of Brigham Young, 1801-1844*, comp. Elden J. Watson (Salt Lake City, 1967), pp. 96-97; hereafter cited as *Ms. History*.

6. Dean Jessee, "The Writings of Brigham Young," *The Western Historical Quarterly* 4 (July 1973): 277.

7. See D&C 118:4-5. This revelation was read publicly in Far West on July 8, 1838, and subsequently referred to often by the Mormons. It thus became known to the anti-Mormon Missourians, who promised to make certain it was not fulfilled. Its importance to Brigham is indicated by his copying it in his diary for the period.

8. *Ms. History*, p. 35.

9. *Ms. History*, p. 36.

10. Joseph Smith, Jr., *History of the Church of Jesus Christ of Latter-day Saints*, ed. B. H. Roberts, 7 vols. (Salt Lake City: The Church of Jesus Christ of Latter-day Saints, 1948), 3:339; hereafter cited as *HC*.

11. *Ms. History*, p. 42.

12. Woodruff, 2 July 1839.

13. Leonora Taylor to John Taylor, 9 September 1839. Reprinted in Ronald K. Esplin, "Sickness and Faith, Nauvoo Letters," *BYU Studies* 15 (Summer 1975): 427.

14. Susa Young Gates, "Brigham Young as Missionary," *Juvenile Instructor* 63 (1928): 307.

15. *Ms. History*, p. 50.

16. Journal of Heber C. Kimball, 14 September 1839, Church Archives.

17. *Ms. History*, p. 61.

18. Ibid., p. 57.

19. Ibid., pp. 57-58.

20. Ibid., 22 November 1839, pp. 58-59.

21. Ibid., p. 52.

22. Ibid., 2 February 1840, p. 67.

23. Ibid., p. 69.

24. Woodruff, 17 January 1840.

25. John Taylor to Leonora Taylor, 30 January 1840.

26. Woodruff, 2 March 1840.

27. Wilford Woodruff to Willard Richards, 31 March 1840.

28. Wilford Woodruff to Willard Richards, 3 April 1840.

29. *Ms. History*, p. 70.

30. *HC*, 4:132.

31. Diary of George A. Smith, 21 May 1840, typescript from holograph, George A. Smith Papers, Church Archives.

32. Ibid., 16 August 1840.

33. Ibid., 21 October 1840.

34. Ibid., 17 September 1840.

35. Heber C. Kimball to Vilate Kimball, 19 September 1840.

36. John Taylor to Leonora Taylor, 19 September 1839; see also Esplin, p. 433.

37. John Taylor to Leonora Taylor, 30 January 1840.

38. Ibid., pp. 10-11.

39. Woodruff, 11 May 1840.

40. Woodruff, 26 June 1840.

41. Ibid., 19 February 1840.

42. *HC*, 3:276-77.

43. Brigham Young to Willard Richards, 10 June 1840.

44. Brigham Young to Willard Richards, 17 June 1840.

45. Certificate, 20 May 1840, Brigham Young Papers, Church Archives.

46. *Ms. History*, 12 July 1840, p. 79.

47. Note, "Conf., Oct. 6, 1840," Brigham Young Papers, Church Archives.

48. *Ms. History*, p. 81.

49. Heber C. Kimball to Vilate Kimball, 19 August 1840, Church Archives.

50. Woodruff, 7 August 1840 and 8 November 1840.

51. Ibid., 6 December 1840.

52. Quorum of the Twelve Minutes, 11 February 1851, Church Archives.

53. "Great Salt Lake Municipal High Council Minutes," 27 January 1849, Brigham Young Papers, Church Archives.

54. Woodruff, 14 June 1840.

55. Ibid., 18 May 1840.

56. *Ms. History*, 8 November 1840.

57. Heber C. Kimball to Vilate Kimball, 25 May 1840.

58. Smith, 13 July 1840.

59. Ibid., 26 June 1840.

60. Woodruff, 18 May 1840.

61. *HC*, 4:325.

62. Woodruff, 3 April 1841.

63. *HC*, 4:325.

64. *HC*, 4:335.

65. Woodruff, 15 April 1841.

66. James B. Allen, *The Man — Brigham Young* (Provo, Utah: Brigham Young University Press, 1974), p. 2.

67. *HC*, 4:120.

68. *HC*, 4:125-26.

69. *HC*, 4:161-62.

70. B. Young and W. Richards to The First Presidency, 5 September 1840, Church Archives.

71. *HC*, 4:227.

72. *HC*, 4:251.

73. See *HC*, 4:345-47.

74. D&C 126.

75. *HC*, 4:403.

76. Diary of Brigham Young, 1840-1844, Brigham Young Papers, Church Archives.

77. Diary of Brigham Young, 1837-1845, Brigham Young Papers, Church Archives.

Notes to Chapter 3

1. Susa Young Gates, in collaboration with Leah D. Widtsoe, *The Life Story of Brigham Young* (New York: Macmillan Company, 1930), p. 362.

2. Ray B. West, Jr., *Kingdom of the Saints: The Story of Brigham Young and the Mormons* (New York: Viking Press, 1957), p. 41.

3. *Journal of Discourses*, 26 vols. (London: Latter-day Saints' Book Depot, 1854-86), 1:313, 20 February 1853; hereafter cited as *JD*.

4. *JD*, 9:364-65, 31 August 1862.

5. *JD*, 4:297-98, 29 March 1857.

6. Journal of William C. Staines, 29 April 1846, Church Archives.

7. *JD*, 12:270, 16 August 1868.

8. Joseph Smith, Jr., *History of the Church of Jesus Christ of Latter-day Saints*, ed. B. H. Roberts, 7 vols. (Salt Lake City: The Church of Jesus Christ of Latter-day Saints, 1948), 5:412; hereafter cited as *HC*.

9. *Manuscript History of Brigham Young, 1801-1844*, comp. Elden J. Watson (Salt Lake City, 1967), pp. 16-17; hereafter cited as *Ms. History*. Brigham Young discussed his momentary wavering and quick repentance in a speech to the Saints in Salt Lake City, 29 March 1857; see also *JD*, 4:285.

10. *JD*, 10:363, 13 November 1863.

11. D&C 107:24.

12. *Ms. History*, pp. 118, 120.

13. *JD*, 5:96, 2 August 1857.

14. Brigham Young to David P. Smith, 1 June 1853, Brigham Young Papers, Church Archives.

15. Speech given 30 July 1843, at Pittsburgh, recorded in *Ms. History*, p. 140.

16. *Ms. History*, p. 143. Italics added.

17. *Ms. History*, p. 148, 26 August 1843.

18. *Ms. History*, p. 156, 10 December 1843.

19. Joseph Smith to Emma Smith, 4 April 1839, Joseph Smith Papers, Church Archives.

20. Diary of George A. Smith, 15 May 1843, typescript from holograph, George A. Smith Papers, Church Archives.

21. D&C 121:41, 44.

22. *Ms. History*, p. 169, 27 June 1844.

23. Quoted from Wilford Woodruff's journal in *HC*, 7:195.

24. Brigham Young to Vilate Young, 11 August 1844, Brigham Young Papers, Church Archives.

25. *Ms. History*, p. 171, 16 July 1844. For an excellently detailed and judicious treatment of the uncertainties surrounding the question of proper authority on Joseph's death, see D. Michael Quinn, "The Mormon Succession Crisis of 1844," *BYU Studies* 16 (Winter 1976): 187-233.

26. Quoted in *HC*, 7:229.

27. Quoted in *HC*, 7:230.

28. Journal of Wilford Woodruff, 8 August 1844, Wilford Woodruff Papers, Church Archives.

29. Diary of Brigham Young, 1837-1845, Brigham Young Papers, Church Archives. For a detailed analysis of this meeting and the other events involved in the succession problem see T. Edgar Lyon, "Nauvoo and the Council of the Twelve," *The Restoration Movement: Essays in Mormon History*, eds. F. Mark McKiernan, et al. (Lawrence, Kan.: Coronado Press, 1973), p. 192.

30. Minutes of "Special Meeting in Nauvoo," 8 August 1844, Brigham Young Papers, Church Archives, pp. 17-18.

31. Ibid., pp. 5, 9.

32. Journal of George Laub, 4 March 1846, Church Archives, p. 91; or see the published version I have edited for *BYU Studies*, Winter 1978.

33. *JD*, 15:81, 8 April 1872.

34. Diary of William Burton, Church Archives. See Quinn, p. 212.

35. Typescript account of testimony of Bishop George Romney, by Mary R. Ross, Church Archives.

36. Manuscript History of the Church, Brigham Young Period, 1844-1877, 9 August 1844, Church Archives; hereafter cited as Ms. History of the Church. This is a forty-seven volume work compiled by clerks and historians under the direction of Brigham Young and others, and written as the work of Brigham Young himself.

37. Manuscript Diary, 1837-45, Brigham Young Papers, Church Archives.

38. Minutes, 6 January 1845, Brigham Young Papers, Church Archives.

39. From the minutes of the "Trial of Sidney Rigdon," 8 September 1844, published in the *Millennial Star*, 5:100 (June 1844 to May 1845).

40. *HC*, 7:386.

41. *HC*, 7:535.

42. *HC*, 7:549-50.

43. *HC*, 7:430-31.

44. Minutes of "Special Meeting in Nauvoo," p. 9.

45. *HC*, 7:240.

46. Manuscript Diary, 1837-45.

47. "Secretary's Journal," 7 August 1845, Brigham Young Papers, Church Archives.

48. Brigham Young to Lucy Smith, 2 August 1845, Brigham Young Papers, Church Archives.

49. *HC*, 7:476.

50. *HC*, 7:256.

51. Ms. History of the Church, 16 and 19 September 1845.

52. Interview in the *Church News*, (9 August 1975), p. 13.

53. Joseph Smith to Emma Smith, 12 November 1838, Research Library and Archives of The Reorganized Church of Jesus Christ of Latter Day Saints, The Auditorium, Independence, Missouri. This version of the letter, with regularized spelling and punctuation, is from *History of the Church of Jesus Christ of Latter Day Saints*, 3 vols. (Lamoni, Iowa, 1897), 2:290-91.

54. Brigham Young to Mary Ann Young, 12 June 1844, photocopy of holograph, Brigham Young Papers, Church Archives; original in possession of Dr. Wade N. Stephens, Brodenton, Florida.

55. Unpublished manuscript, "Brigham Young and Great Basin Economy,"

Church Archives, pp. 5-6; my discussion of this basic difference between Brigham Young and Joseph Smith is essentially a summary of Arrington's ideas.

56. "Journal of President B. Young's Office," 1 October 1860, Brigham Young Papers, Church Archives.

57. *JD*, 1:215, 9 October 1852.

58. *JD*, 3:51, 6 October 1855.

59. Brigham Young to Joseph Young, 9 March 1846, Brigham Young Papers, Church Archives.

60. Brigham Young to Charles C. Rich, 4 January 1847, Brigham Young Papers, Church Archives.

Notes to Chapter 4

1. Brigham Young to Jesse C. Little, 26 February 1847, Brigham Young Papers, Church Archives.

2. Exodus 19:5-6.

3. Joseph Smith, Jr., *History of the Church of Jesus Christ of Latter-day Saints*, ed. B. H. Roberts, 7 vols. (Salt Lake City: The Church of Jesus Christ of Latter-day Saints, 1948), 7:478-80; hereafter cited as *HC*. Volume seven is a compilation by Roberts of various sources, including part of the Manuscript History of the Church, which was compiled under the direction of Brigham Young and written as if in first person. The material I quote from in this chapter is based essentially on the work of Willard Richards, who served closely as President Young's clerk, keeping a daily record in 1844-46.

4. *HC*, 7:468-69.

5. *HC*, 7:464.

6. *HC*, 7:464-65.

7. *HC*, 7:465.

8. *HC*, 7:466-67.

9. *Journal of Discourses*, 26 vols. (London: Latter-day Saints' Book Depot, 1854-86), 4:23, 17 August 1856; hereafter cited as *JD*.

10. Manuscript History of the Church, Brigham Young Period, 1844-1877, 24 January 1846, pp. 18, 20, Church Archives; hereafter cited as Ms. History of the Church. This is a forty-seven volume work compiled by clerks and historians under the direction of Brigham Young and others, and written as the work of Brigham Young himself.

11. Manuscript History of Brigham Young, 9 October 1846, as taken from original manuscript, Church Archives; hereafter cited as Ms. History.

12. Ms. History, 20 December 1846.

13. *William Clayton's Journal* (Salt Lake City: Clayton Family Association, 1921), pp. 189-201.

14. Journal of Thomas Bullock, 27 February 1845, typescript from holograph, Church Archives.

15. See T. Edgar Lyon, "Some Uncommon Aspects of the Mormon Migration," *Improvement Era* 72 (September 1969): 33-40.

16. Clayton, pp. 19-20.

17. Ms. History, 18 February 1846.

18. Clayton, p. 12 (3 April 1846).

19. *On the Mormon Frontier: The Diary of Hosea Stout, 1844-1861*, ed. Juanita Brooks, 2 vols. (Salt Lake City: University of Utah Press, 1964), 1:160. I have regularized the punctuation somewhat for ease of understanding.

20. Ibid., p. 168.

21. Ibid., p. 171.

22. Ibid., p. 172.

23. Ibid., pp. 175-77.

24. Ibid., p. 179.

25. Thomas L. Kane, *A Discourse Delivered Before the Historical Society of Pennsylvania, March 26, 1850* (Philadelphia, 1850), p. 31.

26. Ms. History, 9 August 1846.

27. 2 Nephi 12:2; compare Isaiah 2:2.

28. D&C 49:24-25; this revelation was given 31 March 1831.

29. Included in an address reported in *Church News*, 7 August 1937, p. 5, by Joseph Fielding Smith, Hyrum's grandson, who was then an apostle and Church historian.

30. *HC*, 5:85; this report, verified by the testimony of Anson Call and others who claimed to be present, was made part of Joseph Smith's "History of the Church" in Utah in the 1850s.

31. *HC*, 7:449.

32. *HC*, 7:439.

33. *HC*, 7:548.

34. *HC*, 7:555.

35. *HC*, 7:558.

36. Ms. History, 29 January 1846.

37. Reproduced in Ms. History, 4 January 1846.

38. Brigham Young to the Saints in Camp Creek Branch, 16 September 1845, Brigham Young Papers, Church Archives. This was in response to the first news that mob action had started up against the small Mormon settlements around Nauvoo.

39. Ms. History, 17 March 1846.

40. Ms. History, 2 February 1846.

41. Ms. History, 17 February 1846.

42. Stout, 1:138.

43. Brigham Young to Joseph Young, 9 March 1846, Brigham Young Papers, Church Archives.

44. Brigham Young to Harriet Cook Young, 15 March 1846, Brigham Young Papers, Church Archives.

45. Ms. History, 3 May 1846.

46. Exodus 18:18, 21, 22.

47. Ms. History, 3 May 1846.

48. Ms. History, 16 August 1846.

49. Numbers 11:11.

50. Exodus 32:32.

51. Nels Anderson, *Desert Saints: The Mormon Frontier in Utah* (Chicago: University of Chicago Press, 1942), p. 41.

52. Ms. History, 18 April 1846.

53. Ms. History, 4 May 1846.

54. Ms. History, 7 June 1846.

55. Ms. History, 28 June 1846.

56. Clayton, p. 9.

57. Parley P. Pratt, *The Autobiography of Parley P. Pratt,* ed. Parley P. Pratt (New York: Russell Brothers, 1874), pp. 379-80.

58. Ms. History, 11 November 1846.

59. From a photocopy in Russell R. Rich, *Ensign to the Nations: A History of the Church from 1846 to the Present* (Provo, Utah: Brigham Young University Press, 1972), p. 53.

60. Brigham H. Roberts, *A Comprehensive History of the Church of Jesus Christ of Latter-day Saints,* 6 vols. (Salt Lake City: The Church of Jesus Christ of Latter-day Saints, 1930), 3:67; hereafter cited as *CHC*.

61. Bullock, 28 July 1847.

62. Thomas L. Kane to Brigham Young, 11 July 1850, Brigham Young Papers, Church Archives.

63. Ms. History, 13 July 1846. Italics added.

Notes to Chapter 5

1. Manuscript History of the Church, Brigham Young Period, 1844-1877, 12 August 1846, Church Archives; hereafter cited as Ms. History of the Church.

2. Manuscript History of Brigham Young, 7 August 1846, as taken from original manuscript, Church Archives; hereafter cited as Ms. History.

3. *On the Mormon Frontier: The Diary of Hosea Stout, 1844-1861,* ed. Juanita Brooks, 2 vols. (Salt Lake City: University of Utah Press, 1964), 1:191.

4. Ms. History of the Church, 12 September 1846.

5. Stout, 1:222.

6. This and the following references are from Ms. History, on the dates given in the text.

7. Stout, 1:238 (28 February 1847).

8. Ms. History, 5 February 1847.

9. Stout, 1:232.

10. D&C 136:8-9.

11. D&C 136:28-30.

12. Ms. History, 15 April 1847.

13. *William Clayton's Journal* (Salt Lake City: Clayton Family Association, 1921), pp. 102, 116, 156.

14. Diary of Thomas Bullock, 13 June 1847, typescript from holograph, Church Archives.

15. Ms. History, 8 June 1847.

16. Ms. History, 28 June 1847.

17. Clayton, p. 289.

18. Clayton, p. 290.

19. Clayton, p. 300.

20. Bullock, 18 June 1847.

21. Ms. History, 23 July 1847.

22. Sermon given July 24, 1880, reported in *The Utah Pioneers* (Salt Lake City, 1880), p. 16.

23. Bullock, 23 July 1847.

24. Nels Anderson, *Desert Saints: The Mormon Frontier in Utah* (Chicago: University of Chicago Press, 1942), p. 68.

25. *Journal of Discourses*, 26 vols. (London: Latter-day Saints' Book Depot, 1854-86), 1:133, 6 April 1853; hereafter cited as *JD*.

26. Clayton, p. 291.

27. Bullock, p. 38.

28. Clayton, p. 313 (23 July 1847). Italics added.

29. Bullock, 8 July 1847.

30. Bullock, 28 July 1847.

31. Bullock, 4 September 1847.

32. Parley P. Pratt, *The Autobiography of Parley P. Pratt*, ed. Parley P. Pratt (New York: Russell Brothers, 1874), pp. 400-401.

33. *JD*, 1:108, 8 May 1853.

34. Stout, 1:283.

35. Stout, 1:292.

36. Stout, 1:293.

37. The *Millennial Star* 10 (1848): 88.

38. Ibid., 10:115 (letter to Orson Spencer in England).

39. Stout, 1:293.

40. *A Mormon Chronicle: The Diaries of John D. Lee, 1848-1876*, eds. Robert G. Cleland and Juanita Brooks, 2 vols. (San Marino: The Huntington Library, 1955), 1:7.

41. Lee, 1:59.

42. Lee, 1:39.

43. Lee, 1:64.

44. *JD*, 12:287, 8 October 1868.

45. Lee, 1:65.

46. Lee, 1:68-69.

47. Pratt, p. 105.

48. Lee, 1:87-88.

49. Lee, 1:89.

50. Lee, 1:90.

51. "Journal of Priddy Meeks," *Utah Historical Quarterly* 10 (1942): 163-64.

52. Lee, 1:110.

53. Brigham Young to William Tanner, 21 February 1867, retained copy, Brigham Young Papers, Church Archives.

54. Diary of S. W. Richards, 6 June 1855, Church Archives.

55. *JD*, 1:108.

56. Orson F. Whitney, *Life of Heber C. Kimball*, 4th ed. (Salt Lake City: Bookcraft, 1973), pp. 389-90.

57. Lee, 1:95.

58. *Frontier Guardian*. 15 September 1849; quoted in B. H. Roberts, *A Comprehensive History of the Church of Jesus Christ of Latter-day Saints*, 6 vols. (Salt Lake City: The Church of Jesus Christ of Latter-day Saints, 1930), 3:351-52.

59. Lee, 1:111-112.

60. Ms. History, 29 September 1849: quoted in Anderson, p. 109.

61. *JD*, 1:46.

Notes to Chapter 6

1. *Journal of Discourses*, 26 vols. (London: Latter-day Saints' Book Depot, 1854-86), 4:32, 17 August 1856; hereafter cited as *JD*.

2. Minutes, "Special Meeting at Nauvoo," 8 August 1844, Brigham Young Papers, Church Archives.

3. Christopher Lasch, *The World of Nations* (New York, 1973), p. 66; an essay originally printed in the *New York Review of Books*, 26 January 1967.

4. *JD*, 8:160, 2 September 1860.

5. "Mormonism and the Secularization of Religions in the Modern World," *BYU Studies* 16 (Summer 1976): 629.

6. Sermon of February 1849, reported in James S. Brown, *Life of a Pioneer* (Salt Lake City, 1900), pp. 121-22; quoted in Leonard J. Arrington, *Great Basin Kingdom: An Economic History of the Latter-day Saints 1830-1900* (Lincoln, Neb.: University of Nebraska Press, 1966), p. 61.

7. Brigham Young to Orson Hyde, 28 July 1850, Brigham Young Outgoing Correspondence — Drafts, Church Archives.

8. Sermon published in the *Deseret News*, 20 July 1850, p. 44.

9. Manuscript History of the Church, Brigham Young Period 1844-1877, 26 November 1849, Church Archives; hereafter cited as Ms. History of the Church.

10. "Norton Jacobs Record," 28 July 1847, typescript in Harold B. Lee Library, Brigham Young University.

11. Arrington, pp. 63, 412.

12. See Milton R. Hunter, *Brigham Young the Colonizer* (Salt Lake City: Deseret News Press, 1940), pp. 63-85.

13. Report published in the *Deseret News*, 25 December 1852, p. 10.

14. *Deseret News*, 4 April 1896; quoted in Arrington, p. 115.

15. Arrington, p. 129.

16. Ibid., p. 130.

17. Brigham Young to Orson Pratt, 14 October 1849, printed in the *Millennial Star* 12 (1850): 141.

18. Arrington, pp. 98-104; the Dickens description was published in his *The Uncommercial Traveler.*

19. Journal History of the Church, 16 September 1855, Church Archives; hereafter cited as Journal History. This compilation was made by the Church Historian's Office, under the direction of Andrew Jenson, in the 1890s; it includes parts of the Manuscript History for the early period.

20. *JD*, 3:6, 16 September 1855.

21. *JD*, 3:122, 8 October 1855.

22. Journal History, 8 June 1856.

23. Arrington, p. 155.

24. Brigham Young to Franklin D. Richards, 30 September 1855, retained copy, Brigham Young, Brigham Young Papers, Church Archives.

25. Brigham Young to Edmund Ellsworth, 30 September 1855, retained copy, Brigham Young Papers, Church Archives.

26. Wilford Woodruff to Orson Pratt, 30 September 1856, *Millennial Star* 18 (1856): 794-95.

27. *JD*, 4:113, 5 October 1856.

28. Wallace Stegner, *The Gathering of Zion: The Story of the Mormon Trail,* American Trail Series (New York: McGraw-Hill Book Co., 1964), p. 250. The original essay, "Ordeal by Handcart," appeared in *Collier's,* 6 July 1956, pp. 78-85; it was rewritten and expanded by Stegner for his book.

29. Stegner, "Ordeal by Handcart," p. 85.

30. Ibid.

31. Journal of Patience Loader Archer, typescript of original, Harold B. Lee Library, Brigham Young University, p. 87.

32. From "Mr. [John] Chislett's Narrative," published in T.B.H. Stenhouse, *The Rocky Mountain Saints* (New York, 1873), p. 317.

33. *JD*, 4:69, 2 November 1856.

34. *JD*, 4:62, 2 November 1856.

35. Sermon printed in *Deseret News,* 10 December 1856.

36. Published in *A Believing People: Literature of the Latter-day Saints,* eds. Richard H. Cracroft and Neal E. Lambert, 2d ed. (Salt Lake City: Bookcraft, 1979), p. 107.

37. Arrington, p. 162.

38. Secretary's Journal, 7 April 1857, Brigham Young Papers, Church Archives; hereafter cited as Secretary's Journal.

39. Ibid., 24 July 1857.

40. Ibid., 12 July 1857.

41. Ibid., 20 August 1857.

42. Brigham Young, "Proclamation by the Governor," photographic reproduction in Nels Anderson, *Desert Saints: The Mormon Frontier in Utah* (Chicago: University of Chicago Press, 1942), p. 173.

43. Journal History, 30 August 1857.

44. Anderson, pp. 171-72.

45. *Millennial Star* 19 (1857): 766.

46. The best single source on this material is Juanita Brooks, *The Mountain Meadows Massacre* (Stanford, California: Stanford University Press, 1950).

47. Brigham Young to Isaac Haight, 10 September 1857, Brigham Young Letterbook No. 9, Brigham Young Papers, Church Archives.

48. Anderson, p. 192.

49. Levi S. Peterson, "Juanita Brooks: The Mormon Historian as Tragedian," *Journal of Mormon History* 3 (1976): 52.

50. Office Journal, 27 January 1857, Brigham Young Papers, Church Archives.

51. *JD*, 11:281, 23 December 1866.

52. Ms. History of the Church, 30 September 1857.

53. *JD*, 5:294, 6 October 1857.

54. Journal History, 18 October 1857.

55. Quoted in Arrington, p. 181.

56. Journal History, 25 February 1858. This source located in Preston Nibley, *Brigham Young: the Man and His Work*, 4th ed. (Salt Lake City: Deseret Book Co., 1960), p. 323.

57. Ms. History of the Church, 15 August 1858.

58. Journal History, 6 January 1858; Nibley, p. 325.

59. Cited in Arrington, p. 188.

60. Arrington, p. 196.

61. Cited in James B. Allen and Glen M. Leonard, *The Story of the Latter-day Saints* (Salt Lake City: Deseret Book Co., 1976), p. 313.

62. *Letters of Brigham Young to His Sons*, ed. Dean C. Jessee (Salt Lake City: Deseret Book Co., 1974), p. xx.

63. Samuel Bowles, *Our New West* (Hartford, Conn., 1869), p. 215.

64. Fitz Hugh Ludlow, *The Heart of a Continent* (New York, 1870), p. 373.

65. See Leonard J. Arrington, "The Settlement of the Brigham Young Estate, 1877-1879," *Pacific Historical Review* 21 (February 1952): 1-20.

66. Office Journal, 28 January 1857.

67. Arrington, *Great Basin Kingdom*, p. 410.

68. Ibid., p. 411.

69. Brigham Young to the editor of the *New York Herald*, 10 April 1873; cited in Nibley, pp. 490-92.

Notes to Chapter 7

1. This vision is described by Brigham Young, among other times, in a sermon given 6 April 1853, where he also prophesied concerning some of the temples of the future that would have one central tower and "on the top, groves and fish ponds." See *Journal of Discourses*, 26 vols. (London: Latter-day Saints' Book Depot, 1854-86), 1:133; hereafter cited as *JD*.

2. *JD*, 19:93, 19 August 1877.

3. Journal of Wilford Woodruff, 25 July 1847, Wilford Woodruff Papers, Church Archives.

4. Sermon of 4 February 1849, reported in James S. Brown, *Life of a Pioneer* (Salt Lake City, 1900), p. 119.

5. *JD*, 4:24-25, 17 August 1856.

6. A historian of engineering, Allen Comp, has done the most thorough research on the building of the tabernacle; a copy of his unpublished paper is in the Church Archives.

7. Quoted in Preston Nibley, *Brigham Young: the Man and His Work*, 4th ed. (Salt Lake City: Deseret Book Co., 1960), p. 429.

8. Journal History of the Church, 10 October 1875, Church Archives; hereafter cited as Journal History. This compilation was made by the Church Historian's Office, under the direction of Andrew Jenson, in the 1890s; it includes parts of the Manuscript History for the early period.

9. See *JD*, 5:205, 12 October 1856.

10. *JD*, 16:46, 18 May 1873.

11. Secretary's Journal, 29 January 1857, Brigham Young Papers, Church Archives; hereafter cited as Secretary's Journal.

12. Ibid., 7 March 1857.

13. Ibid., 14 February 1857.

14. Ibid., 10 March 1857.

15. "Eighth General Epistle of the Presidency of the Church," *Millennial Star* 15 (19 February 1853): 113-14.

16. *Millennial Star* 30 (10 October 1868): 643.

17. Brigham Young to Horace Eldredge, 16 February 1871, retained copy, Brigham Young Papers, Church Archives.

18. *JD*, 7:280-81, 7 October 1857.

19. Secretary's Journal, 2 March 1857.

20. Elizabeth Wood Kane, *Twelve Mormon Homes*, ed. Everett Cooley (Salt Lake City, 1975), p. 101. This journal, written as letters to Mrs. Kane's father, was first published, by him, in 1874.

21. Quoted in Nibley, p. 379.

22. George A. Smith to George Q. Cannon, 2 January 1863, George Q. Cannon Papers, Church Archives; quoted in Nibley, p. 382.

23. Richard F. Burton, *The City of the Saints and Across the Rocky Mountains to California* (1861; New York: Alfred A. Knopf, 1963), pp. 262-64.

24. Quoted in Nibley, p. 366.

25. Secretary's Journal, 6 September 1860.

26. *JD*, 8:284-85, 7 June 1860.

27. *JD*, 8:288-89, 7 June 1860.

28. Nibley, p. 361.

29. Ibid., p. 361-62.

30. *JD*, 13:147, 11 July 1869.

31. Ernst Benz, "Mormonism and the Secularization of Religions in the Modern World," *BYU Studies* 16 (Summer 1976): 638.

32. *JD*, 3:203, 17 February 1856.

33. *JD*, 9:305, 15 June 1862.

34. *JD*, 9:167, 26 January 1862.

35. Cited in Nibley, p. 414.

36. Journal History, 28 November 1873.

37. *The Galaxy* 2 (1866): 381; cited in Arrington, p. 255.

38. *JD*, 12:54, 26 May 1867.

39. Brigham Young to John W. Young, 5 February 1867, Brigham Young Letterbook 9, Church Archives, pp. 340-42.

40. Reported in Samuel Bowles, *Our New West* (Hartfort, 1869), p. 260; cited in Arrington, p. 237.

41. See Leonard J. Arrington, *Great Basin Kingdom: An Economic History of the Latter-day Saints 1830-1900* (Lincoln, Neb.: University of Nebraska Press, 1966), pp. 246-250; and also Arrington's *From Quaker to Latter-day Saint: Bishop Edwin D. Woolley* (Salt Lake City: Deseret Book Co., 1976), pp. 432-444.

42. Arrington, *Great Basin Kingdom*, p. 255.

43. Ibid., p. 234.

44. Charles S. Peterson, "A Mormon Village: One Man's West," *Journal of Mormon History* 3 (1976): 11.

45. Ibid., p. 12.

46. Leonard J. Arrington, Feramorz Y. Fox, and Dean L. May, *Building the City of God: Community and Cooperation Among the Mormons* (Salt Lake City: Deseret Book Co., 1976), p. 2.

47. Arrington, *Great Basin Kingdom*, pp. 146-48.

48. Brigham Young sermon, 18 May 1855, "Addresses, n.d., 1844-55," Brigham Young Papers, Church Archives.

49. See *Building the City of God*, p. 70.

50. Ibid., p. 75.

51. Brigham Young sermon, *Deseret News*, 18 October 1857.

52. From remarks of 6 and 8 April 1869, reported in *Deseret News*, 26 May and 16 June 1869; cited in *Building the City of God*, p. 99.

53. Cited in *Building the City of God*, p. 111.

54. Quoted by Lorenzo Snow in his sermon, 21 April 1878, *JD* 19:347.

55. Cited in *Building the City of God*, p. 157.

56. James B. Allen and Glen M. Leonard, *The Story of the Latter-day Saints* (Salt Lake City: Deseret Book Co., 1976), pp. 364-366.

57. *Great Basin Kingdom*, p. 338.

58. D&C 104:13, 15-18.

59. *Great Basin Kingdom*, p. 339.

60. *JD*, 18:354, 6 April 1877.

61. John R. Young, *Memoirs of John R. Young* (Salt Lake City, 1920), pp. 226-27.

62. Cited in *Building the City of God*, p. 293.

63. Evan Z. Vogt and Ethel M. Albert, eds., *People of Rimrock* (Cambridge, Mass., 1966), p. 28.

64. See Moses 7:62-64.

65. *Building the City of God*, pp. 362-64.

66. *JD*, 12:186-87, 24 June 1868.

67. Brigham Young to Albert Carrington, 10 September 1875, retained copy, Brigham Young Papers, Church Archives.

68. Brigham Young to Albert Carrington, 11 December 1872.

69. *JD*, 19: 232, 8 October 1877; cited in Allen and Leonard, p. 375.

70. *JD*, 10:252, 6 October 1863.

71. George A. Smith to John Henry Smith, 3 January 1875, Church Archives; cited in Nibley, p. 512.

72. Brigham Young sermon, 1 January 1877, St. George Temple Book, Church Archives.

73. Ibid.

74. *JD*, 18:356-57, 6 April 1877.

75. Cited in Nibley, pp. 534, 537.

76. Cited in Nibley, p. 538.

77. Cited in Nibley, pp. 536-37; at President Young's suggestion, many others of the School of the Prophets, as well as himself, wrote burial instructions.

Index